Gothic Europe
1200–1450

Arts, Culture and Society in the Western World
General Editor: Boris Ford

This major new series examines the arts and culture of Western civilization within the social, economic and political context of the time. Richly illustrated, each book is structured around a concept of the age as a whole, integrating the different arts into a single analytical portrait of it. Music, literature and drama will be as important to the argument as architecture and the visual arts. The books will give readers their bearings in the cultural landscape via its major landmarks; but, more particularly, they will also examine the artistic activity of the age for what it can tell us of the preoccupations and priorities of the society that produced it.

Now available:

The Enlightenment and the Age of Revolution 1700–1850
John Sweetman

Gothic Europe 1200–1450
Derek Pearsall

Gothic Europe

1200–1450

Derek Pearsall

An imprint of **Pearson Education**

Harlow, England · London · New York · Reading, Massachusetts · San Francisco
Toronto · Don Mills, Ontario · Sydney · Tokyo · Singapore · Hong Kong · Seoul
Taipei · Cape Town · Madrid · Mexico City · Amsterdam · Munich · Paris · Milan

Pearson Education Limited
Edinburgh Gate
Harlow
Essex CM20 2JE
England

and Associated Companies throughout the world

Visit us on the World Wide Web at:
www.pearsoneduc.com

First published 2001

ISBN 0-582-27638-1

British Library Cataloguing-in-Publication Data
A catalogue record for this book is available from the British Library

Library of Congress Cataloging-in-Publication Data
Pearsall, Derek Albert.
    Gothic Europe 1200–1450 / [Derek Pearsall].
      p. cm. — (Arts, culture, and society in the Western world)
    Includes bibliographical references and index.
    ISBN 0–582–27638–1 (ppr) — ISBN 0–582–27637–3 (csd)
    1. Civilization, Medieval. 2. Europe—History—476–1491. 3. Europe—History—15th
century. 4. Europe—Church history—600–1500. 5. Church and state—Europe—History.
6. Art, Medieval—History. 7. Art, Gothic—Europe. I. Title. II. Series.

CB351 .P37 2000
940.1—dc21   00–058046

10 9 8 7 6 5 4 3 2 1
05 04 03 02 01

Set by 35 in 10/12pt Sabon
Produced by Pearson Education Malaysia Sdn Bhd
Printed in Malaysia

Contents

General Introduction

In these days of ever greater specialisation, few people who write about the arts venture beyond their particular field, and virtually none dare to stray over the boundary into an adjacent art. This is a serious loss, for the arts in any age are bound to share common ideals and characteristics and they emerge, after all, from the same society even if they address somewhat different audiences. And thus they can illuminate each other, both through their similarities and contrasts.

This series of ten volumes aims to present and study Western civilisation as expressed in its arts, including the social and economic soil from which these arts rose and flourished. The scope (but not necessarily the titles) of these volumes is as follows:

The Greek World
The Roman World
Early Medieval Europe (from the late Empire to *c*.950)
Romanesque Europe (*c*.950–*c*.1200)
Gothic Europe (*c*.1200–*c*.1450)
The Renaissance (*c*.1400–*c*.1600)
Baroque Europe (*c*.1575–*c*.1750)
The Enlightenment and the Age of Revolution (1700–1850)
The Romantic Age (*c*.1800–1914)
The Twentieth Century

The series as a whole does not resemble an encyclopedia of the arts, with chapters on the separate arts. Built around a concept of the age and its distinctive civilisation, the central argument of each volume is illuminated by a discussion of individual artists and their works, including popular culture; and of how, by looking at their social roles, their conventions and symbolism, and their formal structures, these works of art may best be understood and enjoyed.

Finally, the series provides a social, political and economic context for these works, and examines the artistic activity of the age for what it can tell us of the preoccupations and priorities of the society that produced it.

BORIS FORD

Preface

I began this book with a certain degree of scepticism about its title, and about the integrity of both the chronological period and the geographical region that was implied in that title. Surely, I said to myself, the two-and-a-half centuries from 1200 to 1450 have no reality as a 'period' in referring to any historical set of happenings with an ascertainable beginning and end, nor does the term 'Gothic Europe' mean anything, strictly speaking. They are part of a convenient shorthand way of dividing up the past so that talking about it can be divided up among different people. The danger of dividing up the past thus is that these 'periods' will come to be thought of as realities, as if they existed. The ways of guarding against this danger are either not to do it, or to keep reminding oneself and one's reader of the arbitrariness and artificiality of the proceeding. I began by proposing to take the latter of these options, and in this way to make use of a well-known and attractive term as the opportunity for an argument about the pleasures and pains of periodisation; 'Gothic' would be both the subject as well as the title of the subject.

It is maybe in the nature of such enterprises that I grew more persuaded, as I went on, that there was a possibility of talking about 'Gothic Europe 1200–1450' in a way that would recognise the arbitrariness of the dates assigned to the period without nagging continually about its non-existence. There are, after all, only different ways of organising the historical record in an intelligible way, and this is one of them. It is one of the better ones, and I defend it in the opening pages of Chapter One.

Also, I became more convinced that it was possible to point to 'works of art', as we call them, that were produced during the period of 'Gothic Europe' such as are distinctly different from what was produced before and after. Such works of art will be the nucleus of the study (Chapter Three): the Gothic cathedral, the Gothic illuminated manuscript, and the medieval romance-narrative of love and chivalry. Setting the political, social and cultural circumstances for these works will be the principal business of the first two chapters.

Chapter One will outline the geographical, political, social and economic circumstances which provide the substructure of artistic production, while Chapter Two will concentrate on the needs and desires to which these works catered, with particular reference to the principal patrons of the arts: the church, the court and the city.

The last two chapters will suggest, first, something of the divisions already existing within the hierarchically ordered world of Gothic Europe, and the evidence in the arts of the disturbance created by those divisions, and, finally, the manifestation in the arts of processes and pressures towards new forms of self-identification – of nations, communities, classes, persons, and artists. If Chapter Three is a celebration of the 'climax art' of Gothic Europe, full of tonic majors, Chapter Four introduces discordant notes, unexpected modulations, fragmentations, alternative perceptions. Found first as elements within the prevailing harmony – grotesques in church ornament, obscene drolleries in the margins of illuminated books of hours, realistic genre-scenes in religious plays – these begin to absorb more and more attention, contributing to the characteristic late Gothic restlessness of design. Finally, in the manner of a tying-up of themes, Chapter Five revisits the whole period in terms of an exploration of processes of self-identification. The concentration will be on works of art as an expression of new or different kinds of individuality, artistic self-consciousness and sense of nationhood.

I flatter myself that the book thus has a shape of its own, with a large dome (Chapter Three), perhaps the Millennium Dome of the Gothic Moment, under which are displayed the great achievements of Gothic Europe; two anterooms (the briefing rooms), to prepare one for the understanding of these achievements and to make one ready for the moment of epiphany; and two rooms to enable one to recover from, revisit, and re-evaluate the experience (the debriefing rooms).

France is central to the account throughout, as is proper, and is given an appropriate amount of attention. England is given a disproportionately large amount of attention, and other countries, apart perhaps from Italy, are proportionately neglected. There has been an attempt to keep Europe (that is, western Europe, Catholic Europe) in mind throughout and, though there are passages of purely formal and stylistic aesthetic analysis, to concentrate on the dynamic relation between cultural need and cultural production. Detailed accounts of specific 'case-histories' are introduced to balance the broader general survey that aims at the necessary coverage. The narrative, within its separate sequences, is broadly but not systematically chronological, and there is frequent revisitation, from different points of view, of themes, works and artists previously treated. The effect, it is hoped, will be one of multiple perspectives and not mere confusion.

It is in the nature of such a wide-ranging book that its debts cannot be individually acknowledged, and I want to take this opportunity to thank all those scholars (most of them find a place in the Guide to Reading) whose work I have plundered. I can only express the hope that in the areas of scholarship with which I am least familiar I have not made too many blunders. I am grateful to Barrie Dobson, who has read the whole typescript of the book in draft, for saving me from many such blunders, and to Christopher Norton for his expert reading of the section on the Gothic cathedral and many patient corrections of my misunderstandings. I am also grateful to Katharine Horsley, at present a graduate student at Harvard, who has given me much help in the preparation of the final text and the seeking out of the pictures; to Faith Perkins, who has indefatigably tracked the pictures to their sources and obtained permissions and to Natasha Dupont who has patiently seen the book through its final stages. I should like to pay tribute, too, to the late Boris Ford, who laid the plans for this series and asked me to write the book. Among his many gifts, he had a gift for getting things done.

List of Illustrations

Colour Plates

Figures (black and white)

Map

Genealogical Tables

Notes on the Colour Plates

PLATE I

Chantilly, Musée Condé MS 65 (*Très Riches Heures du Duc de Berry*), fol. 9v. September, from the Calendar sequence. French, 1411–16.

A monthly calendar of saints' days and feast-days was the first item in a book of hours, and it came to be illustrated with scenes of the Labours of the Months, developed in the fifteenth century as full-page miniatures. They were an opportunity to experiment with non-religious scenes of courtly and rural activity in well-realised landscape settings. The painters of this manuscript, the Limbourg brothers, included in each picture one of the châteaux associated with the Duke of Berry or his family. Here, for September, with its grape harvest, is shown the château at Saumur. The miniature was left unfinished, and the lower third, with its stocky figures and genre detail, was completed by Jean Colombe in about 1485. *Text references: pp. 61, 164.*

PLATE II

Bourges Cathedral, interior, from the west.

Bourges was part of the second great wave of building in the Gothic style as it spread from the Ile de France in the early thirteenth century. The choir was begun in 1195 and in use by 1232, and the cathedral completed by 1285. In following the new three-storey ordering of the nave (arcade, triforium, clerestory, omitting the tribune arcade below the triforium), the Bourges master has left the arcades at a great height, creating a soaring interior that has no rival in its sense of spaciousness. *Text references: p. 79.*

PLATE III

Salisbury Cathedral, general view from the north-west.

Built in a single campaign, 1230–66 (the tower and spire were completed in 1285–1320), Salisbury is perhaps the most harmoniously pleasing of English cathedrals. Some of the pleasure is due to the excellent prospects that may be obtained across the uniquely wide and tranquil close that surrounds the cathedral; some too to John Constable's famous paintings of 1823 (now in the Victoria and Albert Museum in London) and 1831 (now in the National Gallery in London). *Text references: pp. 83, 89, 91.*

PLATE IV

Chartres Cathedral, rose-window and other windows in the north transept. *c.*1230.

The fleurs-de-lys of the royal arms of France, repeatedly displayed in the rose, suggest that these windows were a royal commission. The centre of the rose-window depicts the Virgin Enthroned; the lancets below show Melchizedek, David, St Anne with Mary in her arms, Solomon and Aaron. *Text references: pp. 76, 79, 91, 108, 112–14.*

PLATE V

Simone Martini, Annunciation, altarpiece. Commissioned for Siena Cathedral, and now in the Uffizi Gallery in Florence. 1333.

An early example of the lyricism, refinement and sensitivity of the new 'International Gothic' style. Mary's frightened gesture as she shrinks back is a daringly expressive innovation for the period. Yet the delicately modelled figures are set in an almost airless gold void. *Text references: pp. 117, 208, 215.*

PLATE VI

Orvieto, Museo dell'Opera del Duomo. Reliquary of the Sacred Corporal by Ugolino di Vieri and assistants. Enamel on silver-gilt. 1337–38.

At a mass in nearby Bolsena in 1263, a priest who doubted the Real Presence in the eucharist was answered by a miracle, when the host at the moment of consecration began to bleed profusely. The blood stained the corporal (the cloth on which the host is placed after the consecration), a miracle which played a major part in the establishment of the Feast of Corpus Christi soon afterwards. The miraculously stained corporal-cloth was transferred to the newly built cathedral at Orvieto. The magnificently canopied and pinnacled reliquary (139 cm high) has twelve panels, of which these four show the Bishop of Orvieto receiving the relic, pilgrims at the shrine, and (lower two) the Last Supper and the Washing of the Feet. *Text references: pp. 135–6.*

PLATE VII

Brussels, Bibliothèque Royale MSS 9961–2 (the Peterborough Psalter), fol. 14r. *Beatus* page. 1299–1318.

This manuscript is a remarkable example of Gothic book design, in which all the elements of text, decoration, miniature and border have been integrated into a harmonious whole. The *Beatus* page is the page on which the first psalm begins (*Beatus vir*, 'Blessed is the man') and it is usually a showcase for the artist's talent. The initial miniature shows David playing his harp. In the margins are animals and birds, and men working and playing, and in the bas-de-page a vigorous deer-hunting scene. *Text references: p. 151.*

PLATE VIII

Paris, Musée Jacquemart-André MS 2 (the Boucicaut Hours), fol. 65v. The Visitation. 1405–08.

The Boucicaut Master's consummate mastery of landscape and aerial perspective is balanced by reminders of the profound devotional significance of the meeting of Mary and Elizabeth. Two angels follow Mary, one carrying her train, as if she is already the Queen of Heaven, the other carrying her prayer-book. Golden rays symbolise the descent of the Holy Spirit. The scene, for all its compelling appeal to the senses, is 'staged' within a proscenium of grassy and tree-strewn ledges, drawn out-of-scale. *Text references: pp. 165, 212.*

List of Abbreviations

BL	British Library, London
BN	Bibliothèque Nationale, Paris
Bodl.	Bodleian Library, Oxford
CUL	Cambridge University Library
EETS, OS, ES	Early English Text Society, Original Series, Extra Series
fol.	folio (leaf, with two sides, recto and verso)
MS	manuscript
r	recto (i.e. the side of the folio on the right side of the opening)
v	verso (i.e. the side of the folio on the left side of the opening)

Acknowledgements

The publishers would like to thank the following for permission to reproduce illustrative material:

The Warden and Fellows of All Souls College, Oxford, for fig. 2; Biblioteca Ambrosiana, Milan/Scala for fig. 56; Bibliothèque Nationale de France for figs 46, 55 67; Bibliothèque Nationale de France/Roger-Viollet for fig. 69; Bibliothèque Royale de Belgique for plate VII; Bodleian Library, University of Oxford, for figs 47, 51, 53; British Library for figs 3, 49, 50, 52, 57, 58, 59; By permission of the Feoffees of Chetham Hospital & Library, Manchester, for fig. 48; Campo Santo, Pisa/Scala for fig. 65; Cathedral Treasury, Tournai/ Bildarchiv Foto Marburg for fig. 34; Château de Saumur, Chantilly/Musée Condé/Roger-Viollet for plate I; La Documentation Française for fig. 12; San Gimignano, Collegiata di Santa Maria Assunta/Fotographia Lensini for fig. 64; Sonia Halliday & Laura Lushington Photographs for figs 28, 29; Clive Hicks Photograph Library for plates II, IV and for figs 9, 11, 13, 14, 16, 17, 18, 20, 21, 22, 25, 27, 33, 35, 36, 38, 39, 41, 42; Institut Amatller D'Art Hispanic, Barcelona, for fig. 23; A.F. Kersting for plate III and for figs 15, 24, 43; Kunsthistorisches Museum, Vienna/AKG London/Erich Lessing for fig. 4; Dean and Chapter Lincoln Cathedral for fig. 66; All rights reserved, Metropolitan Museum of Art, New York, Cloisters Collection 1954 for fig. 54; the Bequest of Michael Dreicer 1921 for fig. 61; Musée du Louvre/Roger-Viollet for figs 6, 68; Musée des Beaux Arts, Dijon/Lauros-Giraudon for fig. 32; Musée Jacquemart-André, Paris/Bridgeman Art Library for plate VIII; Museo Arqueológico Artistico Episcopal Vich/Institut Amatller D'Art Hispanic, Barcelona, for fig. 5; Museo Civico, Milan/Bridgeman Art Library for fig. 60; Museo dell'Opera del Duomo/Scala for plate VI; Museo dell'Opera Metropolitana, Siena/Scala for fig. 30; National Gallery, London, for figs 8, 62, 63; National Gallery, Prague/AKG London/Erich Lessing for fig. 31; Pierpont Morgan Library, New York, for figs 26 (MS M. 638, f. 3), 45 (MS

M. 638, f. 23v); Scala for fig. 37; Scrovegni Chapel, Padua/Scala for fig. 70; J.C.D. Smith for fig. 40; Uffizi Gallery, Florence/Scala for plate V; Victoria & Albert Picture Library for fig. 7; Dean and Chapter Winchester Cathedral for fig. 44; Württembergische Landesbibliothek/Bildarchiv Foto Marburg for fig. 1.

While every effort has been made to trace owners of copyright material, we take this opportunity to offer our apologies to any copyright holders whose rights we may have unwittingly infringed.

1

'Gothic Europe': The Political and Economic Order

Why 'Gothic'?

'Gothic' in 'Gothic Europe' signifies a period when the style of architecture that later came to be known as 'Gothic' was dominant. It was a style of architecture so innovative and extraordinary, so powerfully visible still, especially as it is manifested in the great cathedrals of western Europe, that it is not surprising that it has given its name to a whole period. This is not to say that it is easy to define: as Ruskin said, in 'The Nature of Gothic', defining 'Gothicness' is like trying to define the nature of red when there is only purple and orange to work with.[1] The extension of the term to sculpture and painting and the decorative arts was natural enough, given that the display of those arts was mostly in architectural contexts (the carved figures in and on church buildings, the paintings in glass, on the walls and on altarpieces) or incorporated architectural motifs (the canopies and pinnacles of 'Gothic' illumination).

Some scholars have attempted to find the character of Gothic architecture, subjectively defined in terms of delicacy, fineness of detail, restlessness, mobility, in the non-visual arts such as literature. In a passage made famous for English medieval literary scholars by the quotation from it in Charles Muscatine's book on *Chaucer and the French Tradition*, Arnold Hauser offers a version of what has become a common generalisation about Gothic art:

> The basic form of Gothic art is juxtaposition. Whether the individual work is made up of several comparatively independent parts or is not analyzable into such parts, whether it is a pictorial or a plastic, an epic or a dramatic representation, it is always the principle of expansion and not of concentration, of co-ordination and not of subordination, of the open sequence and not of the closed geometric form, by which it is dominated. The beholder is, as it were, led through the stages and stations of a journey, and the picture of reality which it reveals is like a panoramic survey, not a one-sided, unified representation, dominated by a single point of view.[2]

Muscatine has no difficulty in finding these elements of 'co-ordinateness and linearity' in Chaucer's *Canterbury Tales*, as well as 'a second typically Gothic quality, the tension between phenomenal and ideal, mundane and divine, that informs the art and thought of the period'. These ideas of 'Gothic form' are widely current, and offer many temptations to make analogies between the arts, and particularly to argue from the aesthetic of visual form in architecture and art to the aesthetic of verbal and non-visual form in literature. Anyone writing about the different arts and their interaction and mutual influence within a certain period will want to make use of these and similar analogies. But the dangers of merely subjective impressionism are obvious, and one has to remain aware of the slippery nature of such analogies and the illusory foundation on which they are constructed. However, for the use of 'Gothic' as a periodising term, and as a means therefore of labelling all the forms of art produced within the period so designated, there is every justification.

'Gothic' was first introduced by Giorgio Vasari (1513–74) in his *Lives of the Italian Painters* as a term to describe the kind of old-style architecture that he despised.[3] Admiring the architecture of Filippo Brunelleschi (1377–1446) and the painting of Raphael (1483–1520), and considering the recent painting, sculpture and architecture of northern Italy as a 'renaissance' of classical art, the only kind of art to be admired, he dismissed the architecture of the previous centuries as barbaric (*maniera barbara*). It was, said Vasari, in the famous philippic against the Gothic style in the Introduction to the *Lives*, in the 'German' (*todeschi*) style or 'the Gothic manner' (*maniera de' Gotti*). Vasari had a theory that the architecture he despised was actually invented by the historical Goths (who surged across Europe in the fifth century and, under Alaric, sacked Rome in 410). A report on Roman antiquities presented by a member of Raphael's circle to Pope Julius II says that the pointed arches and overarching ribbed vaults were imitations of the northern forests where the barbarians constructed rude shelters by leaning trees together. Earlier Gothic (what is now called Romanesque) was meanwhile presumed to imitate the caves and grottoes in which these primitive people had lived even before they hit upon the idea of bowers under spreading leafy branches.

Abuse was heaped upon this Gothic architecture in the sixteenth and seventeenth centuries. Sir Henry Wotton, in *The Elements of Architecture* (1624), comments upon pointed arches thus:

> These, both for the natural imbecility of the sharp angle itself, and likewise for their very uncomeliness, ought to be exiled from judicious eyes, and left to their first inventors, the Goths and Lombards, among other reliques of that barbarous age.

At the same time, buildings continued to be restored and extended, skilfully and lovingly, in the Gothic style. San Petronio in Bologna had its nave rib-vaulted in 1646–58, Saint-Germain-des-Prés in Paris in 1644–45, and Saint-Etienne in Caen and Saint-Nicholas in Blois at around the same time. Lincoln College, Oxford, had its 'fourteenth-century' Gothic chapel built in 1631, and the Gothic fan-vault above the stairs leading to the hall of Christ Church, Oxford, dates from 1640. Engravings in books of architectural history such as Dugdale's

History of St Paul's Cathedral (1658) reflect the love of Gothic. All of this is before Gothic was restored to official favour in the late eighteenth century as the perfect expression of a 'natural' aspiration after the divine. This was the analogy favoured in Goethe's eulogy of Strassburg Cathedral (1772): 'It rises like a most sublime wide-arching Tree of God, which with a thousand twigs, a million twigs, tells forth to the neighbourhood the glory of God'. It was not long before Gothic was canonised as the supreme architectural style, anatomised and classified (the supreme accolade) into its different periods ('Early English', 'Decorated', 'Perpendicular', for instance, in Thomas Rickman's *Attempt to discriminate the Styles of Architecture in England from the Conquest to the Reformation*, 1817), and adopted on a massive scale for new building, ecclesiastical and secular.

Meanwhile, of course, Gothic had also taken its 'Gothick' turn, first in a patronising and playful manner in 'Gothick' novels like Horace Walpole's *Castle of Otranto* (1764), full of vaults, crypts, tombs, painted windows, gloom and dark pomp, and then in a more seriously ridiculous manner in the novels of 'Monk' Lewis and Ann Radcliffe. Samuel Johnson, as a representative of neo-classical rationality, had celebrated the robustness of the ordinary, of truth to nature and the centrally human. The Gothic novel was in some sense a reaction against this, a return of the repressed, a tantalising visitation of the grotesque horrors that lay in the shadow of the Enlightenment. The pervasively religious presences of the Gothic novels – the ubiquitous monks and ruined chapels and suggestions of mysterious supernatural powers – provide one of the links with the past of Gothic, and indicate the nature of some of the spectres that haunted an age of reason (and that remained unappeased in the later literature of vampirism and postmodern schlock-horror).

The familiarity of the Gothic style in architecture, and the visual impact of its many surviving monuments, make it an appealing term to use to identify, if not to characterise, the period in which it was dominant. The exact definition of the chronological extent of that period could vary. If it were being defined in terms of architecture alone, 'Gothic Europe' would begin in 1144, with Abbot Suger, and end in the sixteenth century, sprawlingly, as neo-classical architecture spread from Italy northwards. It would begin early in one part of Europe and end late in other parts (Portugal, England). But though the history of architecture provides the initial justification for the use of the term Gothic, there is no reason to give it too solitary a prominence in arbitrating upon chronological divides. 'Gothic Europe' may be acknowledged to be a convenient periodising term, and 1200–1450 inevitably to some extent an arbitrary slice out of the flux of time, but there are a number of ways in which 'Gothic Europe 1200–1450' can be claimed to have, for 'non-Gothic' reasons, a definable identity and integrity.

Why 1200–1450?

We begin with what defined the Europe we are speaking of. It was the Europe of Latin Christendom, extending north-west to newly Christianised Iceland,

Map 1: Europe, about 1360.

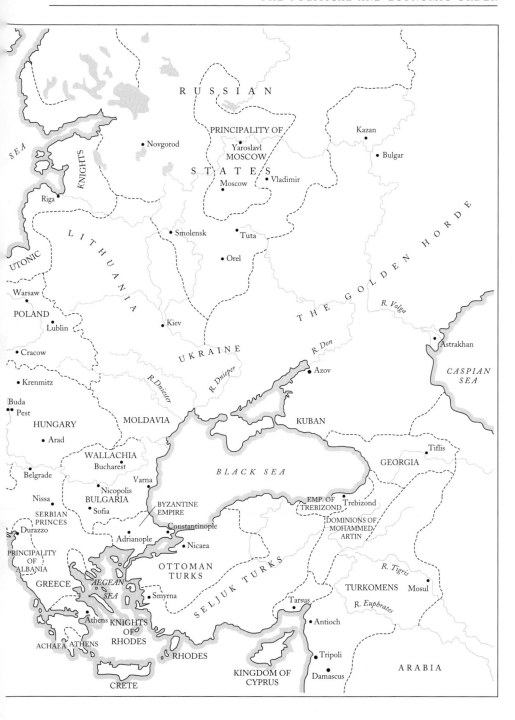

R U S S I A N

SEA

PRINCIPALITY OF

Kazan

Novgorod

Yaroslavl
MOSCOW

Bulgar

S T A T E S

KNIGHTS

Moscow

Vladimir

Riga

LITHUANIA

Smolensk

Tuta

THE

GOLDEN

HORDE

UTONIC

Orel

R. Volga

Warsaw

Kiev

POLAND

Lublin

UKRAINE

R. Don

Astrakhan

CASPIAN
SEA

Cracow

R. Dnieper

Krenmitz

R. Dniester

Azov

Buda
Pest

MOLDAVIA

KUBAN

HUNGARY

Arad

Tiflis

WALLACHIA

Bucharest

BLACK SEA

GEORGIA

Belgrade

Varna

Nissa

Nicopolis

BULGARIA

Sofia

EMP. OF
TREBIZOND

Trebizond

SERBIAN
PRINCES

BYZANTINE
EMPIRE

DOMINIONS OF
MOHAMMED
ARTIN

Durazzo

Constantinople

PRINCIPALITY
OF
ALBANIA

Adrianople

Nicaea

R. Tigris

GREECE

OTTOMAN
TURKS

SELJUK TURKS

TURKOMENS

Mosul

AEGEAN
SEA

Smyrna

R. Euphrates

Athens
KNIGHTS
OF
RHODES

Tarsus

ACHAEA ATHENS

Antioch

RHODES

Tripoli

ARABIA

KINGDOM OF
CYPRUS

Damascus

CRETE

south-west to the disputed borders with the Moors in Spain, north-east and
east to the Slavic kingdoms beyond Poland and Hungary, under the Eastern not
the Roman Church, and south-east to the borders of the Eastern or Byzantine
Empire. The Eastern or Greek Orthodox church had its headquarters in the
imperial capital of Constantinople and claimed, like the Western or Roman
church, from which it had finally split in 1053, to be the only true church. Since
differences between different Christian sects are often as fiercely maintained as
differences between Christians and non-Christians, the Byzantine Empire and
the church of which the Patriarch in Constantinople was the head were almost
as alien to the west as the Muslim Turks. The earlier crusades to recover the
Holy Land inspired some fitful cooperation, but the sack of Constantinople by
the crusading armies in 1204 during the Fourth Crusade confirmed the hateful
division, defining western Europe as an identity through the oppositional structuring of what it was not, whether Turk or apostate. A further barrier between
east and west was erected in the north, where the Mongol invasions of Russia
acted to seal off a region that had previously been open to economic and
cultural contact with the west. Relationships between the west and Byzantium
improved spasmodically during the next two-and-a-half centuries, but it was
again events in the east, the seizure of Constantinople by the Ottoman Turks
in 1453, and the flight of scholars and the spread of Byzantine Greek learning
to the west, that led to a new definition of western Europe. It was not only
what happened within western Europe during the years 1200–1450 that makes
it capable of being talked about as 'Gothic Europe', but also what happened
in the east to make the west 'the west'.

The Byzantine Empire and the Turks

The Byzantine Empire had declined from the peak of its power (*c*.1025), when
it controlled all Asia Minor and nearly all the Balkans. The Turks were pressing upon its borders, and though they were temporarily discomfited during
the First Crusade, which culminated in the capture of Jerusalem in 1098 and
the slaughter of all its Muslim and Jewish inhabitants and the setting up of the
Latin kingdom of Jerusalem, they soon regrouped and united under Saladin
to reconquer Jerusalem in 1187. Meanwhile, adventures in 'Outremer', as it
was called ('the overseas'), had given a tremendous stimulus to trade, chiefly
conducted by Venice, but also Genoa and Pisa. The carnage of 1204, when
the armies of the Fourth Crusade turned aside to sack Constantinople, was
prompted by Venetian trading rivalry as well as religious fervour and the
prospect of holy looting among the renegade Christians. A Latin empire was
set up, the Western church installed, and much land in the Balkans and across
the Bosphorus annexed. The Byzantines held on in western Greece and reoccupied Constantinople in 1261, but their shadowy empire remained a prey
to exploitation by the fleets of Venice and Genoa, as well as by the Turks,
and portions of it were occupied and garrisoned by the west to protect trade
and crusading routes. The island of Rhodes was occupied by the Knights of

St John (the Knights Hospitallers), a crusading order set up for this purpose (another was the Knights Templars, suppressed by the French king in 1312), right up until the end of the Middle Ages (1522).

Crusades continued spasmodically, though not many reached the Holy Land. The Emperor Frederick II had some temporary success in 1228–29, negotiating with the Muslims to have himself crowned in Jerusalem in 1229 (no one was there to crown him in any official capacity, so he crowned himself), but the city was reoccupied in 1244. This led Louis IX of France, shamed by the compromises and greed of his predecessors, to launch a new crusade in 1248. Well-organised and well-financed, the crusading army landed in Egypt, but got no further. Louis IX tried again in 1270, but died on the way at Tunis. This, the Eighth Crusade, was effectively the last. From now on, the pope would concentrate on promoting crusades against western heretics (the Albigensian crusade launched by Innocent III in 1209 against the Cathars of southern France set a bloody precedent) or against those who opposed the wishes of himself and his allies (the clergy could be taxed to pay for such 'crusades', and those who died received plenary absolution).

The Turks, after stemming the advance of the Mongol hordes (who at one point in 1241 raided to the borders of Hungary), picked off the Crusader strongholds one by one. Acre fell in 1300 and the Ottoman Turks got their first foothold in Europe at Gallipoli in 1354. Murad I (Shakespeare's Amurath) set up a Turkish court at Adrianople, and though he himself was killed in battle against the Serbs under Prince Lazar Hrebeljanovic at Kossovo in 1389, the Serbs were defeated, and the Emperor John V asked the west for help. A large and splendid expedition led by John, son of the Duke of Burgundy, proved a fiasco and its army was annihilated at Nicopolis in 1396. The Turks were at the gates of Vienna, but a reprieve came in 1402 when they were set upon in the east by the Mongol Timur (Marlowe's Tamburlaine) and the Sultan Bajezid I was killed. Constantinople was temporarily saved, but Byzantium was now no more than a Turkish vassal (only the Serbs held out) and the 'fall' of Constantinople in 1453 was like the falling of an over-ripe fruit.

The Holy Roman Empire, Italy, and the Papacy

The dissolution of empires is the story too in other parts of Europe, sometimes into elements that were to resist recomposition for many centuries, sometimes into the nation-states that first became recognisable in the later Gothic period. Central and central southern Europe had been ruled by the sprawling Holy Roman Empire in the eleventh and twelfth centuries, dominated by Germany, first under the Ottonian emperors and then under the Emperor Frederick I, Barbarossa (1152–90). Frederick had extended the effective powers of the Empire, as distinct from its nominal suzerainty, into northern Italy and even to Rome, where his challenge to the papacy, then at the height of its medieval power, over rights to the investiture of the clergy (and the claims meantime to the temporalities, that is, the profits from the lands and endowments accrued

Table 1: Chronological list of Holy Roman Emperors, Hohenstaufen to Habsburg

1152–90	Frederick I, Barbarossa, house of Hohenstaufen
1190–97	Henry VI, house of Hohenstaufen
1198–1218	NO EMPEROR
1218–50	Frederick II, house of Hohenstaufen
1250–54	Conrad IV, house of Hohenstaufen
1254–73	INTERREGNUM
1273–91	Rudolf I, house of Habsburg (not crowned)
1292–98	Adolf of Nassau (not crowned), deposed
1298–1308	Albert I, house of Habsburg (not crowned)
1308–13	Henry VII, house of Luxemburg
1314–47	Louis IV (Ludwig IV), King of Bavaria, house of Wittelsbach
1347–78	Charles IV, King of Bohemia, house of Luxemburg
1378–1400	Wenceslas (Wenceslas IV, King of Bohemia 1378–1419), house of Luxemburg
1400–10	Rupert of the Palatinate (not crowned)
1411–37	Sigismund, King of Hungary
1438–39	Albert II, house of Habsburg
1440–93	Frederick III, house of Habsburg

to that office) had ended inconclusively. But Frederick died by drowning on crusade in Asia Minor in 1190 and his successor, Henry VI, died in 1197, leaving an infant son, and the civil wars that followed tore Germany apart. That infant son, early crowned King of Sicily, became emperor as Frederick II in 1218, and Frederick had some success in reasserting imperial power, mostly from his base in southern Italy. He was skilful in his negotiations with the Muslim east when on crusade and had an unusual career as a patron of the arts and sciences, but his struggles to maintain imperial power in Italy against the papacy (he was frequently excommunicated by Gregory IX, pope 1227–41) were undone by his death in 1250.

Frederick II was succeeded as emperor by his eldest son Conrad IV (1250–54), but his illegitimate son Manfred inherited control of large parts of southern Italy. The Empire was in effect divided and, after the death of Conrad in 1254, for many years in disarray. The pope moved swiftly to expel the Hohenstaufens from the south and re-exert papal influence there: he invited Charles of Anjou, the brother of Louis IX of France, to take the throne of Sicily and Naples in opposition to Frederick's son Manfred, thus beginning a century of Franco-papal alliance which was very deleterious to the authority of the papacy. Manfred died in 1266, and the last of the Hohenstaufens, Conradin, was executed by Charles of Anjou at Naples in 1268. The bloody rebellion of the 'Sicilian Vespers' in 1282, when the whole French population on the island was massacred, led to the further invitation to Peter III of Aragon to take the throne of Sicily. There were now two foreign powers with a foothold in the south. Papal influence had been reasserted and the fortunes of the Guelph or pro-papal party in Italy restored, but constant feuding in the kingdoms of Naples and Sicily brought damage to public order and authority, impoverishment to the economy of a region that had been one of the granaries of Europe, and the decline of a culture that, under the Norman kings and Frederick II, had been richly receptive to Muslim scholars and Byzantine influences. Sicily and Calabria have never fully been restored to the economic and cultural prosperity they once enjoyed.

What was bad news for the south of Italy and for the prospects of Italian unification was very good news for the city-states north of Rome. They enjoyed the looseness of the suzerainty exerted by the papal power in the south and the imperial power in the north, and used them as flags of convenience to suit their own purposes. Florence followed mostly the party of the Guelphs, the northern cities mostly the policies of the Ghibelline or pro-imperial party. It was from this situation that the Italian city-states and duchies – Florence, Siena, Pisa, Genoa, Venice, Milan – gained their tremendous economic vitality, the freedom to respond to competition and innovation that made them the economic tigers of their day, unhampered by the traditional restraints of an institutional church or a feudal aristocracy. Economic prosperity had its technical, scientific and cultural spin-offs, and the Italian city-states were a ferment of innovation upon which Europe was to draw for centuries.

Nothing about any of this was peaceable: feuding and fighting went on all the time, and there were slumps as well as booms. The Bardi and Peruzzi banks collapsed in 1340 (partly because Edward III of England defaulted on his loan-repayments), and in Florence and Siena trade declined. Florentine relations with the papacy, now in Avignon, became strained, and at one time the city was preparing to defend itself against papal forces while under inter-dict (one of the notorious papal 'crusades') and also facing a revolt of poorly paid textile workers, the *ciompi*, at home. The centre of prosperity shifted to the north, where the eastward expansion of Venetian trade, with Turk and Christian alike, proceeded apace, and where Milan established itself as a great trading entrepôt with the transalpine lands. The ambitious Lombard Duke Gian Galeazzo Visconti, who had seized power in Milan in 1385 after having his uncle Bernabò murdered, threatened at one point to take over the whole of northern Italy, and Pisa, Siena, Perugia and Bologna all accepted his lordship; he was about to attack Florence when he died of plague in 1402. The inter-city wars fell into the hands of mercenary soldiers who would hire themselves out to the highest bidder under their leaders or *condottieri* and so, even-handedly, maintain an equilibrium in which no city could become all-powerful. Municipal rule had now everywhere fallen into the hands of oligarchies or powerful families, in smaller cities – Verona, Modena, Ferrara, Padua, Mantua, Cremona – as well as large. Florence was ruled by the Medicis from 1434, even though nominally still a republic; Milan had its duke, and Venice its doge, a head of state elected for life (though usually at a very advanced age). War broke out between Milan and Venice in 1423 and lasted till 1445, fought mainly between the *condottieri* Niccolò Piccinino and Francesco Sforza (who was supposed to be fighting for Venice but went over to the Milanese three times to improve his 'take'). The peace of Lodi (1454) held for a while but by the end of the century Italy had become a battleground for the two super-states France and Spain. None of this much affected Italy's cultural pre-eminence.

The papacy had meanwhile gone into serious decline. It had been energetic in the thirteenth century in enlarging its territorial influence and supporting the new orders of friars, and the volume of its business – the hearing of appeals, appointments to benefices, arbitrations, international diplomacy – had enormously increased, particularly under Innocent IV (1243–54). But its resources were overstrained and its reputation, with its immersion in worldly affairs and institutional activities, was precarious. When the unworldly Pope Celestine V resigned after four months in 1294 (he was the ninth pope in eighteen years), he was succeeded by Boniface VIII, who attempted an unprecedented extension of the papal power. His bull *Unam Sanctam* proclaimed the secular authority of the papacy; he invented the Jubilee year of 1300 to bring everyone to Rome; he tried to centralise the papal bureaucracy and to compel payment to Rome of fees for admission to all high clerical office and for every document and privilege, and of the first year's income from every benefice. Philip the Fair, King of France, found much in this to be against his interests: there were developments in contemporary French political thinking towards the idea of the state as itself an absolute entity and not the personal fief of the king, and one over which the king ruled with sovereign authority. In later years Marsilius of Padua was to produce in Paris the *Defensor Pacis* (1324–26), arguing for a secular state in which the church was kept to its strictly sacerdotal function in the administration of the sacraments and the saying of mass. On the horizon was the idea of the 'national church' (something that Richard II came to favour), the church subject to the political authority of the national monarch.

All this was in the future. Philip's immediate response to the papal denial of the royal right to tax the clergy was to engineer the election of the French-born Clement V as Boniface's successor in 1305 and to welcome the new pope to Avignon, a papal fief under French sovereignty, when he sought refuge from the inevitable hostility of the Roman populace.

So began a luxurious 'Babylonian captivity', during which the papal court at Avignon became renowned for extravagance and corruption. None of the succeeding six popes, all of them French (of 134 cardinals created at Avignon, 113 were French), was eager to move back to Rome, which was turbulent with the rivalries of local families, economically backward (the only industry was religious tourism) and much less comfortable than Avignon. The pious Gregory XI (elected 1370) nevertheless moved back to Rome in 1376, and when his successor, the Italian-born Urban VI, elected in 1378, turned out to be unsympathetic to French interests, an antipope, Clement VII, was installed in Avignon. This was the beginning of the Papal Schism, in which the already tarnished reputation of the papacy suffered further as the two pontiffs waged war against each other and competed in using the spiritual prerogatives of their office in order to grant favours to rival supporters. The Schism lasted till 1415, by which time Benedict XIII had succeeded Clement VII (d. 1394) as antipope at Avignon, and a second antipope, John XXIII, had been elected in

1410 in opposition to the current Roman pope Gregory XII. In 1415 Gregory XII agreed to resign and John XXIII was stripped of his name and finally deposed, charged with rape, piracy, murder, incest and sodomy (the more scandalous charges, says Gibbon, in chapter 70 of *The Decline Šand Fall of the Roman Empire*, were suppressed). Benedict XIII was obdurate until 1417, when he was expelled, and Martin V was elected, after an official vacancy at the Holy See lasting two years. All this was brought about under the auspices of the Emperor Sigismund at the Council of Constance (1414–18), which was a new kind of international occasion and, with the Council of Basle (1431–39), generated an important body of conciliar theory (declaring, for instance, the superior authority of a general council of the church even to that of the pope).

In the north, the extinction of the Hohenstaufen dynasty in 1268 led to a weakening of imperial rule. From this time on, the emperor was elected by seven German electors – the archbishops of Mainz, Trier and Cologne, the King of Bohemia, the Count Palatinate of the Rhine, the Duke of Saxony, and the Margrave of Brandenburg – and these were only a few of the many semi-autonomous jurisdictions in the area supposedly the nucleus of the Empire. There were also independent kingdoms contiguous to the east in Austria, Poland and Hungary. The emperor was by no means a shadow, and the emperors of the Bohemia-based House of Luxemburg at times exerted considerable influence, as during the early years of the rule of Wenceslas IV, King of Bohemia 1378–1419 and Emperor 1378–1400 (when he was deposed for incompetence), and during the long reign of Sigismund, Emperor 1411–37. But the Holy Roman Empire did not have a solid power-base till the Habsburg King of Austria Albert II united in himself in 1438 the Hungarian, Bohemian and German crowns and established the dynasty that was to last till 1806.

France and England

The Anglo-Norman kingdom, or Angevin Empire, as it is sometimes called, was the consequence of the conquest of England in 1066 by William, Duke of Normandy. During the twelfth century it was enlarged by the addition of Aquitaine, a large duchy in south-west France, from the inheritance of Eleanor, the queen of Henry II, so that by the time of his death (1189) it included most of north-west and south-west France and much of the central southern region. The French kings had been meanwhile securing their control of the royal domain around Paris and negotiating suzerainties over adjacent fiefdoms and tributary counties. Thus strengthened, Philip Augustus (1180–1223) began to nibble away at the territories of the Angevin Empire as central control began to loosen under Richard I (1189–99) and John (1199–1216), and by 1204 the whole of north-west France except for a small area around Calais was in French hands. This, the English loss of Normandy, was a decisive moment in establishing the independent identity of the two future nation-states. The

Table 2: Kings of England: Plantagenet and Lancaster

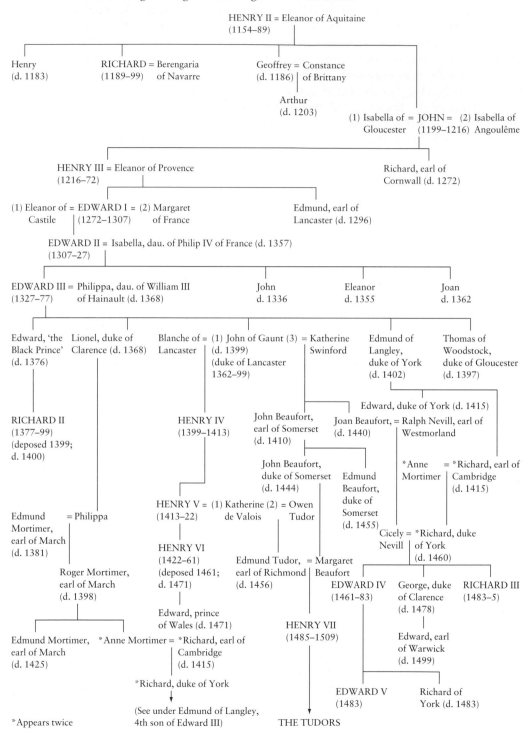

Table 3: Kings of France: Capetian and Valois

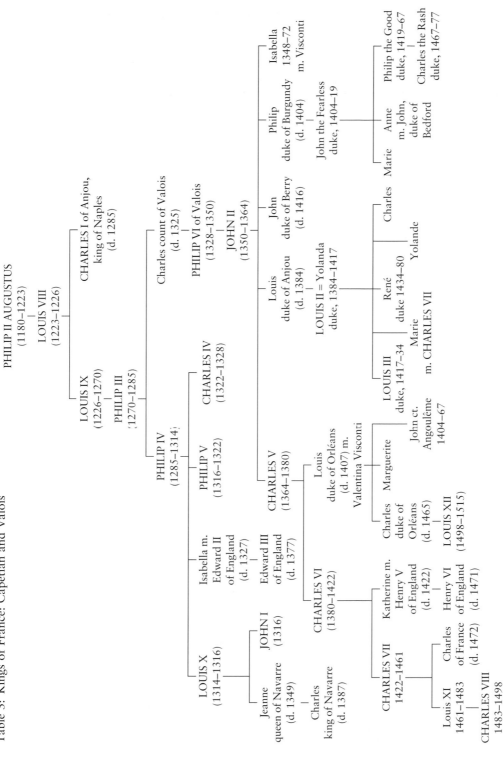

Anglo-Norman dialect of French was to remain the language of court, government and the ruling class in England until the middle of the fourteenth century, but there was no doubt that England was now a separate country (though it still held and paid homage to the French king for Aquitaine).

Philip Augustus also extended French control over the south of France, taking advantage of the Albigensian crusade to introduce French troops into the territories of Raymondin, the formerly very powerful Count of Toulouse. Louis IX (1226–70) continued the programme of expansion and consolidation, his ambitions for France and for a 'religion of monarchy' assisted by his own personal piety and by the convenient collapse of the Hohenstaufen power in Germany. Philip IV (Philip the Fair, 1285–1314) felt confident enough to challenge Pope Boniface VIII (who had been responsible for Louis IX's canonisation), and he installed Clement V at Avignon in 1309, almost as if he were playing the quasi-imperial role of a new Charlemagne. But his death, and the death within fourteen years of four successors (his eldest son, his grandson, and his two younger sons), meant the end of the house of Capet and the passing of the throne to his nephew Philip of Valois (Philip VI, 1328–50). This in turn opened the throne of France to the claim of Edward III of England, whose mother Isabella was the daughter and sole surviving child of Philip IV. The English king was not slow to prosecute his claim, and so began the long Hundred Years War (1337–1453).

England during the thirteenth century had been occupied with other conflicts. First there was a struggle over papal privileges of taxation and clerical patronage between King John and Pope Innocent III, who placed England under interdict or general excommunication (1208–13), which meant that no mass could be said or baptisms, marriages or burials solemnised. There was conflict too between John and his barons, ending with the signing of Magna Carta (1215), a document in which the rights of the barons in relation to the royal power were for the first time written down. (Similar concessions, with the same emphasis on legal-style written instruments, were being wrung from feudal rulers in Hungary, Spain and Poland.) John had to compromise and give way on both issues: he was perhaps before his time in his conception of the royal prerogative. His son, Henry III, succeeded as a minor and reigned a very long time (1216–72): he was a noteworthy patron of the arts and rebuilt magnificently the choir of Westminster Abbey, but the later part of his reign was disturbed by baronial revolts led by Simon de Montfort, who won a victory at Lewes (1264) only to be defeated and killed at Evesham a year later (1265). The barons were aggrieved at the manner in which Henry III had filled his court with French followers, his own and those of his queen, Eleanor of Provence, and at the neglect of the barons' interests and of what they perceived to be their role in the royal government and counsels. Edward I (1272–1307) demonstrated, not for the first or last time, the importance of war against other countries as an effective way of articulating royal authority over the barons, and he had great success in asserting English power in Scotland and in Wales, which he annexed, seizing the crown of the Welsh princes and declaring his eldest son Prince of Wales. War was his *métier*, and he was good at it; he also used parliament skilfully to ensure that no breach opened up between him and his barons, knights and large burgesses; and he also used the story of King Arthur, and associated himself with it, as did his grandson Edward III, as a way of adding to the mystique of royal power.

Edward II's reign (1307–27) was unfortunate. Scotland was lost to Robert Bruce at the battle of Bannockburn (1314), and the barons were up in arms again in outrage at the power the king gave to upstart favourites. The reign ended in civil war, in which Edward's queen Isabella took the side of the barons, and in his own deposition and murder. His son, succeeding at the age of fourteen as Edward III (1327–77), was soon 'busying giddy minds with foreign quarrels' by making claim to the throne of France.

At first the war went all England's way. Territorial lordships such as Burgundy, Brittany and Anjou were happy to see French power weakened, and neighbours such as the kings of Navarre, the Gascon counts of Armagnac, and the Flemish city-states had the opportunity of profitable alliances of convenience. The English won spectacular victories at Crécy (1346) and Poitiers (1356) against superior but poorly commanded French forces. John II, King of France (Jean le Bon), was captured at Poitiers and kept in luxurious confinement in England, and a huge ransom was imposed at the Treaty of Brétigny (1360). English power was at its peak, and now soon began to decline. Payment of the ransom was held up, and the new king, Charles V (1364–80), practised a cautious diplomacy and avoided pitched battles. English authority, asserted through military success but never properly established 'on the ground' in effective forms of local government, melted away, and incursions and *chevauchées* such as that of John of Gaunt, Duke of Lancaster, the king's younger son, in 1373 were no more than plundering raids. The death in quick succession of Edward III's eldest son and most successful military commander, Edward the Black Prince, in 1376, and of Edward III himself in 1377, and the succession of the nine-year-old Richard II, broke the back of the English military enterprise. Richard developed a policy of peace with France, one of the things, along with the usual neglect of their counsels and their *amour propre*, that turned the great magnates against him and led to their brief imposition upon him of a humiliating 'committee of protection' in 1388. Having resumed his regality in 1389, Richard began to operate the levers of power more skilfully, took revenge upon his enemies one by one, exercised the other nobles with unlosable wars in Ireland, and was on the verge of establishing a uniquely personal autocratic rule when he made the fatal error of confiscating the Lancastrian estates to the crown on the death of John of Gaunt in 1399. Gaunt's exiled son returned at once to claim his inheritance and, when he saw his opportunity, the throne, as Henry IV.

In France there had been a time of prosperity, cultivation of the arts and building works by royal patrons, extension of the royal power, and a theatricalisation of the monarchy in the use of insignia amd costume and in the introduction of public ceremonies and rituals associated with royal entries and appearances, feasts and burials. Charles V's three brothers, Louis, Duke of Anjou, John, Duke of Berry, and Philip (the Bold), Duke of Burgundy, were fully involved in these displays of magnificence (which Richard II made some attempt to emulate), but the reign of Charles VI (1380–1422) was soon shadowed by his first bout of madness (1392) and by the increasing power of the Duke of Burgundy. The territory in east-central France he had been assigned by his father John II in 1363 was not inconsequential, but it became a European-scale power-base when he married Margaret, the daughter of the Count of Flanders and Artois, in 1384 and succeeded to those immensely wealthy lands. It became possible for the Duke of Burgundy to think of himself not as France's greatest tributary but as a sovereign and equal ruler. The struggle for power that accompanied Charles VI's decline was brutally evidenced in the treacherous murder in 1407 of Louis, Duke of Orléans, the king's brother, by Philip's son John the Fearless (Jean sans Peur), who had succeeded to the dukedom in 1404, and then in the terrible revenge exacted through the murder of Duke John by partisans of Charles the Dauphin (Dauphin was the name given to the French king's eldest son) in 1419. The civil strife between the Burgundians and the Armagnacs (named after Bernard d'Armagnac, the father-in-law of Louis of Orléans's son Charles) was a vitally important factor in the success of Henry V's campaigns in France in 1415 and 1417–21, and the Anglo-Burgundian alliance was the framework of English military strategy in France until 1435.

Henry IV had been preoccupied with civil strife and rebellions against his usurpation (he had a claim to the throne as the grandson of Edward III, but a less strong one, technically, than the descendants of Edward III's second son Lionel – and Richard II's 'abdication' was a very doubtful business). Henry V, on his accession in 1413, determined on the familiar policy of uniting doubtful friends by pitting them against a common enemy and by reasserting an English claim to the French throne in which national identity would be strengthened, and also symbolised and expressed in his own royal person. The Agincourt campaign of 1415 was a brilliant success and won him the support he needed at home, including the all-important financial support, to embark in 1417 on a full-scale reconquest of Normandy and of the whole of northern France including Paris. The Treaty of Troyes (1420) was imposed upon the ailing Charles VI, providing for the succession to the throne of both kingdoms of Henry's issue by his marriage to Katherine, Charles VI's daughter. This was the nine-month-old Henry VI's inheritance when his father died suddenly on campaign in France in 1422, and he was indeed crowned King of France in Paris in 1431, though not before Joan of Arc had crowned Charles VII (1422–61) in 1429 in Reims, the ancient place of coronation of the French kings. Joan of Arc was captured and burnt in 1431, and English fortunes were maintained for a while by the faithful lieutenancy of John, Duke of Bedford, the king's uncle and Regent in France, but the defection of the Duke of Burgundy, Philip the Good, in 1435 and the death of Bedford in the same year were the end of English hopes. The rest was a succession of defeats for the demoralised English armies, and expulsion from all except Calais by 1453, while Philip of Burgundy turned his attention to the provinces on his Dutch and German borders.

The Hundred Years War

The Hundred Years War was the classic case of war in the period of 'Gothic Europe', and in some respects it was not an unusual set of events. It would be possible to regard these centuries as the time when Europe was learning to do without fighting as a normal form of life, but war was still endemic, and in some border-areas such as the Pyrenees and Westphalia and northern England it went on more or less all the time. War was the occupation of knights: it was the thing that they were taught and the thing that they were good at. If they were deprived too long of the opportunity to pursue their profession, they became discontented; tournaments and jousting were enjoyed, but they were not a substitute for the real thing, nor were the sporadic raids in which western knights joined with the knights of the Teutonic Order in their 'crusade' against the Slavonic populations ('the heathen') of Lithuania and Russia. Fighting was not a safe activity, but it was not, for the fully armed knight, a very dangerous one, and the prospects of capture were not alarming, since confinement would be comfortable while a ransom was raised. Relations between knights on opposing sides were usually cordial, and they probably felt closer to each other than to the ordinary soldiers on their own side. It was these ordinary soldiers who did the real fighting and got killed in large numbers; many of them were mercenaries, and there were often soldiers from one country, such as Scotland, fighting on both sides. There was usually no systematic policy of wasting a conquered territory, and damage to the economy was localised: there was more to fear when the soldiers were unemployed and would form themselves into 'free companies', marauding gangs preying upon the country-side and demanding protection money.

The monetary aspects of wars such as the Hundred Years War are puzzling. War brought in money, from plunder and ransoms, but this went to a very small segment of the population, and there was no continuing source of revenue such as might come from a peaceably settled conquered territory. It was very costly to wage war, and Edward III bankrupted the Italian banks as well as his own exchequer in trying to cover his expenses. Parliament and the clergy and the people (in so far as they had a voice) were always complaining about the levies that were demanded to pay for the wars. Yet they nearly always paid them, and it has to be acknowledged that economic explanations are not enough to account for the prevalence of war. War was not on the whole profitable, but fighting was popular, and successful wars were very popular indeed. There are many expressions of enthusiasm for the glory of battle and the honours to be won, and the echoes of the romances of chivalry in Froissart's eulogies of the loyalty and comradeship of knights in arms are not hollow.

Yet there remains something unusual about the Hundred Years War. It was in some ways an extraordinary, and extraordinarily lengthy episode in European affairs. France, the most advanced and wealthy country of northern Europe, and the acknowledged power-house of northern European culture, was held to ransom for over a hundred years by a northern kingdom that was smaller and less wealthy, and in many ways culturally dependent on France.

London was by far the largest city of England: its population was about 50,000, and those of the next largest cities, York, Norwich, Bristol, were no more than 8,000. This was in comparison with Paris, where the population was over 100,000, and of course with the several cities of Italy – Genoa, Florence, Venice – which were about the same size as Paris (and, if one were to look further afield, with Baghdad, which had a population of a million at this time, though with admittedly a different relation to the surrounding rural economy). To the French, the constant depredations of the English marauding and invading armies must have appeared in the same light as the Scottish raids and threats of open war appeared to the English (or the Viking invasions, in an earlier century, to all the northern coastlines). The advantage of the English over the French was always a highly centralised monarchy which was able to keep close control over its compact sea-fenced property, and which was able repeatedly to weld the baronial class into unity through the prospect of glory and plunder in wars with the ancient enemy. Hostility to the French was the glue of English national sentiment and was to remain so at least until the Napoleonic wars. The English monarchs also had one great asset over the French in the sphere of war finance, that is, the ability to impose heavy customs duties on the enormously profitable export of raw wool from England to Flanders and other industrial centres.

Spain and Portugal

In the Iberian peninsula, the story of the twelfth century is of the gradual encroachment of the Christian kingdoms of the north upon the Moorish lands to the south and east. The two peoples had continued to live in amity, and indeed with a large Jewish community as well, and though the later thirteenth century saw an increasing hardening of attitudes against both groups, Spain for a long while escaped the intolerance that had begun to show itself against the Jews in other countries, and the great Spanish scholar Raimundo Lulio (Ramon Lull, 1225–1315) was still at the end of his long life trying to maintain a dialogue between Christian, Jewish and Arabic learning.

But the decree of the Fourth Lateran Council of 1215 that Jews must henceforth wear a distinctive form of dress was a sign of change, and persecutions long practised began to increase, particularly in those countries where the Jewish population was small, such as England, from which the Jews were eventually to be totally expelled in 1290. France followed, decreeing the expulsion of its Jews in 1306. In eastern countries such as Poland, Austria, Bohemia and Hungary, where the Jewish population was large, a measure of protection was granted to them by the state (if only so that they could be more successfully exploited as moneylenders, financiers and providers of capital). Spain did not expel its Jews until 1492, the same year that the Moors were made to evacuate Granada, their last stronghold in Spain, and the same year that Spanish colonisation began in the Americas. The intensified persecution of the Jews in the twelfth and thirteenth centuries, scattered and sporadic as it was, was in part a domestic version of the religious exaltation, hatred and greed that inspired the Crusades (riots against the Jews in York in 1190 coincided with the declaration of the Third Crusade), but it was also a means through which a developing apparatus of papal and royal power could articulate itself in opposition to a readily located and demonised 'other'.

The decisive defeat of the Moorish Almohades came at Las Navas de Tolosa, 70 miles east-north-east of Córdoba, in 1212, and Ferdinand III of Castile (1217–52), having united the kingdoms of Castile and León in 1230, seized Córdoba in 1236 and Seville in 1248, leaving only the territory around Granada in Moorish hands (where it stayed until 1492). King James of Aragon (1213–76), who succeeded to the throne at the age of five, began a campaign of reconquest in the east as soon as he was old enough (1227), attacked and seized Mallorca in 1229 and the whole area around Valencia by 1245. The Portuguese meanwhile pushed south and took the last Moorish coast-town in 1249. Resettlement took different forms. Alfonso X ('the Wise') of Castile (1252–84) prided himself on ruling over a multiracial culture, and Aragon, too, open to the east through its great cosmopolitan seaport in Barcelona, did

Table 4: Rulers of Aragon and Castile

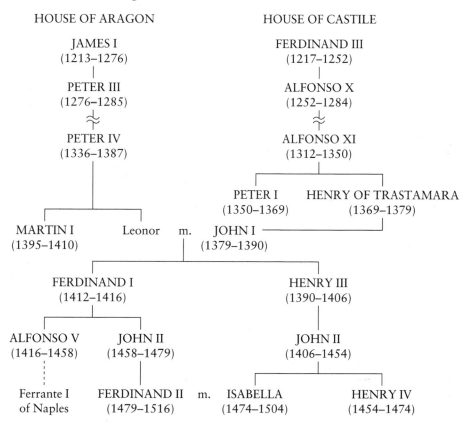

not discourage cohabitation. But in Castile, after Alfonso's death, the Moorish population was gradually dispossessed and driven out, the land reverted to pasture and became sparsely populated, and large areas were given over to a frontier-style ranching economy. The Moors had been better at agriculture, building, trade, textiles and metalwork. They had lived in better houses and finer cities. They had more libraries and were better read. They were better philosophers, physicians, poets, musicians, artists. The Christian attempt to absorb their culture had not been a matter of tolerance but of self-interest. Bigotry and intolerance earned their reward in economic and cultural decline. The great achievement of Castilian culture in the fourteenth century might be thought to be the decision of Pedro the Cruel (Peter I) to order the restorers of the Alcázar in Seville to respect its Mudéjar or Arabic character.

Aragonese involvement in Sicily was a distraction, and the country was particularly severely hit by the Black Death. Catalonian trade plummeted, banks collapsed, and Barcelona, which had been at the peak of its prosperity between 1282 and 1348, went into decline. Economic difficulties created unrest which, as often, vented itself in pogroms against the Jews, which spread across the country in 1391. Castile, meanwhile, prospered in wool and wool-related industries, and did not suffer so much from plague as from the civil wars that followed the death of Alfonso XI in 1350. In the struggle for succession between his legitimate and illegitimate sons, Pedro (Peter) the Cruel and Enrique (Henry) of Trastamara, there was much foreign involvement, as England and France observed what was to become a familiar practice in later centuries, of fighting out their wars on other people's territories. The Black Prince won a brilliant victory for Pedro the Cruel at Najera in 1367, but the French commander Bertrand du Guesclin won a comprehensive and decisive victory for Enrique at Monteil in 1369. Enrique prospered: his attempt to take over Portugal failed, but his successors absorbed Aragon in 1412. John of Gaunt, Duke of Lancaster, married Costanza (Constance), the daughter of Pedro, in 1372 and declared himself King of Castile and León, but his expedition to claim his inheritance in 1387 was a failure. This was not an unusual experience for John of Gaunt, who, though the most powerful man in England for much of his career, was endearingly unsuccessful in most that he attempted. However, his daughter Philippa married King John I of Portugal in 1387, establishing an alliance between the two countries which was to remain loosely in place for many centuries.

Portugal had been formally independent since 1179, when it was perhaps the first compact unified kingdom in Europe. Except during the reign of King Dinis (1279–1325), a poet and patron of learning who made Portuguese the official language, it lay in the shadow of Castile until the accession of the new Aviz dynasty and John I in 1384 and the decisive battle against the Castilian invaders at Aljubarrota in 1385, won with the help of English archers. John I's son became known as Prince Henry the Navigator: he was at Ceuta, in Morocco, when it was taken in 1415, and sent ships to seize Madeira in 1419 and the Azores in 1427. Portuguese ships passed Cape Bojador in West Africa in 1434 and Portugal became for a century or so a world power.

Agriculture, Labour, Famine, Plague

Agriculture was the principal source of wealth (in the form of lands and rents) in the Middle Ages, and arable farming the sole activity of the vast majority of the population. It was a life of grinding subsistence for the peasant-cultivators, and not made easier to bear by the obligations of labour and other services due to manorial lords and of the payment of tithes to the church. Most peasants lived in poverty, or extreme poverty, and a bad harvest meant starvation for many. There were occasional outbreaks of rebelliousness, usually at the imposition of some new tax or at the prospect of some change for the worse in the unbearableness of their condition, but no ferment of continual discontent at oppression and exploitation. The strength of ties of family and community, the general acceptance of social hierarchy and inequality as something ordained by God, the impossibility of perceiving any alternative, as well as the more obviously repressive apparatus available to the lords and landowners, kept society stable.

But the period 1100–1300, particularly in northern Europe, was a time of comparative prosperity, when the margin between subsistence and surplus became slightly broader, that is, when the peasant economy could sustain the lives of families and the exactions to which they were subject and still retain a small surplus for sale on the market. The climate of western Europe was experiencing one of its periodic mild optimums (which was to last till about 1300, when the Baltic Sea started to freeze over again, and a 'Little Ice Age' began), and the different states and regions were settling into a belligerent equilibrium; the days of being perpetually on a war footing against the threat of invasion, by barbarians from the east, or Muslims from the south, or Vikings from the north, were over. So there was much agricultural and economic development, estate improvement, new settlement and population growth all over western and northern Europe in the twelfth and thirteenth centuries. In agriculture, there was the introduction of the iron plough, of the three-field crop-rotation system, and of a new yoke that made it possible to use horses as draft animals and for the transport of heavy materials. Water-mills and windmills sprang up all over the country for the grinding of corn, waterways were made navigable, forest, heath, bog and other marginal land were brought under cultivation. There was new settlement of lands to the east of Germany in Brandenburg, east Prussia and Silesia, and expansion of sheep-farming in the hilly areas of Wales and northern England and northern Spain. Hundreds of little market-towns grew up in England to serve the needs of the thousands of villages and hamlets where the working population lived. Harvests in Europe doubled between 1000 and 1300, and so did the population. England's population more than doubled in the twelfth century and by 1294 it is guessed (guess-work is all that is available) to have reached five-and-a-half million, a level that it did not reach again until Tudor times.

But expansion brought its problems. The yield from marginal lands was not self-sustaining, over-exploitation of land left it exhausted, and productivity was not sufficient to keep pace with the rapidly increasing population. By the end of the thirteenth century there is clear evidence in northern Europe (Italy and Spain are excluded from most of this account) of agricultural depression. There was worse to come. In northern Europe, in the three years 1315–17, there was a succession of fierce winters and bad harvests, followed by a murrain which killed off the draft animals, oxen and horses, which represented such a huge investment for peasants. This was the Great Famine. The usual crop-yield was so small that even a slight reduction was disastrous, and many people died from starvation and in the epidemic of amoebic dysentery that followed the famine, young children and the old first and then the working people. The situation was so bad, and the people so poor, that landowners could not take advantage of the higher prices caused by shortages (there was no one who could pay higher prices) and even had to lower rents if they wanted to get rents at all. There was much social disruption and bad behaviour – theft, disorder, hoarding, speculation.

The Black Death of 1347–49, though it caused much greater loss of life and affected the whole of Europe, was in some respects no more serious in its economic consequences than the Great Famine, and in fact led to something of an economic boom. A boat returning from a Genoese trading post in the Crimea put into the Sicilian port of Messina in October 1347 with a crew of dead and dying men, their bodies swollen and blackened. The mysterious disease that afflicted them, which had already swept through India and the Middle and Near East, spread rapidly from the east via the trading routes that the great Italian mercantile cities of Venice and Genoa maintained with the Levant. So began, in Europe, the outbreak of bubonic plague called in its own day 'the death' or 'the great pestilence', but now commonly referred to as the Black Death. It soon spread to the rest of Europe, and came ashore on the south coast of England in June 1348. There were other outbreaks of plague in subsequent years (every summer brought the threat of plague) but the Black Death was exceptional: in terms of loss of life it was the greatest natural catastrophe ever to strike Europe and Asia.

The disease began with swellings in the groin and armpits and soon the whole body broke out in black blotches and sores. Death usually came after three days, often sooner; few who became infected survived. The bacillus that caused the disease lived in the black rats which came in boats from the east and was transmitted by fleas that the rats carried. The disease was spread by flea-bite or, less commonly, by respiratory infection. A third at least of the population of Europe is estimated to have died, in some places (such as Aragon) more, in some places (such as Bohemia) fewer. Close-knit communities, in-cluding religious communities (53 of 93 monks died at the abbey of Bury St Edmunds) as well as villages, suffered particularly severely, though of course the inevitable association of poverty with poor straw-thatched dwellings and rats put poor people more at risk. Yet death was more of a leveller in 1347–49 than in 1315–17, and the experience (for those who survived) of a totally natural disaster, whose effects were swift and inevitable, was easier to bear than the grinding down and unequal burden of slow starvation. There was no outbreak of debauchery, no breakdown in public order, not even any of the descent into morbidity that later historians thought must be a consequence of such a disaster. On the contrary, there was a renewed sense of the value of the religious life (as a refuge from and consolation for such horrors), an increase in ascetic practice, and a flood of religious endowments.

As for the economy, it received, paradoxically, a boost, and there was for a time, patchily, a greater prosperity for those who survived. The longer-term effects were more complex, and will be treated in Chapter Four. The general economic effect of the Black Death was to loosen manorial ties by encouraging estate workers to go off in search of the higher wages which were now available because of the shortage of labour. Employers and landowners tried to resist these developments, and to restrict mobility and wages, and these oppressive restraints were triggers for popular revolt in France (the Jacquerie of 1358) and England (the Peasants' Revolt of 1381), but they had in the end no choice. The labour market was becoming more powerful than the webs of customary obligation that had characterised the old manorial economy, and the already increasing practice of commuting estate services for money rents assisted in the process. While wages rose because of the shortage of labour, prices fell, and then stabilised, because of the surplus in production. The acreage under cultivation shrank, but it was the best land that remained, only the marginal land which had been ploughed during the days of overpopulation being aban- doned. The proportion of arable land shrank, and much more land was given over to viticulture (in the south) and stock-raising to cater for the expanding urban populations. The Black Death did not cause all these changes – they had been taking place before – but it did accelerate them and consolidate their effects.

Trade and Industry

The profits from agricultural lands and rents were the traditional income of the landowning ruling class. Such profits were reliable and stable, but neither quickly arrived at nor readily convertible into cash. Trade was much the more conspicuous agent of economic growth, therefore, in the Middle Ages, and to a lesser extent industry. The expansion of trade in these centuries is spectacular, nowhere more so than in the Mediterranean, where by 1300 Venice had state- run galleys sailing to the Black Sea, Syria, Egypt, Tangier, Marseilles and Barcelona. Genoa was not far behind. The ports in the eastern Mediterranean were outlets for the export of fine Levantine fabrics – damask (from Damascus), muslin (from Mosul), gauze (from Gaza) – and also staging-posts for the large overland trade from the east in silks and spices and slaves (there were still slaves in Florence and Venice, and Genoa counted 2,000 slaves in a census of 1458, nearly all of them women from the Levant used as household servants). Marco Polo was not the only Venetian to travel to China, though he stayed there longer than most (fifteen years, from 1275 to 1290, at the court of the Mongolian Emperor Kublai Khan in Peking, called then Khambalik); trade was an even more compelling motive than curiosity, and during this century of the 'Mongolian peace' (c.1250–c.1350) traders penetrated further east than ever before.

Developments in late medieval maps were chiefly the product of the needs of trade, and had little to with any more abstract or intellectual desire to 'know' about the world. Cassiodorus in the sixth century had valued cosmography because it enabled one to locate places named in the scriptures, and Roger Bacon, in the early thirteenth century, still argued for geographical knowledge as necessary to the conversion of pagans as well as for trade. Medieval maps such as the thirteenth-century Hereford Map (in Hereford cathedral) remained theoretical propositions about the ordering of God's creation; the only maps that provided near-exact outlines of coasts – that are at all like modern maps – were the 'portolans' or navigational maps carried by medieval sea-travellers, with every inlet, islet and haven marked. The *Travels of Sir John Mandeville*, written in French in the mid-fourteenth century, and one of the most widely known and translated books of the later Middle Ages (Columbus carried a copy on his journey to find 'the Indies'), reflects these different ideas of travel, being itself derived from books (the author, if he existed, never left his library) that provide just that mixture. It is at once a goggle-eyed catalogue of the marvels of the east (Amazons, anthropophagi, pygmies, people with one eye, or with no head and their eyes in their shoulders, or with a face but no facial features, or with ears that hang down to their knees, or with an upper lip so large it can act as a sun-shade) and also a compendium of practical information about pilgrim-routes and pilgrim-places, with a summary of the main tenets of the Muslim faith, perfectly dispassionately presented.

Much of the business of the Italian cities was entrepôt trading and banking, but Florence had a large cloth-making industry, and Milan and the cities of the Po valley developed specialised and high-class textile manufactures. Italy was at the centre too of technological development. Fine glass for tableware and windows was manufactured in Italy, and spectacles (eye-glasses) were first invented in Tuscany in the 1280s, the advance upon lenses, which had been in use for some time, being not so much in the science of optics as in the technology of glass-making. Now one could read for a lifetime, and the market for books increased. Paper was first manufactured on any scale in the west at Fabriano in 1276 (though it was in Moorish Spain by 1150 and across the French border in Hérault in 1189), and both supply and demand expanded dramatically in the fourteenth century. The growth of the cloth industry saw a vast increase in the consumption of cloth, especially linen-cloth for shirts, underclothes, sheets, towels, handkerchiefs (introduced into England by Richard II, it is said) and napkins; the throw-outs made linen rags, and linen-rags made paper. Another Italian technological innovation was the mechanical clock, which made its first appearance on a church in Milan in 1309 and was perfected in 1364 by Giovanni de' Dondi, a professor at Padua. 'Merchant-time' had to be much more exact than the old 'church-time', told by the tolling of bells at the canonical hours: a bargain might be lost through a missed appointment. Also closely connected with the development of trade and commerce was the introduction of Arabic numerals (by an Italian mathematician) and the invention of double-entry book-keeping (by an Italian accountant). Systems of banking, credit, bills of exchange, marine insurance (why wasn't 'The Merchant of

Venice' insured?), all had to be invented, and it was in the commercial and banking centres of Florence, Siena, Genoa and Lucca that they first came in.

All such trade looked to the south and the sea, and Florence itself acquired a sea-borne trade after the conquests of Pisa (1405) and Leghorn (1421). Milan, however, looked to the north and to the trade on the far side of the Alps that in the thirteenth century followed the overland routes to the great fairs of Champagne at Provins, Troyes, Bar-sur-Aube and Lagny-sur-Marne. These fairs acted as temporary market-places, for a week or a month or two, for a trade that was not yet sufficient to maintain a permanent merchant settlement in any one place. They were conveniently spread through the year and often associated with some famous shrine so as to take advantage of the streams of pilgrims. The Chartres fairs were the largest and most famous, but there were many others situated along the waterways between Provence and the Low Countries, the Rhône, the Saône, the Seine, with easy access to the large centres of population nearby, Nîmes, Lyon, Paris, Beauvais, Arras. To these fairs came Scandinavian furs, English wool, Lombard silks, Spanish leather, Genoese armour and swords, Venetian jewels and laces, German linens, and spices, drugs and dyestuffs from the east. Lesser fairs operated on the same basis in relation to local markets and in other countries.

The development of the Champagne fairs during the twelfth and thirteenth centuries had much to do with the policy of the independent counts of Champagne, who welcomed merchants and guaranteed safe-conduct. They began to decline when Philip IV (Philip the Fair, Philippe le Bel) acquired Champagne in 1284 and introduced a system of taxation. The fairs shifted to the Low Countries, where Bruges and Antwerp became the principal marts of western Europe. Bruges in particular became a great international trade-centre, shipping cloth and wool from England, grain, timber, metals and furs from the Scandinavian countries, wines and spices from the south, and specialised goods like alum, woad and dye-stuffs, essential for the textile industry. Most of the trade began to be carried by sea, and piracy and privateering became another important source of profit. Careful regulations had to be drawn up within what was becoming a large body of 'merchant law' to try to prevent rival merchants operating in league with hired pirates. England was necessarily active in this sea-borne commerce, having established its wool-staple (port licensed with a monopoly on the import and onward trading of English wool) at Calais (sometimes at other Channel ports), but it was a small player in a commerce dominated by Italian, Flemish and German merchant-adventurers. The tenacity of these Italian merchants in pursuing profit in alien northern countries where they were often made extremely unwelcome is remarkable. Italian merchants were expelled from France in 1311 by Philip IV, and two were murdered on the London streets – Nicholas Sardouche in 1371 and Janus Imperial in 1379 – by the hired thugs of their English rivals.

Flanders was the great industrial centre of northern Europe, and cloth-making of all kinds its principal industry. Bruges, Ypres and Ghent (in the north of Flanders) and Lille and Courtrai (in the south) developed during the thirteenth century a fledgling capitalist economy, with a wealthy patriciate of investors, a number of well-organised and powerful guilds of masters, and a large, poorly paid work-force. Arras and Brussels (in nearby Artois and Brabant) shared in the general prosperity, the former especially after the invention by one of its masters of the art-industry of woven tapestry in the 1320s, catering for the luxury trade. Flanders dominated the politics of the region, and foreign countries, England and France, were frequently drawn into its affairs. Philip IV intervened in the long-running civil war (1297–1328) between the patricians and the guilds, but was humiliated by the townsmen at the battle of Courtrai in 1302, much to the glee of the English. The struggle continued under the burgher-leaders Jacob van Artevelde and his son Philip, but the townsmen were finally crushed by Philip of Burgundy at Rooseborke in 1382 with the slaughter of 20,000 Flemish artisans. The Flemish cloth-making industry was already in decline, much of the trade having been taken over by indigenous rural cloth-making centres, for instance in western and northern England.

The trade of northern Europe and the Baltic was dominated by the Hanse, a league of merchants in cities and seaports stretching from Dinant in Brittany to Stockholm, and centring on Lübeck, the most important of the German Baltic ports that formed the nucleus of the league. As they extended their influence eastward during the thirteenth century, the Hanseatic merchants worked closely with the Teutonic Knights, a crusading order vowed to the expulsion of 'the heathen' from Lithuania and Russia. Rostock was incorporated in 1218, Danzig in 1224, and by the end of the thirteenth century the island of Gotland, off the coast of Sweden, and its port of Wisby, had become a great northern market-place and a clearing-house for architectural and decorative styles as well as trade-goods. The power of the Hanse, which was enforced through trade embargoes that could oblige Scandinavian kings to adapt their trading policies to suit the merchants, was well demonstrated in the Treaty of Stralsund (1370), which provided that no Danish king was to be elected by the council of the estates without the approval of the Hanse. Margaret, the daughter of the Danish King Valdemar who made this treaty, united Denmark and Norway (by her marriage to Hakon VI of Norway) when she became regent in 1387, and she invaded and conquered Sweden in 1389. The pan-Scandinavian kingdom set up at the Union of Kalmar in 1397 was a formidable grouping, and seized Gotland in 1409, but beyond that it did not seriously challenge the power of the Hanse.

NOTES

1.   John Ruskin, 'The Nature of Gothic', in *The Stones of Venice* (1851; ed. J.G. Links, New York, 1960).
2.   Charles Muscatine, *Chaucer and the French Tradition: A Study in Style and Meaning* (Berkeley and Los Angeles, 1957), pp. 167–8, quoting Arnold Hauser, *The Social History of Art* (New York, 1951), pp. 272–3.
3.   The next two paragraphs, on the history of 'Gothic', draw especially upon George Henderson, *Gothic* (Harmondsworth, 1967), pp. 179–200.

2

The Social Machinery of Cultural Production: Church, Court and City

There are other imaginable sources for the encouragement and patronage of cultural production in Gothic Europe than the three that will be treated here. 'Popular' culture may seem the most obvious, and the absence of any account of it a serious omission. There is something to say on the subject, but generally speaking it is not until the fifteenth century that popular culture breaks into the record. It is, in its evidences, a late medieval phenomenon, and will be dealt with in a later chapter. For the moment, the church, court and city are the scene.

The Church

THE CHURCH'S POWER AND WEALTH

By the mid-fourteenth century, the church was a gigantic multinational corporation dedicated primarily to the preservation and extension of its own institutional wealth and privileges. It overshadowed everything. It was, first of all, an overwhelming physical presence. In a city, the cathedral would be by far the largest building, and would overtop the next highest building that was not also a church by hundreds of feet. It would be the centre of urban life, commerce and ritual, and its priests and canons and clerks would be a significant and wealthy part of the local population. In the city around, there would be churches in almost every street, and a parish organisation to support them: the city of London, in an area of about a square mile, had about 120 parish churches, while York, with barely a quarter of London's population, had 40.

The church was also a dominating economic presence. In most countries of western Europe it was by far the largest single landowner – in England, a third of the cultivable land was owned by the church – and because of its nature as a permanent institution, without heirs, its landholdings always increased, never decreased. The quality of organisation on a great monastic estate was superior to anything that might be found in the secular sphere: the administrators were all educated men; they had no personal financial ambition to interfere with their ambition for institutional accumulation; and they could plan ahead on the basis of year upon year of secure capital investment. The Cistercian *latifundia* or sheep-ranches of northern England and the Welsh marches were at the heart of the English wool economy and its remarkable prosperity in the thirteenth and fourteenth centuries.

Finally, there was the immense social and mental control that the church exerted over everyone's lives, above all through the parish, the central ecclesiastical institution for most people at most times. The year's and the day's rhythms were organised according to the church's calendar of feast-days and the tolling of its bells. Communion and confession were obligatory at least once a year, and the latter obligation was a means through which the whole mental life of the individual could be supervised. There was no inner life but that which was to be interrogated by the faithful Christian for its sinfulness, and no scintilla of mental activity but was recorded in the book of life to be brought in evidence at the Last Judgement. It was a better system of control than any that might readily be devised, since it manifested itself as a form of social self-discipline and was enforced through an overwhelming fear of damnation rather than through simple clerical coercion.

There were many who inveighed against the worldliness of the church and its apparent commitment to its own economic aggrandisement. The centuries saw a steady and understandable increase in anticlericalism and in hostility to the established order of the church. Churchmen were not, however, specially corrupt: there was almost, indeed, a kind of inevitability about the development of the church as a business operation. Monasteries were built and maintained on the basis of endowments, usually of land: it was vital that those estates should be properly managed and their profits maximised. There was no essential difference between the performance of the *Opus Dei* by singing and chanting day and night in the monastic church and the performance of God's work by riding out to see to the hedging and ditching, drainage and planting of the monastic estates. The notable black (Benedictine) abbots of fourteenth-century England tended to be great managers, like Henry of Eastry at Christ Church, Canterbury, or Thomas de la Mare at St Alban's, rather than pious holy men. But it is easy to see how an observer might wonder whether the special mission of the monastic orders, to act as witnesses to the faith by withdrawing from the world and devoting their lives to praising God, was not in some way compromised. 'How shall the world be served?' says Chaucer's Monk, speaking through Chaucer's ironically mediating voice (*Canterbury Tales*, General Prologue, line 187), and indignantly repudiating the accusation that his hunting and love of fine food constitute a betrayal of the monastic ideal, but in speaking of 'the world' he rather gives the game away.

So it was with the friars, orders founded with the purpose of bringing the Gospel to the poor and the outcast, with brothers of the order living the same lives as those to whom they ministered – mendicant, possessionless, rootless, wandering. In their earlier days they would hold valiantly to these principles, especially those who had been urged on by the example of St Francis: friars would often live in lean-to shanties in slum areas, and affiliations with universities would be refused if they seemed to be offering a regular and well-supported life. But as time went by, endowments inevitably accumulated, and larger and larger churches were built so that friars could carry on their necessary mission of preaching. The Franciscan order entered into excruciating debates, and splintered repeatedly, over the question of the exact kind of absolute poverty which was practised by Christ and to which they were vowed, and it seemed only sensible and practical to most of them to accept a degree of financial stability rather than risk going out of business. So friars were in the market for every financial benefit to be obtained from their profession. People wanted to confess to friars because they were the elite of the priesthood, and also because they would not be there next week, as would the parish priest, to check that the penances they had enjoined had been performed. To offer a contribution to the friars' order was the natural next step, and thereafter it became very difficult to distinguish between a gratuitous charitable gift and a 'payment' for a service so courteously rendered and so painless to the recipient. People wanted friars to perform marriage and burial services; they wanted to be members of the friars' lay fraternities; they wanted to be buried in the grand new mendicant churches. It all cost money, and the friars grew wealthier and wealthier.

Parish priests were unhappy about this, as they watched the sources of their small emoluments drying up because the friars offered a better 'deal', even the tithes which were their right being diverted to their rivals. But they had their opportunities too. Chaucer describes his ideal Poor Parson, in the General Prologue, as one who does not, like so many others, rush off to London and there obtain an easy living saying masses in a chantry chapel for the souls of the rich departed. These chantry chapels (see Fig. 44) were a consequence of one of the church's most successful innovations – the invention of Purgatory. The need for a purgatorial place had been evolving slowly over many centuries as the character of the period between death and Last Judgement became increasingly open to negotiation, but the first use of the word *purgatorium* to designate a place of punishment is in 1170 in Petrus Comestor, and the first important dogma concerning purgatorial or cleansing punishment after death was declared in 1274. It is an innovation that could be construed as an attempt to temper the harshness of the church's eschatology of sin and punishment and to offer the hope that there would be some place of purgatorial preparation for heaven after death which would not be so hard to qualify for as heaven (limbo, also invented in the twelfth century, could likewise be seen as a kindly refuge for miscarried and aborted foetuses). But it was also, as it turned out, a money-maker on a vast scale, because now priests could be paid fees to say masses for the soul in purgatory so as to expedite its progress and shorten its time of pain. So many masses, so many fewer years of future pain for oneself or present pain for a dead father or mother. Hence the proliferation of chantry chapels in the fourteenth century, and the increase in the private ownership of church space.

Another innovation was the introduction of indulgences. By the thirteenth century, Christ and his saints, it was decided, had built up an enormous 'treasury of merit' and it was possible to draw on this budgetary surplus of goodness so as to grant to people who were truly sorry for their sins some remission or reduction of physical penance such as might normally be imposed – fasting, vigils, self-flagellation, barefoot pilgrimage, whatever it might be. The idea of indulgences, which was like transferring money from an inexhaustible deposit account to a permanently overdrawn current account, quickly caught on, and received a great boost when Pope Boniface VIII declared 1300 a jubilee year and granted a plenary indulgence – complete remission of the penance due for sins – to everyone going on pilgrimage to Rome in a proper state of penitence. Now, agents were to go round distributing these indulgences to any they found to be properly contrite; if the beneficiaries wished to make a charitable contribution to the work of the church, well and good. But the agents came to be called 'pardoners' and it was inevitable that ordinary people would begin to think that offering money was the means to obtain an indulgence. The pardoners, who had an eye to personal profit as well as the swelling of the church's coffers, were not quick to disabuse them. They began indeed to claim that they could offer, not just remission of penance by indulgence, but pardon for sins committed, and even to pretend, like Chaucer's Pardoner, that they could grant, for money, the equivalent of plenary absolution. It was a very successful scam because it was so satisfactory to all the parties involved – the church, the pardoner and the ordinary person. Everyone was happy, except presumably God, and in the end certainly Martin Luther, who was finally pushed into indignant objection when Pope Julius II, anxious to raise the money to meet the soaring costs of the rebuilding of St Peter's in Rome, sent John Tetzel round the cities of Europe claiming to grant pardons not only for sins committed but for sins that the recipient might commit in the future.

THE CHURCH: INSTITUTIONALIZATION, REFORM AND CHANGE

These were the very obvious ulcers on the body of a church which for centuries commanded the loyalty of the vast body of believers. The medieval church's success in this is much more remarkable than its eventual fragmentation. What had made its success possible was its capacity, as an institution, to absorb and channel the periodic waves of fervour and desire for the true apostolic life, the true *imitatio Christi*, that are the history of religion in these centuries. The process of absorption and canalisation begins before our period, in the great Cluniac reforms of the Benedictine order in the tenth century, then in the papal reforms of the eleventh century under Pope Gregory VII (1073–85), and most significantly in the Cistercian movement of the twelfth century (the order was founded at Cîteaux, in Burgundy, in 1098). In each case, a renovation from within offered a renewed energy and conviction to the belief that the church was holding to its mission. The Cistercian monks rejected pomp and wealth and the world, went out into the wilderness to establish their new communities, devoted a portion of their time to manual labour, and stripped their churches of extraneous ornament. There were resentments of course: the older Benedictine orders took time to become accustomed to their upstart brothers, and St Bernard, the charismatic and powerful promoter of the Cistercian order, made many enemies. But for a time, the Cistercians, and attendant smaller orders of monks and canons (Carthusian, Premonstratensian, Victorine), seemed to offer, on this earth, the answer to the young man's question to Christ, 'What shall I do that I may possess eternal life?' (Matthew 19:16).

By 1153, the Cistercians had 350 houses all over Europe; by 1270 they had 671. In 1200 the order was still in its golden age, but as endowments poured in and estates accumulated and churches grew larger, it became increasingly locked into the economic order. It was the friars who now took over the spearheading of the church's spiritual mission and who now bore most urgent witness to its truth. The message of St Francis (1181–1226) was not an easy one for the church to absorb, and in many ways he was an uncomfortable reminder that the Christ of the gospels was not at all like his representatives now on earth. Francis was born Giovanni Bernardone, son of a wealthy cloth-merchant, but he rejected his father and his wealth in a spectacular ceremony, and offered a revolutionary alternative to the money-grabbing that was taking over so many lives and making so many of the poor poorer: Christ's ministers should imitate Christ in their lives and be like his apostles in going forth without bag or baggage to beg their bread and minister to all who were needy. Christians should behave like Christ. The simplicity of his summons was irresistible, and a new religious order of 'Little Brothers' or 'Friars Minors' (*Fratres Minores*) was established in 1210, with a final revised written rule approved by Pope Honorius III in 1223. By 1282 the Franciscans had 1,583 houses all over Europe. Another order of friars was founded in 1217 by St Dominic (d. 1221), the 'Friars Preachers' (*Fratres Praedicantes*), with a preaching and teaching mission and a particular responsibility for the extirpation of heresy (whence their nickname, *Domini-canes*, 'the bloodhounds of the Lord'). The Carmelite and Augustinian (Austin) friars followed soon after.

Sustained in its spiritual mission by these waves of fervour, the church was at the same time establishing itself as the institution that has come to be thought of and taken for granted as 'the medieval church'. Canon law had been codified by Gratian (*c*.1140), the universities had started up as great engines for the production of biblical commentary and theology, and papal power was at its peak. Pope Innocent III, the greatest of medieval popes (1198–1216), was himself no theologian: his immensely popular *De miseria conditionis humanae* ('Concerning the misery of the human condition') is a stale, sour and shallow piece of contempt-of-the-world propaganda, written in 1195 and designed to advance the claims to papability of the then Lotario dei Segni. But he was the first pope to state explicitly that he stood as Peter's successor and Christ's lieutenant and that all the princes of the world owed him homage. Towards the end of his pontificate, he called a council whose mission was to eliminate heresy, reinforce the faith, reform morals, uproot vice, and establish virtue, truth and universal peace. In the decrees of his Fourth Lateran Council of 1215 and in other administrative measures introduced by himself and his energetic successors Gregory IX (1227–41) and Innocent IV (1243–54), the church became what it was to be. Celibacy was strictly imposed for the first time on the priesthood, the number of sacraments was fixed at seven, the mass was put in its final form, the articles of faith were established as dogmas that must be believed, communion and confession were made compulsory for all Christians.

All these moves could be understood as ways of improving the spiritual state of the Christian community; but they are also the means through which the church's power over that community was articulated. Orthodoxy must be defined in the most absolute way, not so much because it *matters*, theologically, as because the rooting-out of unorthodoxy, defined as what the church has defined it to be, offers an immediate and practical and generally tolerated means of exercising authority. Where in the twelfth century there had been public debates between Christians and Cathars or between Christian and Jews (Maimonides, the outstanding Hebrew scholar of the west, died as late as 1204), now there was the Albigensian crusade to exterminate the Cathars (*Albigenses*, 'people of Albi'), the increasing persecution of the Jews, the first burnings of heretics. The university-trained clerical elite, meanwhile, became separated from the clerical proletariat (the vast mass of parish priests and clerks), and the clergy as a whole became separated from the lay community. The priest now turned his back on the people at the consecration of the host, so that the eucharist became more of a priestly mystery than a shared communion. The mass was said in a tongue that few of the lay congregation could understand, and translation of the scriptures was discouraged or forbidden. Only the priests could interpret the scriptures; truly, the priesthood constituted 'the church'.

These developments were under way in the thirteenth century, and even before his death there are signs that St Francis was disappointed at the way his new order was becoming entangled in the affairs of bishops and universities. The conflict between the Spirituals (advocates of strict adherence to the rule of poverty) and the Conventuals began as early as 1230 with the disagreement over the building of the great Franciscan double church (upper and lower) at Assisi, a spiritual citadel that Francis might have wanted torn down immediately as a point of principle. But the friars nevertheless retained their reputation as the spiritual vanguard of Christendom for much of the thirteenth century, and contributed in a major way, the Franciscans especially, to the development of affective devotion.

A movement had begun as early as the twelfth century to concentrate the thoughts of Christians less on the legalistic framework of the doctrine of the Atonement (such as the 'trick' that must be played on Satan through the Incarnation so as to circumvent his legal claim to man's soul after the Fall) than on the debt of love and gratitude that man owed to Christ for his voluntary loving sacrifice on the Cross. The movement was associated with a greater emphasis on the intrinsic value of human feeling – when it was directed towards the right ends – in the theology of St Bernard. Images of the Crucifixion began to take on a more pathetic air, as Christ's body, instead of standing four-square with the feet separately nailed on little platforms, slumped realistically from the suspending nails into a poignant S-curve and was then incorporated into more extravagant dramas of grief and pain (Figs 1, 2, 3 and 4). Language

Figure 1: Stuttgart, Württembergische Landesbibliothek MS Bibl.fol. 23 (the Stuttgart Psalter), fol. 27r. North French, *c*.820–30.

The older form of Crucifixion picture: Christ is crucified with four nails, almost appearing to stand upon the cross, with eyes wide open and arms calmly extended as if in triumph. Crucifixion pictures appear in psalters because of the typological reading of the psalms as prefigurations of the life of Christ. The text here is Psalm 22:18, 'They divide my garments among them [*diuiserunt sibi uestimentum meum*, in the text above, from Vulgate Psalm 21:19] and for my raiment they cast lots', cf. Matt.27:35. This scene is shown in the lower part of the picture. The lion and the unicorn are from a later verse of the same Psalm (22:21). The Roman soldier on the left is the centurion of Mark 15:39.

Figure 2: Oxford, All Souls College MS 6 (the Amesbury Psalter), fol. 5r. English, *c*.1250.

The Crucifixion here is a more emotional scene of human suffering. Christ's head lolls to one side, his eyes are closed, he hangs from the cross, blood trickles from his wounds, and the feet are nailed with one nail, more painfully, together. Yet the emotion is contained, and there is a serenity in the formal grieving poses of the Virgin and St John. The cross is represented as a tree, with a lopped branch as the cross-piece. Above, God the Father holds the Holy Spirit. To the left is the Church and to the right the Synagogue, cast down by Christ's victory on the cross; below, Adam rises from the tomb, revivified by Christ's blood trickling down from the cross.

Figure 3: London, BL MS Add.38116 (the Huth Psalter), fol. 11v. English, *c*.1285.
In this more developed Crucifixion picture, Christ's suffering is emphasised, for the purposes of affective meditation, by showing the three nails being hammered in simultaneously with the forcing onto his head of the crown of thorns, the piercing of his side (Longinus, the blind soldier who wielded the lance, according to the story in the Apocrypha, is shown pointing to the eye cured by the miraculous blood that spurts from Christ's side), and the holding up of the sponge with vinegar. Christ's body slumps in the 'Gothic' S-curve, and there is further drama in the eager and ugly faces of the onlookers (the dark faces and hooked noses are characteristic of contemporary representation of Jews). Yet the Virgin and St John remain comparatively serene.

and images lingered upon this suffering humanity, and the cult of the Virgin, which was not new, was intensified so as to provide a witness for Christ's tender babyhood (in nativity scenes) and humanity. A Madonna and Child of the pre-Gothic period shows the child seated on the lap of the Virgin but otherwise unattached to her, as she gazes intently before her, out of the picture, regardless of her son, meditating on the mystery of which she is part and the prophecy which has come to pass (Fig. 5). In the fourteenth century she becomes more human, radiant with maternal pride, entwining gazes with her son and some-times visited by even more touching displays of feeling (Fig. 6).

It was a Franciscan author, though not the famous scholar St Bonaventure (d. 1274) to whom it was deeply indebted and long attributed, who compiled in about 1340 the *Meditationes vitae Christi* (Meditations on the life of Christ), an enormously influential work, translated and adapted into many languages, in which the whole life of Christ is told as the story of a man who lived as a man and suffered all that a man could suffer. The detailed, realistic and largely uncanonical account of the Crucifixion, in which every necessary circumstance of the lengthy process of events leading up to the terrible torment on the Cross is elaborately and graphically laid before us, is the climax of the work. It was the source-text for much late medieval devotion to the humanity of Christ, and provided the materials for the representation of the Passion in the mystery plays.

Devotion of this kind, with its debt to the Franciscans, drew in many holy lives in the later Middle Ages, but it was mainly a form of private devotion, fostered by the church as a kind of piety that would not interfere, as St Francis had threatened to do, with the imperative of institutional consolidation and expansion. The movement towards renovation, the urge to return to the pristine state (*ad pristinum statum ire*), had again been absorbed, contained, channelled. But it was now exhausted, and the mendicant orders were mired in scandal and controversy: jealousy of their success, fear of their influence, disillusion at their worldliness and their betrayal of their high ideals, combined to create a powerful anti-mendicant movement in which they were vilified as the arch-conspirators of Antichrist against the church. They were Satan's 'fifth column'. And by this time the church had lost whatever flexibility it had had to make part of itself these cyclic movements towards renewal and reform. There were a series of such movements in the fourteenth century, but they were pushed out to the edges of the church's life where they could embarrass no one, or else were expelled altogether.

Figure 4: Rogier van der Weyden, Calvary Triptych. Altarpiece (central panel 102 × 70 cm). Vienna, Kunsthistorisches Museum. Netherlands, *c.*1430–40.

An example of a late medieval Crucifixion, with a fully humanised Christ shown in the midst of his suffering within a complexly articulated landscape scene. The realness of the scene (contradicted only by the airborne angels) reinforces the emotional identification of the observer with the realness of Christ's suffering. St John and the Virgin look on in grief; the donor pair kneel on the other side. In the wings are St Mary Magdalen and St Veronica.

Figure 5: Vich, Museo Arqueológico Artistico Episcopal. Virgin and Child, from an altar-frontal. Spain, twelfth century, first half.

The Virgin, seated within a mandorla supported by four angels, gazes intently before her, out of the picture, as does the infant Jesus, both rapt in contemplation of the mystery of which they are part. There is no human contact between them.

Figure 6: The Virgin and Child, donated to the church of Saint-Denis by Jeanne d'Evreux, Queen of France, in 1339. Silver-gilt. Height (including base) 69 cm. Now in the Louvre.

The Madonna poses in an elegant S-curve, and the infant Jesus reaches his hand out affectionately to touch her face. She stands upon a pedestal engraved with an inscription relating to the donor and with various scenes from the lives of Mary and Christ. This little statuette is one of the high points of the Parisian goldsmith's art in three-dimensional Gothic.

The church was now a different kind of organism, its character made newly transparent in the Avignon papacy of 1309–78. It was not only an elaborately bureaucratised institution in itself but, by the fourteenth century, fully integrated, through its officers, in the administrative and bureaucratic systems of the state. The increasing apparatus of government and the burgeoning civil service needed educated men, and it was the church that provided them. Bishops in particular, with the unique authority that they wielded throughout Western Christendom, became the essential hinges between church and state. In England, where there were so few bishops (seventeen) compared with France and Italy, and the few that there were therefore so comparatively wealthy, this was above all true. Where in the thirteenth century most bishops in England were still monks and scholars, by the mid-fourteenth century more than half of them had trained in canon law and held administrative posts in the government. This was partly due to the powerful influence of Pope John XXII (1316–34), who favoured canonists as bishops rather than theologians and who kept a sharp watch, throughout Europe, on episcopal appointments (which he of course had to approve). Archbishops of Canterbury, too, tended less to be men renowned for their piety and dedication to the church's spiritual mission than servants of the state, much involved in day-to-day politics, like Thomas Arundel (archbishop 1396–1414) and Henry Chichele (1414–43). The close ties of church and state are evident too in appointments at lower levels. In England, a promising bureaucrat would be appointed to a benefice not so that he could perform the attached priestly office but so that he could receive the emolument and so save the government money. If the benefice were worth £50 a year, the state could pay the holder perhaps an extra £5 a year and meanwhile the office could be discharged to a vicar for £5 a year. The holder of the benefice, being a member of the clergy, would now avoid normal forms of taxation. A valued public servant could hold a number of these benefices as a 'pluralist', much as a modern businessman holds directorships of several companies. In France it was less easy to be provided to a benefice in such a way, and a lot of anticlericalism came from embittered clerics who had taken government jobs and were poor. In England, though, it made for a dangerous harmony of church and state.

This is the framework in which the rise of mysticism and the spread of heresy might be seen. Of the evidences of these developments in the later Middle Ages, there will be more to be said later.

THE UNIVERSITIES

'University' is a rather misleading term if we apply it in its well-developed and well-defined modern sense to the amorphous groupings of the Middle Ages. But if we understand it to mean gatherings of teachers and students who get together so that the former can impart instruction to the latter and give them degrees to prove that they have absorbed it, we shall not be so far misled. Universities began as gatherings of masters and their students, setting themselves up independently of the monastic and cathedral schools which had a virtual monopoly on higher level education up till 1150. The first university, if we exclude the professional schools of law and medicine in Italy, was at Paris, which came into existence in the late twelfth century as masters and students gradually detached themselves from the cathedral school of Notre Dame. The subjects of study were the seven liberal arts – grammar, logic, rhetoric, arithmetic, astronomy, geometry and music – and then, after admission to the degree of master of arts, theology and canon law. The university was the training-ground for the elite who would go into the church, whether as priests, canonists or administrators, into law, or into lay administration. Whatever the final vocation, theology was the dominant discipline, and every student was a clerk in minor orders or in the making.

The organisation at Paris was loose and fissiparous, and Oxford's first growth probably came from an exodus from Paris in 1167, just as Cambridge began with a migration from Oxford in 1209. At first there were just dining-halls, hostels and hired lecture-rooms at Oxford, but the first colleges (University, Balliol, Merton) were founded in the thirteenth century, followed by Exeter (1314), Oriel (1324–26) and Queen's (1341), while at Cambridge, which was always less important than Oxford during the Middle Ages, the only thirteenth-century foundation, Peterhouse, was succeeded by King's Hall (c.1316), Michaelhouse (1324, later absorbed in Trinity College), Clare (1326), Pembroke (1347), Gonville Hall (1349) and Trinity Hall (1350). A migration to Stamford in 1334 by a group of Oxford masters ('the Stamford secession') was suppressed with the help of the crown – perhaps one answer to the question as to why there were only two universities in England in the Middle Ages, and yet three in Scotland and fifteen in France. There were, it is true, cathedral schools at London (St Paul's), Salisbury, Exeter and Lincoln offering a range of university-level courses.

So too in France, a number of 'universities' were at most *ad hoc* conglomerations of faculties. At Orléans, for instance, there was a law school and a school of arts, grammar and rhetoric, while Montpellier, in the extreme south, was famous for its school of medicine, at which both Arabs and Jews taught, at least until the end of the thirteenth century. In Italy, where there was a long tradition of secular education, the Parisian model did not pertain. Bologna was established in the twelfth century by students who paid teachers so that they might acquire the means to a lucrative and prestigious career. It was the greatest university in Europe for the teaching of law, both civil or Roman law, from the code of Justinian, and canon law, as codified in the encyclopaedic *Decretum* of Gratian (c.1140) and the additional *Decretals* of successive popes. Italy had a host of other smaller 'universities', some of them no more than municipal schools of law, like the Inns of Court in London, but some famous, like Padua, which was founded by an exodus from Bologna in 1222 and became notable as a centre of Aristotelian and independent thought: a Jew was given a doctorate in medicine there in 1409. In the south there was the medical school at Salerno, the most famous in Europe, open to some extent to the much more advanced medical science of the Arabs. Spain was exceptional in its universities in that all the early ones were royal foundations, endowed from the ecclesiastical contributions to the king's exchequer: Palencia (1208–9) and Valladolid (*c*.1250) in Castile; Salamanca (*c*.1227–28) in León, raised to the greatest university in Spain by the endowments of Alfonso X (the Wise) of Castile in 1254, after León had been absorbed into Castile; Lérida (1300) in Aragon; Lisbon (1290, moved to Coimbra in 1308–09) in Portugal. Germany looked mostly to Paris and northern Italy, but there were many new foundations in the later fourteenth century – Prague (1348), Cracow (1364), Vienna (1365), Erfurt (1379), Heidelberg (1385) and Cologne (1388).

At Paris, to which most great masters found their way at some point in their career, the theological curriculum set the framework for the rest of Europe. It was gradually put in order and systematised during the late twelfth century, especially by Stephen Langton (d. 1228), who later became Archbishop of Canterbury and was the opponent of King John. But the coming of the friars transformed both Paris and Oxford (and led to much controversy between them and the secular masters). The Dominicans opened a *studium generale* at Paris in 1229 and the Franciscans followed in 1231, and they proceeded to establish biblical study and theology on much firmer ground by systematising annotations and glosses. This was particularly the work of the Dominicans Hugh of St Cher and Albertus Magnus, who taught at Paris in 1245–48. Alexander of Hales, an Englishman who was the greatest Paris master of his time, became a Franciscan in 1238 as the order swept Paris. In Oxford the friars gave the same powerful impetus to learning. The secular master Robert Grosseteste (his name, surprisingly, does not refer to the size of his head), later Bishop of Lincoln, was the master of the Franciscan school at Oxford and also for a while chancellor of the university. He made moves to strengthen scriptural understanding through the study of Hebrew and Greek and of science. The Franciscan Roger Bacon, who taught at Paris in 1240–47 as well as at Oxford, was very active in denouncing the irrational and unscientific nature of traditional scholarship, though without putting much that was solid in its place.

The translations into Latin of the Arabic texts of Aristotle, and of the commentaries on his works by Arabic scholars such as Avicenna and Averroes, put Christian thinkers to a new task of bringing theology and biblical interpretation into conformity with the principles of rational thought. Things needed explaining. The Dominican Thomas Aquinas, who taught at Paris in 1252–59, was the scholar who had the greatest confidence in the capacity of the mind to build a bridge from reason to faith, and he showed this confidence in academic debate by encouraging his students to offer questions of their own ('quodlibets', from Latin *quodlibet*, 'what you will') for *disputatio*. Of course, we may presume that such freedom of the intellect was under the necessary constraint of arriving at answers that were consonant with the faith – a *quodlibet* on the question of the existence of God or the immortality of the soul was unlikely to come up with a negative conclusion – but the advance in intellectual respectability was very great. There is also a serene good sense about Aquinas which is perennially refreshing. 'Thou shalt not boil a kid in the milk of his dam' (Exodus 23:19) was a text that frustrated traditional commentators. It had absolutely no useful literal meaning for the Christian: it was absurd, and typological allegory had to be fetched from afar to come to the rescue. St Augustine explained it as a prophecy that Christ would not die in the Slaughter of the Innocents, but later commentators were reluctant to throw overboard the literal sense so completely. It was a matter of hygiene, explained the Jewish scholar Maimonides; it was out of concern for the animal's feelings, suggested Aquinas, amiably enough.

Aquinas was entranced by the Aristotelian metaphysic of matter and form (things have material being as the materialisation of an informing form – a kind of metaphysical DNA), and he tried to develop from it a more sophistic-ated account of the relation of the body and the soul ('the soul, as pure form, actualizes the body as its matter from the first moment of its creation') and a metaphysic of the unity of forms. This was too much for less refined intellects: it seemed to make the soul an intellective principle, which was hard to square with Christ's teaching. Aquinas's opinions were also too close for comfort to those of Siger of Brabant, who taught at Paris in 1260–69 and who truly seemed to promote the autonomy of reason. Consequently 219 theses, mostly Siger's but including a few by Aquinas, were condemned by the ecclesiastical authorities of the university of Paris in 1270. Aquinas left Paris for good and died soon after (1274); condemnation of Thomism was not revoked until 1325.

What his successors tried to do was to preserve some freedom for intellec-tual enquiry and a rational metaphysics by declaring certain kinds of question to be off-limits. The Franciscan John Duns Scotus (taught at Paris in 1303–08) liberated scholastic philosophy (but in the process destroyed its reason for existence) by reducing the number of truths of the faith – like the doctrine of the immortality of the soul – that could be proved by natural reasoning. Only faith was pleasing to God on such matters, and faith sufficed. William of Ockham (d. 1349), who studied at Paris and taught at Oxford from 1318 before he was summoned to Avignon in 1324 to answer for his views, went further. He denied all contact between the speculative mind and the world of non-material being: the mind can only deal with what it perceives, and ab-stract concepts exist therefore only as words, mere names. The rigour of his reasoning got him into trouble, partly because the placing of God outside the mind's terms of reference seemed, paradoxically, to give a more central role to human consciousness: it was all there was, apart from blind faith. Ockham's views were condemned in 1337, after he had fled from Avignon in 1328 to live under the protection of the Emperor in Munich, but there was no going back to the pure Thomist synthesis once the new epistemology of signs had separated philosophy from theology. There remained some small area of free operation for natural philosophy as a form of science, such as was exploited by Ockham's fellow-exile in Munich, Marsilius of Padua, with his secularist political philosophy (in the *Defensor pacis*), or by Nicholas Oresme (d. 1382), Bishop of Lisieux, who attacked astrology and translated Aristotle's scientific works into French.

But all orthodox theology could do now was to try to contain the virus that Scotus and Ockham had released. There was no longer any rational basis for faith, only the necessity of faith and the acceptance of the unknowability of God in his arbitrary and absolute omnipotency. God must be free: there is nothing in man's power of reason to prove that he is fair, just and reasonable. 'Nominalism', as it was called (words are mere names), as opposed to Realism (the mind has access to non-material realities), dominated and generally sterilised late medieval thinking. It opened the door to fideism, and the readiness to test faith by multiplying dogmas that were offensive to reason; to a retreat into the ecstatic oblivions of mysticism (as in the English *Cloud of Unknowing*) and the emotional transports of affective devotion; and to a good deal of anxiety on the part of thoughtful writers like Chaucer and Langland about the precise capacities that were left to be allowed to human free-will.

RELIGIOUS WRITING

The local church was by far the largest building that most people would encounter, and the only 'work of architecture'; the things it contained – sculptured figures, carvings, paintings, stained glass, gold and silver altar-vessels and reliquaries, embroidered vestments – were the only 'works of art' they would know. Almost everything beautiful that was made was made in the service of religion or using religious subjects. In addition to churches and their contents, religion also provided the doctrinal subject-matter, the narratives and the imagery, and sometimes the means of production, for books of hours and psalters, devotional objects, paintings and icons, alabasters and ivories, for the use of layfolk. All such works and works of art will receive attention later, in Chapter Three, but for the moment it is the overwhelming importance of the church in written culture that will be the subject.

The church no longer had a virtual monopoly on writing, as it had in the pre-1200 monastic era, and commercial scribes and workshops gradually took over much of the work of manuscript-production, but the vast mass of writing that was produced was always to do with religion. Pretty well every piece of secular vernacular writing from the Middle Ages has been conned exhaustively, and much of the religious writing in the vernacular has been studied, but meanwhile the libraries of Europe bulge still with unpublished and unstudied religious writings in Latin: theological expositions, biblical commentaries and glosses and postills (continuous glosses with text-*loci* inserted) – many of these surviving in the form of students' lecture notes (*reportationes*) – tracts, treatises, biblical paraphrases, sermons, preaching manuals, collections of preaching *exempla*, saints' lives, penitentials, manuals of confession, *summae, quaestiones, distinctiones* (concordances of key-words).

It is difficult to find any form of writing, even in the vernacular, where the church and the clergy have not left their traces. A poet in the throes of unrequited sexual passion will beg his lady for mercy and pray for grace in the manner enjoined upon the penitent, while a hymn in praise of the Virgin Mary will appropriate in a startling manner the imagery of sexual desire. A poem will begin in the manner of a *chanson d'aventure* (song about something that happened by chance) with the speaker going forth alone into the country so that he may make complaint to his beloved, but it is not long before it becomes clear that his beloved is the Virgin Mary. A woman speaker will appropriate the discourse of sexual love in the same way to express her devotion to Christ. Chivalric romances, whilst ostensibly dedicated to secular aristocratic rites of passage and tests of value, are full of priests, hermits and confessors, and the Grail is introduced into the monastic redaction of the Arthurian cycle of romances so as to make explicit the nothingness of secular chivalry in relation to the quest for spiritual truth. Even in the *fabliaux*, coarse comic tales of sexual intrigue among the bourgeoisie and petty bourgeoisie such as gave great delight to the French courts and to the sophisticated audiences of Boccaccio and Chaucer, the clever trickster will usually be a clerk, or friar, or student-clerk, and the surroundings of the tale will be full of signs of the church's presence. When Nicholas and Alison, in Chaucer's Miller's Tale, have managed to get her jealous husband out of the way and jump into bed together, their nocturnal progress is punctuated by the tolling of the bells in the local friary, calling the brothers to their early morning prayers.

Classical writings, being themselves pre-Christian or non-Christian, might seem to be exempt from this universal clericalisation, but it gave great pleasure to medieval exegetes to find a Christian meaningfulness even in writings that were non-Christian. Virgil was almost an honorary proto-Christian because of the interpretation of his prophecy in *Eclogue IV* of a new age under Augustus and the birth of a certain *parvus puer* as a foretelling of the birth of Christ. The classical gods and goddesses were either euhemerised (interpreted as primitive deifications of real persons who once lived) or allegorised as representations of various kinds of human predisposition (lecherousness in Venus, or aggressiveness in Mars, for instance) or treated as personifications of the influences exerted upon human lives by the planets of the same names. Ovid's *Metamorphoses* was widely read – the least Christian text one could imagine – but commonly in the allegorised form of the *Ovide moralisé*, where the stories mostly became how-not-to warnings against the indulgence of inordinate or disordered desire.

The Italians became classicisers before anyone else (which is another way of saying that the 'Renaissance' began early in Italy), and Boccaccio's *Teseida* (completed 1339–41) is a full-scale twelve-book classical epic of Theseus, with the epic motifs and supernatural apparatus of Virgil and Statius and all the appearance of a meaningless charade. It is noteworthy that when Chaucer adapted Boccaccio's poem as his Knight's Tale he removed much of the classicising allusion and treated the gods as planetary influences, integrating the poem not into a Christian universe but into a moral, stoic, Boethian universe deliberately made compatible (as was the fifth-century stoic *Consolation of Philosophy* of the Christian Boethius upon which he drew) with Christianity. So profound was Chaucer's immersion in the mentality of the Christian faith that it was apparently impossible for him to conceive of a world that was meaningful and that was not at the same time Christian. When he came to write *Troilus and Criseyde*, likewise set in pre-Christian times, he could not forebear giving to Troy's inhabitants a consciousness informed by medieval Christian experience – of contrition and penitence, for instance, in Pandarus's advice to Troilus about how to behave in love. At the end, the pressure and the logic of Christian experience works in a different way, and forces Chaucer to reject the world of the poem as illusory and to urge his readers to turn to Christ; he gives the poem meaning by denying its meaningfulness.

These are special cases of the power of religion to penetrate non-religious forms of discourse. Elsewhere, the writing most directly associated with the church's purposes is readily recognisable. There is a mass of homiletic writing, in Latin and all the vernaculars, whether sermons for delivery or treatises for reading, that offers instruction in the elements of the faith and exhortations to good behaviour. Didactic works list and explain the seven sacraments, the seven works of spiritual mercy, the seven works of corporal mercy, the petitions of the Paternoster, the articles of the Creed. Latin religious drama is essentially an extension and additionally theatricalised version of the liturgy, but vernacular religious drama (and there is little other vernacular drama that survives in written form) is best seen as a product of the church's mission to preach and instruct, though in this case in a more entertaining way. Vernacular plays based on the story of the bible (mystery plays) or on the lives of saints (miracle plays) or on allegories of good and evil in their struggle for man's soul (morality plays) were widely popular throughout Europe, but little survives in written form from before the later fifteenth century.

Much religious writing is in the form of witnesses to the faith and stirrings to devotion. The lives of the saints are endlessly rehearsed as exciting exemplary stories of faith and fortitude in the face of persecution. They usually end in a martyrdom, and much graphic detail, especially with the female virgin-martyrs like Katherine, Margaret and Juliana. Many of the hundreds of saints whose lives were celebrated have been removed from the Roman calendar because of uncertainty about whether they existed, or certainty that they didn't, but the Middle Ages was comparatively unworried about such matters. As one hagiographical compiler explained, he had no information on the lives of some of the saints whose lives he was recounting, and so in such cases he would provide for them, through God's grace, such lives as they would have lived and would be instructive for others.[1] Large new compilations of lives of the saints were being made in the thirteenth century, a great age of systematisation, by far the most successful being the *Legenda aurea* of the Dominican Jacobus de Voragine (*c.*1280), which was translated, adapted, excerpted, amplified and imitated in every European language. In England, one of the earliest major works in the vernacular was the *South English Legendary*, a collection of saints' lives first composed in the south-west, perhaps at Gloucester, about 1280, which was disseminated in many manuscripts throughout the country, with additions of local saints as appropriate (a reminder of how saints' lives functioned also to advertise particular shrines and to promote pilgrimage-tourism). In its fully developed form the *Legendary* also contained lives of Christ and the Virgin and other matter for the non-saints'-day feast-days of the church (the *temporale*, as opposed to the *sanctorale*). It is possible that these, and the saints' legends as well, were read out in church on the appropriate days, so that the lay congregation would understand at least something of what was going on, but it is more likely that they were used independently by preachers or intended simply to be read by the layfolk as part of the day's devotions.

Miracles of the Virgin worked in the same way as saints' legends, as witnesses to the power of faith to defeat the devil and win salvation. They tended even more towards extravagance, to the recounting of lives that are so heinously sinful that only damnation seems possible but that are redeemed through one tiny act of charity, one forgotten tear of compassion, and through the unlimited power granted to the Virgin to act as mediatrix of mercy in such cases. Often illustrated, such stories operated at a fairly low level of sophistication to suggest that good deeds would be rewarded and that only inveterate hard-heartedness and the refusal of grace cut people off from God's mercy. This was the church's 'good-cop' approach. To set against it there were also the warnings of hellfire, the vivid descriptions of hell's torments, the terrifying vision of the Last Judgement, reminders of the inevitability of death (the *memento mori*), graphically detailed accounts of the physical process of dying. There was sometimes almost more relish in the bleak epigrammatic grimness of the message of mortality than there was in the ministration of hope:

> Erthe toc of erthe erthe wyth woh;
> Erthe other erthe to the erthe droh;
> Erthe leyde erthe in erthene throh;
> Tho hevede erthe of erthe erthe ynoh.[2]

This kind of writing or sermonising (which often has its pictorial equivalents or accessories) worked to make people act in certain ways by appealing to their common sense or their fear or their admiration for heroism or their greed ('How mercy multiplies temporal goods', that is, how charitable acts will be financially rewarded in this world, is the title of a chapter in a book of instruction for the laity by a monk of Canterbury, Dan Michael). It was the propaganda of orthodoxy. Another large body of religious writing was more concerned with the stirring to devotion, and it appealed to a somewhat more sophisticated taste. The Franciscans gave an immense stimulus to this kind of writing, in prayers, songs on the Joys of the Virgin, meditations on Christ's suffering on the Cross, dialogues between Christ and Mary at the Crucifixion (the *Stabat mater*), monologues by Christ from the Cross or in the person of the Man of Sorrows. Such evocations of compassion, grief and joy were meant for participation, and they worked in the same way as pictures of such scenes, and sometimes with them: a picture of the Crucifixion or the Deposition or the Man of Sorrows would be accompanied by a text in which instruction would be given in the 'reading' of the picture so that the observer might draw from the *imago pietatis* the full burden of pity.

Much of this writing was in the form of songs – the Franciscans called themselves the *joculatores Dei* or 'minstrels of God' and sang new words to popular tunes to seduce people to love and pity. They wrote often in Latin, which would be the normal written and often spoken language for a friar

(English vernacular sermons of the thirteenth and fourteenth centuries are often recorded in the form of Latin 'shorthand notes' with the key English passages quoted in full), but they were amongst the earliest to write vernacular lyrics. These lyrics can be seen as ways of seizing the attention of the audience – bursts of song or recitation within a sermon, for instance – but there was also the more extended narrative meditation on the life of Christ for the devout learned reader. The *Meditationes vitae Christi* of the pseudo-Bonaventure have already been mentioned. They were not the only example of the genre: the *Vita Christi* (*c*.1350) of Ludolphus of Saxony (d. 1378), enormously long, amplified in every direction and at every level, was widely disseminated.

LATIN AND VERNACULAR

The movement from Latin to the vernacular took place at different rates in different linguistic communities and in relation to different kinds of writing activity. The English vernacular took longer to establish itself in England than French in France or Castilian in Castile, though England did have an Anglo-Norman vernacular 1150–1350. Some kinds of writing (theology, law, classical scholarship) stayed in Latin until the end of the Middle Ages in England, and longer, but others (history, encyclopaedias, scientific writing, political writing) found their way into the vernacular well before then. History had been the special preserve of the English monasteries, which had the long-term outlook, the library resources, and the contacts with the great and powerful (who used the monasteries as four-star hotels on their progresses and peregrinations) to make a success of it. There was a long-lived school of Latin historiography at the Benedictine abbey of St Alban's from the time of Matthew Paris in the mid-thirteenth century to Thomas Walsingham at the end of the fourteenth: St Alban's was 25 miles north of London and was usually the first stopping-place for the king on the journey north and the last on the way back. The great European encyclopaedias of Bartholomaeus Anglicus (*c*.1280) and Vincent of Beauvais (d. 1264) were written in Latin, but the former at least was in both French and English by the end of the fourteenth century, in English in the translation (1397) by John Trevisa, who had earlier translated into English (1387) the great world-history, or *Polychronicon* (1352), of the Chester monk Ralph Higden.

The single greatest stimulus to religious writing, outside the universities, was the decree of the Fourth Lateran Council of 1215 that every Christian had to confess at least once a year. In order to implement this strategy of reform and control, confession had to be systematised: priests had to know what categories of behaviour were to be deemed worthy of reprobation, and they had to know how to classify according to a clearly organised taxonomy the precise kinds of behaviour that their parishioners would bring before them. What needs to be confessed is not always self-evident. They also had to have some way of judging whether a confession was full, open and truthful, whether reprehensible behaviour was being concealed or disguised in confession and (most difficult of all) whether certain kinds of acceptable sinfulness were being laid claim to in order to mitigate guilt for what was felt to be too terrible to reveal. In order to perform this role, confessors had to have elaborate schematisations of sin, with the seven deadly sins divided into sub-species and sub-sub-species of sinfulness. Treatises on the seven deadly sins lay out a kind of cartographic grid over the body of human experience, so that the exact category of sin can be read off, or, in the medieval metaphor, they describe a tree that is rooted in the fallen body of man and that flourishes in sending forth the branches, twigs and twiglets of sin. The number of twigs of Pride, says Chaucer's Parson, cannot be told: 'There is inobedience, avauntynge, ypocrisie, despit, arrogance, inpudence, swellynge of herte, insolence, elacioun, inpacience, strif, contumacie, presumpcioun, irreverence, pertinacie, veyneglorie, and many another twig that I kan nat declare' (Parson's Tale, *Canterbury Tales*, X.391).

So there was a spate of manuals of confession and treatises on the vices and virtues to educate priests in the proper administration of confession. These were in Latin at first, but in the fourteenth century they began to appear in the vernacular, and were sometimes directed just as much to the penitent as to the confessor. Dominican friars were early active in the production of the necessary manuals of instruction, and two of the most widely disseminated treatises were the *Summa de poenitentia* (1222–29) of Raymund of Pennaforte and the *Summa vitiorum* (1236) of William Peraldus. A French adaptation (1279) of their work by Friar Laurent, Dominican confessor to Philip III of France, became known as the *Somme le Roi* because of its royal connections. These works laid out the schemata of sin, the Linnaean categories; they are the product of an extraordinary faith in the analysability of human sinful behaviour (and an equally extraordinary blindness to the impossibility of any such analysis). There were also manuals of confession, designed to help priests in the day-to-day business of confession. One of the most popular was the *Oculus sacerdotis* (1320–28), 'The Eye of the Priest', of William of Pagula, which not only gave lists of the sins and their remedies (that is, the corresponding virtues) but also incidental bits of advice to expectant mothers (avoid heavy work) and mothers (suckle your own children) and warnings about receiving the confessions of sailors. Be cautious, says William, for the vast number of their sins – piracy, killing merchants, unlawful matrimony – may overstrain the machinery of confession.

When these works got into the vernacular, they became somewhat more relaxed in tone, and began to accommodate little exemplary stories to make the nature of sin more vivid. Robert Mannyng, a Gilbertine canon of east Lincolnshire, added many such stories to his English translation (1303) of the Anglo-Norman *Manuel des Péchés* of William of Waddington (c.1260) to which he gave the title *Handlyng Synne*. The work is in verse, and was probably designed with the laity in mind, since verse was, paradoxically in our eyes, a 'lower', less sophisticated medium than prose. Works of this kind proliferated in the fourteenth century, and far outstripped in bulk the production of all other kinds of vernacular writing put together. They are repulsive enough for the most part: the English *Prick of Conscience* goes into a good deal of detail about the precise degree of torment promised in the after-life to unbaptised infants as well as to the righteous heathen. But they were enormously influential. They shaped, as nothing else did, the way in which people thought about themselves and about their inner lives. They were the materials of their subjectivity. There was no such thing as 'autobiography' except that which was framed as confessional. When Edward III's great lieutenant in the French wars, Henry, Duke of Lancaster, settled himself to prepare for the end, it was in the form of a confession, *Le Livre de Seyntz Medicines* (1354), that he reviewed his life. When imaginative writers came to talk in intimate terms about the inner life of their characters, or of themselves, it was often the confessional form that they chose. Much of the exposition of human behaviour in Jean de Meun's continuation of the *Roman de la Rose* was done as confessional monologue (the speeches of *Faux Semblant*, 'Hypocrisy', for instance, and of *la Vieille*, the old bawd), and when Chaucer came to the 'autobiographical' monologues of the two most vividly realised and fully 'interiorised' characters of the *Canterbury Tales*, the Pardoner and the Wife of Bath, it was to the personifications of the *Roman* that he first turned for inspiration. John Gower designed his whole vast *Confessio Amantis* as the 'confession of a lover' ('himself', as he puts it, 'in another person') to Genius, the priest of Venus, of his sins against the code of Love. It is a mock-penitential discourse, but it was the existence of penitential discourse that made it possible and that gives it much of its incidental power to please and surprise. Thomas Hoccleve, the earliest of Chaucer's fifteenth-century followers, seems hardly able to frame his mind to the writing of poetry except by beginning, in a semi-confessional vein, with the story of his life of sin and tribulation.

Courts and Aristocratic Households

Medieval secular society, outside those cities in which oligarchic forms of government came to be developed, was organised on a pyramidal basis, and at the apex of the pyramid was the court of the monarch or the courtly household of the nobleman. The importance of the latter in relation to the former varied. In England the royal court, because of the highly centralised system of government, was overwhelmingly important. In Germany there were a number of important semi-independent ducal, baronial and episcopal courts, as well as a multitude of princelings whose households and 'castles' were many of them no more than primitive fortified single-hall residences, lacking all comfort and privacy, a mere base for hunting, fighting and feasting. Whatever the extent of their jurisdiction, though, lordships and the lord's 'affinity', or *famulus*, great and small, were the centres of wealth and power. A man could build up his estates by shrewd buying and bargaining and legal know-how as well as force, but he would get only so far without the patronage of his lord.

It was in kingly and ducal courts and aristocratic households that the arts flourished. Medieval chivalric romance, of which more will be said in Chapter Three, came into existence as the celebration of the values to which this society aspired. It was the mirror into which it wished to look, and the construction of the mirror depended on the image which it wished to see. Arthurian romance could be used to glorify the idea of a centralised monarchy and a contented body of magnates, and several English monarchs invoked for their own benefit the idea of Arthur as the great national hero surrounded by his Round Table of loyal knights (some parts of the story, especially those involving Guenevere and Lancelot, were not talked about on such occasions). Edward I held an elaborate 'Round Table' feast and tournament in 1284 to celebrate his conquest of Wales, and Edward III organised one at Windsor in 1358 at which two captive kings, David Bruce of Scotland and John II of France, were put on display.

Romance could also be used to glorify the ancestors of a noble family, or simply provide them when they were lacking: the newly established Anglo-Norman aristocracy in England, conscious of their status as transplants, were keen to commission 'ancestral romances' (*Gui de Warewic* is the most famous) in which suitable forebears might act out traditionally heroic roles. The popularity of 'exile-and-return' romances (such as *Havelok* and *Horn*, in both Anglo-Norman and English), in which the hero is dispossessed and returns to claim his inheritance by force, and of other stories in which a younger son wins through against the odds to fame and fortune, may have something to do with other pressures within courtly households. The law of primogeniture meant that there were many young men of birth without appropriate estates. It is true that a young landless knight who was proficient in arms could make his fortune, as did William Marshall (Guillaume le Maréchal, 1146–1219), who served four English kings in France, Wales, Ireland and England, married successfully, was created first Earl of Pembroke, and had his exploits posthumously celebrated in a famous verse biography in French. But there were many who could only dream of marrying a rich heiress, and romances may have acted to feed such fantasies and to resolve some of the tensions they created in real life.

The nobility, men and women, listened to these romances being read aloud, and later started to read them for themselves. They also surrounded themselves with images and representations of characters and episodes from the romances – wall-paintings, tapestries, illuminated manuscripts, ivory caskets and mirror-cases, tableware and other decorations (Fig. 7). Such objects, now unnaturally sealed in the antiseptic hush of museums and galleries, once had a living reality, we must remember, in everyday visual experience.

MUSIC AND FEASTING

One hears enough of the gentlemen at court who were 'syngynge and floytynge al the day', like Chaucer's Squire, practising their skills in the composition of love-lyrics and serenading their ladies, and much survives of the words and music of art-songs that were written down; but the larger role of music in royal and aristocratic households, whether or not as an accompaniment to feasting, is something that it is easy to lose sight of. The written record can

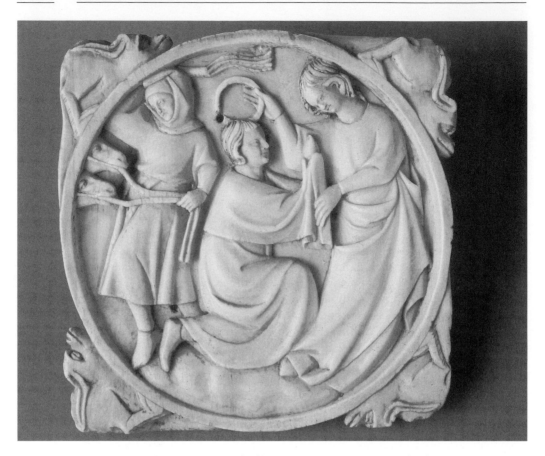

Figure 7: London, Victoria and Albert Museum. Ivory mirror-back.
    These objects in ivory – caskets, mirror-cases, combs – carved with amorous scenes, often in allusion to fashionable love-romances, were very popular in courtly circles. Here a lover offers his heart to his lady, who prepares to place a garland upon his head in token that she accepts him as her lover. Behind the lover a servant holds two horses in check with a whip (an allusion to the consequences of unbridled desire?), and four monstrous crawling creatures square the roundel.

only be brought alive in performance, and performances are rare, and in any case can give only a partial experience of the whole event. But music and feasting were central to court-life – part of the art of good living, like hunting, the 'art of love', and the 'art of war' – and it is worth trying to capture some sense of their importance.
    The best evidence of music at the English royal court is in an unusual record of the feast organised by Edward I to celebrate the knighting of his son in 1306.[3] Ninety-two minstrels were present at the feast, including 19 trumpeters, 6 taborers, 26 harpers, and 22 string-players. These minstrels were

not permanently resident at court, but might stay in service for long spells when they were called. Trumpeters went around with the king to enhance his dignity, 'cornours' (horn-players) blew the night-watches, announced meals, and warned of departure or fire, taborers and fifers served as a dance-band, and the stringmen played like a café orchestra at mealtimes, or in private rooms, or if the king were ill or recovering after blood-letting. Minstrels were specially important at great feasts, where they organised shows and spectacles. Some of them went on campaign too, composing victory songs when appropriate.

By this time, it is true, England was losing contact with music in France, and there is little evidence of the influence of the extraordinary developments in the polyphonic elaboration of the motet that were taking place there. It was perhaps the establishment of choirs at the new royal chapels, such as that of St Stephen's, Westminster, by Edward III in 1348, that, as one factor at least, led eventually to the resurgence of English music under the early Lancastrian kings. During their time, music was one of England's principal glories, and royal patronage played a very significant part. Henry IV was famous for his love of music, and Henry V seems to have taken a special interest in the new forms of elaborated liturgical style, in both words and music, and may have worked with Edmund Lacy, Dean of the Royal Chapel at Windsor (1414–17), and later Bishop of Exeter (1420), to encourage the monk-poet John Lydgate to compose appropriate words to be sung to new musical settings in the Royal Chapel. The Old Hall MS (preserved in the library of St Edmund's College, Ware), the major surviving manuscript of English music of the Middle Ages, was probably made for or in the household of Henry V's oldest brother, Thomas, Duke of Clarence (1388–1421). Clarence's own chapel was where Lionel Power (d. 1445) spent his formative years; he is an important composer, perhaps as important in his way as the much more famous John Dunstable (c.1390–1453), who was in the employ of Henry V's next oldest brother, John, Duke of Bedford, principally in France.

For all of these politically shrewd Lancastrian kings and dukes, as for Charles V of France, music was not only a form of devotion and a source of pleasure, but also well recognised for the part it could play in enhancing the prestige of the royal dynasty through ceremonial. This was true of feasts too: great tournaments had always been accompanied by days of feasting, in which chivalric pageantry would glorify the name and image of the patron of the feast, as in the royal 'Round Tables' of Edward III at Windsor (1344, 1358), or the 'Round Table' of Roger Mortimer at Kenilworth in 1279, or the St George's Day tournament at Windsor in 1349, which (in the year of the Black Death) instituted the Order of the Garter. But the Lancastrians, again, were more ruthlessly single-minded in their propagandist mission. At the coronation feast of Henry VI in 1429, there were 'subtleties' (sugar-confections used as table-decorations) to remind everyone of the dual monarchy to which Henry was heir, and of the blessings of the patron saints, George and Denis, of the two countries. Lydgate wrote verses to explain the meaning of everything, but those present may have had little time left for ideology, given what they were fed:

Here follows the second course: Meat blanched, barred with gold. Jelly divided by the writing and musical notation, Te Deum laudamus. Pig gilded. Crane. Bittern. Rabbits. Chickens gilded. Partridge. Peacock in its plumage. Great bream. White leach [almond gelatine], with an antelope of red carved therein, a crown about his neck with a chain of gold. Flampayne [pie ornamented with pointed pieces of pastry] powdered with leopards and fleurs de lis of gold. Fritters, a leopard's head, with two ostrich feathers. A subtlety, the emperor and the king who is dead, armed, and their mantles of the Garter . . .

And that was just one course of three.[4]

CASTLES AND PALACES

Castles, of course, were still a practical preoccupation for great lords, and continued to perform a primarily defensive function throughout the thirteenth and into the fourteenth century. There was a great stone castle boom in central France and the Loire valley in the twelfth and thirteenth centuries as the kingdom of France expanded its borders and consolidated its territorial claims. Some were later absorbed into Renaissance palaces, but the original purposes of fortification are still impressively evident in such castles as those at Angers, Gaillard, Loches and Tours. Defensive function was here all-important, but the lords of these castles were not immune to fashion, nor free from the desire to demonstrate that they could afford the services of expert workmen, and Gothic detail was often incorporated in chapels and residential apartments within the main fortifications. It was in the central areas of France, too, that the transition from the castle to the château, from the fortress to the palace, took place, in the intervals of the Hundred Years War and after. Such changes and refinements were slower to come into operation in less prosperous regions of feudal Europe and in disputed border-lands where castles were still needed, and sometimes in a hurry, for defence. But even at the eastern frontier of Europe, fortresses were being remodelled on the lines of French buildings as early as the fourteenth century: Prague Castle was restored from 1333, and Karlstein Castle nearby in 1348–65 by Charles IV of Bohemia.

In north-western Wales Edward I was asserting his modest imperial achievement in a series of magnificent castles. Under the direction of his chief military engineer and architect, Master James of St George, who had learnt his art in the service of Edward's ally Count Peter of Savoy, they were built along the line of his advance, beginning in 1277 at Flint and Rhuddlan, and continuing with the two largest, Conwy and Caernarfon, both begun in 1283 (and the former, astonishingly, ready by 1287), and ending with Harlech (begun 1290), square, high-walled, drum-towered, presiding majestically over its little town and bay, and Beaumaris (begun 1295).

Caernarfon has been considered to be aesthetically the most satisfying secular building of its size which the Middle Ages have left to us, but there are other later English castles that are, though less grand, at least just as beautiful in their own way, and mark, like the French châteaux, the transition from defensive function to residential comfort and personal ostentation – Sir John de la Mare's Nunney in Somerset (begun 1373), Michael de la Pole's fortified manor-house at Wingfield in Surrey (c.1385), the beautiful water-landscaped castle at Bodiam (1386) in Sussex, and the great brick manor-house castles of Sir John Fastolfe at Caister in Norfolk (1432–35) and of Sir Ralph Coggeshall at Tattershall in Lincolnshire (begun 1434).

Edward III had to some extent anticipated these later builders in his re-building of the royal castles. Windsor was transformed from a castle into a palace (1350–77), with refurbishing of the royal lodgings on a sumptuous scale. At Eltham Edward built a new range of royal lodgings (1350–59), and he made improvements at King's Langley (1359–77), including the installa-tion of a quite large and well-appointed bath-house with hot running water. He built virtually a new palace at Sheen (1358–70), with much glass and elaborate decoration in the new chambers. Leeds and Rotherhithe were other royal castles where the residential quarters were upgraded, and a completely new and beautifully symmetrical royal castle, all trace of which has now disappeared, was built at Queenborough on the Isle of Sheppey.

Such glimpses as we get of the interiors of these castles (as in the January scene of feasting indoors in the Duke of Berry's *Très Riches Heures*) suggest the great importance of tapestries. Tapestries and painted cloths were much favoured for covering interior walls, especially since they helped to keep out draughts. Their subjects might be biblical or they might be drawn from romance or from such classical stories as those of Troy and Alexander. Some survive, such as the magnificent Apocalypse tapestry made for Louis of Anjou in the work-shop of Nicolas Bataille in Paris (1376–81) from designs by Jan Bandol of Bruges, court-painter to Charles V from 1368 (it is now in the museum at Angers).

Wall-paintings are more subject to destruction (because they cannot be removed) and deterioration, but a few survive. In the great chamber of Longthorpe Tower, near Peterborough, there are the remains of a remarkable series of mural paintings which once covered the walls, window-recesses and vaulted ceiling. They were done about 1330, and include figures of the evangelists and the apostles, and scriptural subjects such as the Nativity, but also subjects of a more general interest – the Seven Ages of Man, the Labours of the Months, the Wheel of the Five Senses and the story of the Three Living and the Three Dead (a *memento mori* in which three young knights confront the corpses they will one day be).

The role of courts and noble households in cultural and artistic patronage and production can perhaps best be illustrated in a series of specific examples.

FREDERICK II, HOLY ROMAN EMPEROR 1218–50

Frederick II (1194–1250), King of Sicily from 1198, King of Germany in 1212, and Emperor in 1218, has earlier figured in this story as a strenuous upholder of imperial power against the papacy and as a versatile crusader who negotiated with the infidel to have himself crowned in Jerusalem in 1229. But he was also a great patron of the arts and sciences, and made Naples, where he founded a university in 1224, into a pan-European cultural centre. Continuing the traditions of his predecessors in the Norman kingdom in Sicily, he maintained close contact with the Mohammedan sovereigns of North Africa and the east, brought their scholars to Italy, and conducted a learned correspondence with their scientists and philosophers. He also used his position as the head of an empire that stretched from the Baltic to the Mediterranean to bring to his court poets and singers from France and Germany, the troubadours and the Minnesinger, and to welcome Theodore the philosopher from Antioch and Michael Scot the scientist from Spain. These two made versions of Arabic works on zoology for the Emperor's use, and were also his official astrologers. His interest in science led him into organising and encouraging experiments that got him a reputation, along with his readiness for dialogue with the Mohammedans, for being a dangerous freethinker. It was said that he had a man shut up in a wine-cask to prove that the soul died with the body; that he had two men disembowelled to show the respective effects of sleep and exercise on digestion; and that he had children brought up in silence to ascertain whether they would speak Hebrew, the original language, as their 'natural' language (the children all died).

Frederick was famous for the lavishness of his entertainment of important foreign visitors, and the English monk Matthew Paris, in his *Chronica maiora*, gives a scandalised account of the four-month series of entertainments, complete with dancing girls, bathing parties, feasting and music, that Frederick laid on at his palace in the Apennines for the visit of Richard of Cornwall, the brother of the English King Henry III, in 1241. He had a great menagerie, in imitation of his Mohammedan contemporaries, and the animals often travelled around with him. In 1231 he came to Ravenna with elephants, dromedaries, camels, panthers, lions and leopards, and took some of them over the Alps to Germany, where they caused a great stir. The animals were sometimes used in his scientific investigations.

Frederick was also an author in his own right: his Latin treatise on falconry, *De arte venandi cum avibus* (The art of hunting with birds) shows a genuine interest in the practical science and exact description of his subject, even though most written observation of nature in his day was highly schematised. Frederick tells us that Aristotle, the great authority on natural history, relied too much on hearsay and must be corrected from personal observation. He himself tried experiments to test whether ostriches' eggs could be incubated by sunlight (they could) and whether barnacle geese were hatched from barnacles (they weren't). The *De arte venandi* was written in Latin, later translated into French, and put out in lavishly illustrated manuscripts, the earliest, most famous and most fully illustrated being the manuscript of the Latin text in Rome, Biblioteca Vaticana MS Pal.lat.1071, with hundreds of marginal pictures of birds and of the practice and equipment of falconry.

HENRY III, KING OF ENGLAND 1216–72

Henry III, who maintained close contact with the Sicilian as well as the French court, was probably the greatest patron of the arts in medieval England, and it was he who established the expectation that the royal court should be the natural centre of cultural life and the fount of artistic patronage.[5] It was not, in Henry's case, literature that was his chief interest as a patron, though he extended his usual generosity to Henry of Avranches, a kind of itinerant professional Euro-laureate who wrote eulogies for a pope, two emperors (including Frederick II), three kings, six archbishops and a dozen or so assorted bishops. He had clearly mastered the art of winning patrons, and he wrote for Henry III lives of St George and St Edward (the latter possibly the Anglo-Norman *Estorie de Seint Aedward le Rei* of 1245) for which he received the handsome stipend of 20s a month in 1243–44. From 1255 he received 3d a day as *magister Henricus versificator*, which, with the regular grant of wine, suggests that he had become almost a court official.

Henry III's patronage of the arts can be seen in two phases. In the early part of his reign he was the benefactor whose generosity assisted the projects of others with money, materials, and other kinds of support: during the period up to 1240 he gave aid for construction purposes to 350 institutions, and a further 170 received precious gold or silver utensils and vestments. After 1240 nearly all his energies and wealth were devoted to Westminster Abbey, to the purchase of every kind of ceremonial and decorative object, to the ennoblement of the shrine of Edward the Confessor, and to the enlargement of the building. Henry's piety and devotion to his chosen saint are unquestioned, as are his extravagance and love of beauty, but emulation too played a part. The reception of the relic of the Holy Blood in 1247 and its presentation to Westminster Abbey seem a direct imitation of the enshrinement of the Crown of Thorns in the Sainte-Chapelle in 1239. Henry's plans for the Abbey were further driven by what he saw of the new building in Paris (the Palais Royal, the Sainte-Chapelle) on a visit to Louis IX in 1254. To all these spurrings, the rebuilding of the Abbey, mostly during 1245–69, at his direct personal instigation, was Henry's answer. It was a revolution: a great monument of religious art constructed under the auspices of a secular connoisseur.

No expense was spared. Purbeck marble was shipped from the new quarries in Dorset for columns and effigies, and at one time in 1253 Henry had 49 marblers and 15 polishers at work in London. A new 'court school' emerged, attracting the best craftsmen from all over the country. To Edward of Westminster, his artistic administrator, Henry sent a constant stream of requests and instructions for building, carving and jewelwork, and he diverted money for the task from wardships and special taxation of the Jews. During the 1240s and 1250s, quite a large part of the national revenue was going into this national monument.

Westminster Abbey occupied much of Henry's energy and wealth as a patron, but he was also keen to decorate his own palaces in the French style. Chambers in Westminster Palace, in Clarendon Palace near Salisbury and in the Tower of London were painted with scenes of the crusading exploits of Richard I, including the famous duel with Saladin, with the story of Alexander, and with depictions of the Labours of the Months and the Wheel of Fortune. Everything has disappeared, and is known only from accounts and descriptions, though some drawings were made of the Painted Chamber at Westminster before it was pulled down in the rebuilding of 1818–19 (later, the fire of 1834 destroyed nearly all the palace but for the Great Hall). The drawings were made by a skilful draughtsman, Charles Stothard (sometimes he was hurrying ahead of the workmen who were tearing the plaster from the walls), and reveal a lavish programme of brilliantly coloured murals – a scene of Edward the Confessor's coronation, a series of personified virtues, each a crowned woman seven feet high trampling on enemies, and an 80 ft band of warlike stories from the bible running round the room. Franciscan visitors in 1322, on an itinerary that had included Notre Dame and the Sainte-Chapelle in Paris and San Marco in Venice, marvelled at its magnificence.

No detail was too small for Henry's attention. He had, for instance, a whole series of extraordinary floor-tiles made by Master William of Westminster, his favourite painter. Some, with figure-designs of Henry and his queen, and also hunting-scenes, were used to floor the new chapter-house of the Abbey (1248–55), later also used for parliamentary assemblies; some were prepared for use in royal residences, with illustrations of the story of Tristan and of the combat of Richard Lionheart as well as individual animals and human heads. A residue from this manufactory was sent by Edward I to Chertsey Abbey in Surrey, where masses were to be said for his queen, Eleanor of Castile, and from where they survive as the most famous evidence of English tile-manufacture.

ALFONSO X 'EL SABIO' (THE WISE), KING OF CASTILE 1252–84

Alfonso X was an enlightened king who made Castilian the official language of his kingdom (the first Romance language to be so dignified) and authorised translations of histories and encyclopaedias in the new vernacular. He prided himself on being a 'King of Three Religions', presiding over a multiracial culture which had lasted for two centuries and in which the Jewish community played an important role in medicine and financial administration. During his reign the church of Santa María la Blanca in Toledo (which still stands, though much renovated) was used by Moslems on Friday, by Jews on Saturday, and by Christians on Sunday. Jews and Arabs played a major part in Alfonso's mid-century renaissance, and among the works he caused to be translated were the Koran and the Talmud as well as the Bible and the *Tresor* of Brunetto Latini. Translations from Arabic scientific books on mathematics, physics, chemistry, medicine, alchemy, astronomy and chess made Castile for a time a leading European centre of learning. Alfonso directed the compilation of the *General Chronicle*, a history of Spain up to 1250, a remarkable work of vernacular learning, though marred as to its reliability by patriotic fervour and the habit of including chunks of epic poetry. He was also keenly interested in legislation and supervised the composition of an encyclopaedia of law, the *Siete Partidas*, which became a textbook for Spanish lawyers. Though he wasted time trying to secure the crown of the Holy Roman Empire, and was also unsuccessful in his attempt to control a turbulent nobility, he was very important as a patron of learning.

The most impressive record of the encouragement that Alfonso gave to writers and artists is in the richly illustrated manuscripts that he commissioned to accommodate the *Cántigas* ('songs') in honour of the Virgin that he had collected.[6] These are not in Castilian but in Galician/Portuguese, which had won a special role in lyric poetry because of the links of Santiago de Compostela (in Galicia) with southern France through the pilgrim routes (Castilian took over in the mid-fourteenth century). Four manuscripts of the *Cántigas* survive, two in the library of the Escorial, near Madrid, one of which (Escorial MS T.j.I) has 1,255 miniatures illustrating the stories of the miracles of the Virgin described in the songs. They are a pictorial encyclopaedia of medieval secular life, people singing, fighting, feasting, riding, building churches, being shipwrecked, being hanged, wrestling, giving birth, playing dice, painting a fresco (the miracle here is that the scaffold collapses but the painter is saved because he was painting the Virgin Mary), fighting bulls, shearing sheep, writing books, frying eggs, ploughing, fishing. The opening page shows King Alfonso pointing to one of the songs on a long scroll being admired by his courtiers. The second miniature has three musicians playing, the king listening, dictating words to two clerics who copy them on scrolls and then transfer them to a large volume from which four singers are singing. It is a representation of the whole process of 'compiling' the book.

CHARLES IV, KING OF BOHEMIA AND HOLY ROMAN EMPEROR 1346–78

Charles succeeded to throne and empire when his blind father, John of Luxembourg (crowned in 1310), died fighting on the French side at Crécy in 1346. During Charles IV's reign, and for a brief time that of his successor, Wenceslas IV (Emperor 1378–1400), Bohemia was the cultural centre of the Empire.[7] The house of Luxemburg had a tradition of patronage both secular and pious. Charles's father had employed the French poet and musician Guillaume de Machaut as his personal secretary and clerk (1323–37), and was rewarded by being made judge in a poetic love-debate, *Le Jugement du Roy de Behaigne* (*c*.1340), in which he must decide who suffers more, the lover whose mate is proved unfaithful or the one whose beloved has died. John's son Wenceslas (the Czech form is Václav), Duke of Brabant, was a patron of the later French poets Froissart and Deschamps. A more distant ancestor was the abbess Kunigunde (1265–1321), who was one of the great female patrons of the arts in late medieval Europe. A friend of the German mystic Meister Eckhart, she played an important part in encouraging female piety and mystical devotion and in commissioning writings celebrating the humanity of Christ.

Charles IV himself brought Bohemia to the height of its international reputation. He preferred diplomacy to fighting, and spent his time and money collecting religious relics, which he housed in Karlstein Castle near Prague. He built the new cathedral of St Vitus and the stone bridge over the Vltava which still stands, laid out the new town of Prague, and founded the oldest university in central Europe at Prague in 1348. To his cosmopolitan court, where French, German, Italian and Latin could all be heard spoken as well as Czech, came the Strassburg painter Nicholas Wurmser, the architect-sculptor Peter Parler, and Petrarch, who wrote an epistle in praise of women, *De laudibus feminarum*, for Charles's third wife, Anne of Schweidnitz. The court was a particular centre for the encouragement of female literacy and piety. When Charles's daughter Anne married the English King Richard II in 1381, it was as much of a catch for him as it was for her. She brought with her the reputation of belonging to a court-culture which was all that was chic in jewellery, sculpture and panel-painting, and she was literate in several languages.

JEAN, DUC DE BERRY (JOHN, DUKE OF BERRY) 1340–1416

Charles V of France and his three brothers, Louis, Duke of Anjou, John (Jean), Duke of Berry, and Philip the Bold, Duke of Burgundy, were the great patrons of the late fourteenth century. Following upon the example of their cultivated father, John II (Jean le Bon), whose taste and connoisseurship were matched only by his incompetence as a military commander, they set up networks of art patronage that had no equal before the Borgias. The Duke of Berry was by any standards the greatest of late medieval patrons, but he was by no means without competitors. He and his brother Philip, in fact, entered into a kind of rivalry in acting as grand patrons of the arts – architecture, sculpture, painting, book-illumination, and the minor decorative arts. Berry hired André Beauneveu, who had distinguished himself as a designer of royal tombs for Charles V in 1364, and as a sculptor and painter for many halls and chambers in Flanders (Ypres, Malines, Courtrai, and later, in 1394, the painted chamber in the market-hall at Valenciennes), to be the general supervisor for the décor of Mehun in 1386. Philip of Burgundy sent his own artistic adviser, Jean de Beaumetz, to Mehun, to see what was going on. The duke had already established the ducal seat at Dijon and begun to bring in artists such as the Dutch sculptor Claus Sluter, who did the portal at the recently founded Carthusian monastery at Champnol and also a tomb for the duke, who planned to be buried there. Another of Philip's importations was Melchior Broederlam of Ypres, who entered his service in 1378 and whose most famous work is in the two surviving wings of a lost altarpiece (1399) now in the Museum at Dijon (see Fig. 32).

Great patrons such as these were in the market not only for magnificent illuminated manuscripts but also for all kinds of *objets d'art*, and Italian merchants such as the Rapondi family set up in Paris to cater for their taste for expensive textiles and jewelled art-objects. Louis of Anjou, for example, owned a silver wine-vessel designed as a garden surrounded by battlemented walls, with trees growing about a fountain in which people are bathing; he also had a golden goblet with rabbits playing in the grass at its base and deer nosing their way between shrubs and trees on the bowl. There was competition in exchanging magnificent gifts, especially at New Year, and a treaty or marriage-agreement would often be sealed with the bestowal of some splendid and irrelevant artefact. The Brussels Hours (Bibliothèque Royale MSS 11060– 61) were given by Berry to Burgundy in 1403/4, and the Belleville Breviary, made by Jean Pucelle about 1325 (BN MSS lat.10483–4), was presented to Richard II on the occasion of his marriage to Isabel, the daughter of the French king Charles VI, in 1396 (Henry IV later used it as a gift for John, Duke of Berry). Individual portraits intended to be recognisable likenesses were introduced into manuscript-paintings as a mark of this new ostentation of ownership.

Ostentation was not everything, however: Berry and his brothers were educated men, with a keen interest in the contents of books as well as their appearance. They encouraged writers, built up libraries, employed reputable scholars as their secretaries and chancellors, commissioned new kinds of scientific and historical work, and employed translators for older Latin texts that had not before been put into French.

The Duke of Berry is most famous now for the magnificent series of books of hours that he commissioned (of which there will be more to say later, in Chapter Three). The Gothic palaces that he built throughout his estates, and that were his greatest achievement in his time, have all but disappeared. Only ruins survive at Mehun-sur-Yèvre and only the great hall of the château at Bourges, but the buildings are remembered more vividly than any reality through the calendar-pictures in the book of hours done for the duke by the Limbourg brothers, *Les Très Riches Heures du Duc de Berry* (1413–16). The pictures of the 'Labours of the Months' show, in the background, the duke's castles at Lusignan (March), Dourdan (April), Clain, near Poitiers (July), Etampes (August), Saumur (September) and Vincennes (December), while other months show scenes of the Palais de la Cité in Paris (May, June). October has a painting of the Louvre so meticulously detailed that the fourteenth-century palace, now completely overbuilt, can be exactly reconstructed from it. Meanwhile, the duke's greatest Gothic extravaganza, the castle at Mehun-sur-Yèvre, near Bourges, is reserved for the dominant foreground of the painting of the Temptation of Christ (maybe with some relish on the duke's part of the irony of the scene).

The fondness for detail in these buildings, and in the representation of them by these greatest of manuscript-painters – the machicolated towers and turrets, the soaring pinnacles and finials – are what make them part of the fashion for 'International Gothic': they look, particularly Saumur (which still stands, though much changed), like fairy-tale castles, or the generic castle that now does duty in Disneyland (Plate I). In its own day, this kind of architecture was thought supremely *à la mode*, and when the English alliterative poet of *Sir Gawain and the Green Knight* (*c*.1390) describes Sir Gawain arriving at a castle that has appeared almost miraculously to him after a long winter journey, it is in terms of the most fashionable contemporary architecture that he presents it. It is all crocketed towers, tall pinnacles with carved finials, chalk-white chimneys, so fine and exquisite that it seems like a cut-out paper pattern in an elaborate table-decoration:

So mony pynakle payntet was poudred ayquere
Among the castel carneles, clambred so thik,
That pared out of papure purely hit semed.[8]

It almost seems that the author had a preview of the Limbourgs' September picture of Saumur! It is also nearly impossible not to remember here Vasari's famous attack on the monstrous and barbarous nature of Gothic art:

> On all the façades [of churches] they build a malediction of little niches [una maledizione di tabernacolini], one above the other, with no end of pinnacles and points and leaves, so that, not to speak of the whole erection seeming insecure, it appears impossible that the parts should not topple over at any moment. Indeed, they have more the appearance of being made of paper than of stone or marble.[9]

RICHARD II, KING OF ENGLAND 1377–99

Berry's contemporary, the English king Richard II, has a great reputation as a patron of the arts, though much of that reputation is built on the actual achievement of his grandfather, Edward III. St Stephen's Chapel at Westminster, a continuation of the work of Henry III, was completed at vast royal expense in 1348 and painted 1352–61 so as to be 'one universal blaze of splendour and magnificence', and Edward introduced a building programme for the royal palaces the organisation of which rivalled that of his great-grandfather. He had an energetic administrator in William of Wykeham (who exercised his own personal patronage in the building of Winchester College and New College, Oxford) as Clerk of the King's Works, and by the end of his reign there were established posts for King's Mason and King's Carpenter and also for royal painters.

Richard II continued the work of his grandfather. He made some expensive additions to Sheen, which was his favourite residence and the one he caused to be demolished in 1395 after the death of Queen Anne. At Eltham he added (1384–88) a new bath-house, a painted chamber, a dancing chamber, a spicery, and a saucery. Much of the time he was working with an organisational machinery that had its own momentum. However, the king's influence was never less than very significant, as is illustrated by the manner in which funds for royal building works were cut off while Richard was more or less in the hands of his opponents in 1388–89 but were released when he resumed power. In 1393 he began the rebuilding of the Great Hall of Westminster Palace, employing the old King's Mason, Henry Yevele, as his chief architect, and Hugh Herland as the carpenter for the great hammer-beam roof, the finest such roof in Europe (still surviving, though now braced with steel). It is Richard's most magnificent legacy, and was completed more or less in time for his deposition there in 1399.

For the rest, Richard's tastes ran to more personal kinds of ostentation, such as may have prompted the commissioning of the Wilton Diptych (now in the National Gallery in London) in the later years of his life (Fig. 8). One panel of this exquisite small devotional object shows Richard as a young man, backed by John the Baptist and the royal saints Edmund the Martyr and Edward the Confessor, kneeling in homage to the infant Jesus, who leans towards him from the arms of his mother in the other panel. She is surrounded by attendant angels, all in daring monochrome blue and all bearing Richard's personal badge, the white hart. It is a startling piece of effrontery, and exudes the atmosphere of elegance, privilege, high affectation and remoteness characteristic of the International Style.

Richard also commissioned expensive gilded bronze effigies of himself and Queen Anne for their tombs in Westminster Abbey, and lavished expenditure on *objets d'art* and clothes. He probably spent more money than any other English king, but much of it was spent, in an attempt to keep up with France, on the import of foreign-made goods. An ivory-mounted looking-glass in a gold frame with enamelled and jewelled roses, ivory caskets with lids showing scenes of courtly dalliance, bed-hangings of blue camoca embroidered with gold, book-covers of red, white and blue satin with silk tassels, were all imported work, as was a white satin doublet Richard had made, decorated with golden orange-trees bearing a hundred silver-gilt oranges, the white satin sleeves hung with 15 silver cockles and 30 mussels and whelks in silver-gilt. The decline of *opus Anglicanum*, the traditional English embroidery, can probably be traced to the taste for imported clothes, while the deterioration in the quality of English illuminated manuscripts (the ones that Richard II commissioned, such as the *Liber Regalis*, a record of his coronation, do not even represent the best that was available) may similarly owe something to the preferment of the French style. A famous story is told of King John II of France, when he was a prisoner in England after being captured at the battle of Poitiers (1356), ordering a book from a London workshop and turning it down when he saw it. Though Richard can be credited with creating an atmosphere of luxury and refinement, and encouraging his own kinds of extravagance in a few others (John of Gaunt's rebuilding of Kenilworth Castle as a lavishly appointed residential palace would be an example), he did less to establish a machinery for the distribution of artistic patronage than did Henry III and Edward III.

The City

Cities were where the greatest cathedrals were built and where aristocratic and royal patronage found much of its fullest cultural expression, in palaces and palatial town residences (*hôtels*) and the works of art they were filled with. Capital cities like London and Paris were dominated by these great buildings and to some extent by the culture they represented and purveyed: the finest secular building in London was the Duke of Lancaster's Savoy Palace (actually just outside the city, on the 'strand' leading to Westminster), and abbots and bishops had their town-houses too, for the occasions when they were in attendance at Parliament – like the Bishop of Ely's fourteenth-century

house in Holborn, with its vast hall and Gothic windows. These buildings have disappeared, the Savoy burnt down by the rebels in 1381, and generally speaking such town-residences have little chance of surviving the upheavals of urban reconstruction. Fine houses in provincial towns can be more fortunate, such as William Grevel's house in Chipping Campden, in Gloucestershire, or the Angel Inn (as it is now) in Grantham, in Lincolnshire, with the latest in oriel windows.

French provincial cities are often equally favoured, sometimes for special reasons: the grandest medieval non-ecclesiastical building in Bourges (which was the home of the French court during its exile from Paris, 1420–37) is the town-house (1443–51) of Jacques Coeur, a native of the city who was a trader, ship-owner and industrialist but who made his fortune as a financier and moneylender and in particular by advancing to Charles VII the money for the reconquest of Normandy in 1449–53. His house is a sumptuous building in flamboyant Gothic style, with an arcaded courtyard, a bath-house, towers and galleries, coats of arms sculpted in stone, no less than four halls, and fancy names ascribed to several of the rooms – 'the chamber of galleries', 'the chamber of the bishops', 'the room of the months of the year' – though not to the counting-house rooms with their desks of green baize. In a fifteenth-century description of Paris, the house or *hôtel* of Jacques Duchié, a *maître de comptes* who died in 1412, sounds like an eighteenth-century stately home. A 'music room' is filled with harps, organs and other musical instruments, a 'games room' with chessboards and gaming-tables. Another room has a display of military gear, banners, bucklers, crossbows, axes, hung on the walls. At the top of the house is a square room with windows through which the city can be viewed.

The castle at Avignon which became the palace and residence of the popes during the 'Babylonian captivity' (1309–76), and of one of the popes during the Papal Schism (1378–1415), is perhaps unique among secular buildings, and represents an interesting confluence of traditions. It has a fortress-like appearance, but the interior was rebuilt and decorated in high Gothic style under Clement VI in the mid-fourteenth century. The new quarters included a spacious personal chamber for the pope, 10 sq.m, well-lit by two large windows, with an enormous fireplace (fires were useful in warding off the 'vapours' that were thought to encourage the spread of plague), and with a polished floor and wood ceiling. The other amenities of the palace included a

---

Figure 8: London, National Gallery. The Wilton Diptych. Panel, 54 × 37 cm. English? *c*.1395?

This delicious devotional object shows Richard II as a young man (perhaps alluding to his Coronation in 1377, when he was ten years old) kneeling to the infant Jesus, who is held in the arms of his mother. She is attended by angels, all of them bearing Richard's personal badge of the white hart (a quite astonishing appropriation of the angelic host to Richard's livery). Richard is presented by St John the Baptist and by the royal saints Edmund the Martyr, King of the East Angles (with the Danish arrow that killed him in 870), and Edward the Confessor.

whole Tower of Latrines, two storeys high, and elsewhere there were frescoes illustrative of courtly diversions such as hunting and fishing, including at least one by Simone Martini, who was artist-in-residence at Avignon for some years. Much would strike a modern observer as inappropriate to the living-quarters of the pontiff, but the worldliness of papal courts cannot be overstated.

But cities had their own specifically civic importance as centres of culture and patronage of the arts. In all parts of Europe, cities, particularly newly emergent trading and commercial cities, were jealous of their privileges, and would do all they could to secure charters from the king or local suzerain to free them from overlordship and establish the area of their own jurisdiction (their 'liberty', as it was called). The king's own relation with the metropolis of his realm – London or Paris, Prague or Brussels (which became the capital of the dukes of Burgundy after 1435) – was often strained; there were suspicions and fears on each side, and yet each needed the other. Cities grew more confident in taking the initiative particularly in those countries, such as Germany, where the superior authority of a powerful 'state' had declined. However, it was in Flanders and Italy that city-culture developed most independently, and it was there that great civic buildings in the Gothic style were provided for by the commissions of a proud and wealthy urban patriciate.

THE CITIES OF ITALY

The cities of central and northern Italy are the power-house of late medieval and Renaissance culture. They have to be understood as centres of dynamic and competing impulses, their glories necessarily precarious and often short-lived. They were not, for instance, as independent as their municipal authorities might have wished. Cities had to have a hinterland and had to gain control over the surrounding countryside – as a source of food, as a barrier for defence purposes, as a means of increasing their tax-base – and this brought them into contact and conflict with the local landowning magnates, who did not take easily to urban forms of control. These magnates were disruptive, and tended to bring their family feuds and alliances into the city (*Romeo and Juliet* is a distant echo of the politics of the Italian city-state) and to assert themselves physically by building great urban towers for purposes of ostentation, as at San Gimignano. The city authorities had to limit the height of these towers so that they were no higher than the town-hall (planning ordinances in modern cities often adopt similar criteria) – one result of which was that town-halls got higher and higher – and use measures to prevent these aristocratic *mafiosi* from holding civic office, like the Florentine Ordinances of Justice of 1293.

But factions would exist whatever precautions were taken, and city-states were in continual political turmoil. They had a 'communal' form of government, but of course class-based: rule in Florence was by a large General Council, consisting of representatives of those families eligible for membership, advised by a committee of priors, partly elected, partly chosen by lot. Any such system was vulnerable to a local 'strong man', an Alcibiades (many citizens might long for one), and seigneurial rule often returned. A powerful image of city and countryside is provided by Simone Martini's painting of Guidoriccio da Fogliano in the Palazzo Pubblico at Siena, in which a gorgeously clad noble-man on a richly caparisoned horse is depicted riding through a landscape marked off by two flanking cities, Montemassi (on the left) and (probably) Sassoforte; the landscape is empty, but central.

Siena had a long period of comparative stability, the Government of the Nine, 1287–1355, during which time the Palazzo Pubblico was built, 1288–1309. The city was very well organised financially, both in raising taxes and in encouraging commerce by tax-exemptions, and had an extensive programme of public works: dams were built for purposes of irrigation, and fountains in the city were supplied by 25 km of underground aqueducts bringing water in from springs outside the city. Though the plans for a grand new cathedral did not work out, as we shall see in Chapter Three, there was much effective regulation of trade, rubbish disposal, hostelries and brothels, and a great hospital was built, Santa Maria della Scala. Ambrogio Lorenzetti did two magnificent frescoes for the Palazzo Pubblico (1337–39), the 'Allegory of Good Government in the City' and the 'Allegory of Good Government in the Country', which depict this ideal of the urban community and the sub-urban countryside. The commune guarantees the security of the surrounding farms, its officers guard the fields against the intrusion of livestock and thieves, a network of lanes and paths between the fields provides access and control. The country is civilised by the town.

As the fourteenth century went on, wealthy people in towns began to decorate their homes with more and more elaborate wall-paintings. A notable example is the Davanzati Palace in Florence, with floral and geometric patterns on the walls of halls and chambers, and friezes above with trees, birds, coats of arms, and illustration in one room of episodes from the thirteenth-century French romance of La Chastelaine de Vergi. Some of the painting is done in trompe-l'oeil imitation of tapestry. Further north, in Trento, one of the rooms in the Torre dell' Aquila, part of the bishop's palace, was decorated (c.1410) with a magnificent series of seasonal scenes showing the Labours of the Months. For April there is a series of scenes of springtime agricultural activity, vertically stacked in the International Style without regard for perspective and separated by rocky coulisses and wattle fences, while January, quite exceptionally (and almost at the same time that the Limbourgs were doing a genre snow-scene for February in the Très Riches Heures du Duc de Berry), shows a fully developed winter snow-scene, with peasants plodding up to their knees through the snow and courtiers, richly apparelled, playing snowballs in the foreground.

All of this display was made possible by the wealth generated by trade and commerce and by the sophisticated new systems of banking and book-keeping. Florence's peak was 1343–78: it had the most magnificent buildings, and commissioned work from the greatest painters and sculptors, though it never created a central 'place' or piazza to match those of Siena or Perugia, a spectacular civic space for processions, ceremonies, plays, preachings, or, in Siena, for the annual horse-race or Palio. In Perugia, the Priors' Palace (Palazzo dei Priori), begun 1290, looks out over a cityscape such as no other western

European city can boast, unless it be the aquatic cityscape of Venice, whose cultural pre-eminence was to come in the late fifteenth and sixteenth centuries, when its power had begun to decline.

But at Florence there was Dante (Dante Alighieri, 1265–1321), active in Florentine politics before being banished from the city in 1302. He was reared in the Tuscan civic tradition, and was interested in political theory, philosophy, theology, cosmology and science as well as intent on writing a great poem in the Italian vernacular. His intention was announced in the Latin *De vulgari eloquentia* and put into practice in the *Divina Commedia*. Dante was, in some sense, 'medieval' in his political outlook, in his distaste for the 'politics of the possible', and in his advocacy of universal empire on the Roman model. He was the product of Florence, but also its nemesis: he consigned 32 Florentines to Hell, and a further 13 from Tuscany, out of a total of 79 distinguished by name; only two of his fellow-townsmen made it to Paradise.

Chivalric culture was strong in Italy, and there was much influence from France, but there was also a sophisticated secular culture such as other European countries were to be a long time in establishing. There were many schools and universities for the training of lawyers, administrators and doctors. The arts of writing letters and speeches were recognised for their practical value, and the interest in such rhetorical arts led naturally to classical theories of eloquence and a renewed attention to classical literature. Giovanni Boccaccio (1313–75) cultivated Dante himself as an Italian 'classic', gave lectures on him, and in his own writing gave expression both to popular urban literary forms (in his poem of *Il Filostrato* and in the tales of the *Decameron*) and also to the learned Latin tradition (in the influential compilations *De casibus virorum illustrium*, 'Concerning the falls of princes', and *De claris mulieribus*, 'Concerning famous women'). The *Decameron* (1348–51) is unprecedented in literature of the Gothic period in the record it gives of contemporary urban life, its social attitudes and customs, beliefs and practices, and the material realities of existence. Much that is revealed in passing of the detail of ordinary life is not easily accessible from other sources. Petrarch (Francesco Petrarca, 1304–74), though he was a friend of Boccaccio (if a relationship composed of condescension on the one part and flattery on the other can be called friendship), despised the *Decameron* as a triviality. He was not a Florentine: he cultivated his ducal patrons in Milan, enjoyed intimacy with power, was adept at self-publicisation and invented 'laureation'. He was a connoisseur of the Latin classics and hunted out and collected manuscripts of classical texts. He also wrote the greatest series of love-poems of the Middle Ages, in the *Canzonieri*, brought to a high level of sophistication the sonnet and the idea of the 'person' of the individual poet, and cultivated a high Ciceronianism in his Latin prose writings (especially in his many letters) which made him the model of the 'humanist'.

More and more, as the Italian city-states were taken over by aristocratic rulers, cultural patronage fell into the hands of a different political class. There were no more 'Allegories of Good Government' set up in civic buildings: the political interests of patrons were now differently and more subtly sublimated, though rarely with any desire to obscure the ostentation of expense. Contracts for paintings specified that so much ultramarine and lapis lazuli and gold leaf, all of them very expensive, should be used, and that the master of the workshop was to do at least the main figures in the composition – maybe because this would make for a 'better' painting, but more immediately because it would enhance the cultural return on the investment. The influence of such patrons is not easily predictable. Sigismondo Malatesta, dictator at Rimini 1430–68, whom Ezra Pound wished in 1923 to recommend to the Italian dictator Benito Mussolini, *Il Duce*, as a model patron of the arts, reconstructed the church of San Francesco with a façade designed by Leon Battista Alberti – it was the first church to incorporate a Roman triumphal arch – and with bas-reliefs by Agostino di Ducci. But he also gave commissions to Pisanello and to Piero della Francesca.

THE CITIES OF FLANDERS

In Flanders, too, it was the pride and wealth of the city burgesses that provided the commissions for great civic buildings in the Gothic style, especially the city-halls of Flanders, such as the Cloth Hall in Bruges (1376–1420) and the Cloth Hall in Ypres, which was completed in 1380 and was the largest building in the Low Countries until it was destroyed in the First World War. The cloth-making towns of northern England did not aspire to comparable buildings until the nineteenth century: the guildhall of the most powerful guild in a provincial city like York, the Merchant Adventurers' Hall (1357), is still an old-fashioned single-hall timber-framed building. The splendid Guildhall of London (1411) was severely damaged in the Great Fire of 1665 and rebuilt virtually from the ground after the Blitz of 1940.

The tastes of the French-speaking aristocracy of Flanders and Brabant were well satisfied by French versions of Arthurian romance, but there are also Middle Dutch renderings, as early as the thirteenth century, that are evidently designed for an aspirant bourgeoisie, much like the contemporary English versions of French romance. Stories from the *chansons de geste* were also popular with this audience, who seem to have been happy with a mixture of heroic, fantastic and broadly comic motifs: the short Charlemagne poem of *Karel ende Elegast* anticipates the novella in many of its witty and imaginative innovations. The masterpiece of thirteenth-century Dutch literature is *Van den Vos Reinaerde* (*c.*1275) of one 'Willem', a brilliant adaptation of the scatological French beast-epic of the *Roman de Renart*. It is hard to think of it satisfying the 'taste' of an audience, or to think of any audience, other than one of clerical drop-outs, that would admit to enjoying it, but it is usually associated with the middle classes. A better guide to bourgeois taste might be the Van Hulthem manuscript of *c.*1400 (Brussels, Koninglijke Bibliotheek, MS 15589–15623), a treasure-house of narrative poems, lyrics, legends and plays (comparable with the London Auchinleck MS of *c.*1330–40, Edinburgh, National Library of Scotland, MS Advocates 19.2.1, likewise designed for an urban client) such as might have provided a book of 'specimens' for an urban customer to choose from in commissioning his own personal compilation. Each text has an indication of the number of lines that it contains, as if for purposes of computing payment.

But the influence of great magnates was a factor in the cities of Flanders as well as in the city-states of Italy. Jacob van Maerlant was the most influential Flemish author of his time, and perhaps the most prolific poet of the Middle Ages (some 250,000 lines of verse are attributed to him), and he made his name writing for Floris V, Count of Holland (1254–96).[10] He did Middle Dutch versions of Virgil and Ovid, of the *Historia scolastica* (bible-history) of Petrus Comestor, of the *Speculum historiale* of Vincent of Beauvais (a vast encyclopaedic history of the world from the Creation to the 1250 crusade of Louis IX), of the lives of Alexander and St Francis, and of the stories of Troy and the Grail, many of them the first adaptations into any vernacular of the central texts of the European Latin tradition. Later in the fourteenth century there was a flourishing court-poetry among Floris's successors at the Holland-Bavarian court at The Hague, involving the participation of career diplomats, civil servants, heraldic officials and chaplains, rather as in contemporary English courts. The mix of courtly and urban in later Flemish literature makes a good parallel for the London poetry of Chaucer and Hoccleve.

Once the Burgundian dukes moved their court to Flanders, they provided much of the richest patronage. Jan van Eyck (*c*.1390–1441), acknowledged in his own lifetime as the greatest Dutch painter of his day, was court-painter for eleven years (1425–36) to Philip the Good at the ducal court at Lille. When the duke moved his court to Brussels in 1435, he was surrounded again by the skilled craftsmen, the entrepreneurs of the arts, the writers, as well as the banks and the moneylenders, who were inevitably drawn to the honeypots of patronage. Even in Bruges, with its long tradition of civic government, the grandest of the town-houses was the Hôtel Gruthuyse, built by the lords of La Gruthuyse 1425–70. Van Eyck's great commissions there were from traditional types of patron, like the altarpiece of the Madonna and Child with St Donatian and St George that he did in 1436 for George van der Paele, a rich canon of St Donatian's church, who appears kneeling before the Child holding his spectacles in his hand.

NOTES

1. Agnellus of Ravenna (ninth century), *Liber Pontificalis Ecclesiae Ravennatis*, quoted and translated in Charles Jones, *Saints' Lives and Chronicles in Early England* (Chicago, 1947), p. 63.
2. From BL MS Harley 2253, fol. 59v. *droh*, 'added'; *throh*, 'grave'; *Tho*, 'then'. For the rest, all one needs to know to understand this quatrain is that *erthe* means (1) the earth, (2) dirt, (3) flesh as dust, and (4) flesh.
3. The detail here is from Constance Bullock-Davies, *Menestrellorum Multitudo: Minstrels at a Royal Feast* (Cardiff, 1978).
4. See John Lydgate, 'The Soteltes at the Coronation Banquet of Henry VI', in *The Minor Poems of John Lydgate*, ed. H.N. MacCracken, EETS, OS 192 (1934), p. 623.

5. Much in the following paragraphs draws upon Elizabeth Salter, *English and International: Studies in the Literature, Art and Patronage of Medieval England* (Cambridge, 1988), pp. 80–92.

6. For these manuscripts, see Christopher de Hamel, *A History of Illuminated Manuscripts* (London, 1986), p. 141.

7. For an account of this period in Bohemia's history, see Alfred Thomas, *Anne's Bohemia: Czech Literature and Society, 1310–1420*, Medieval Cultures, 13 (Minneapolis, 1998).

8. In Malcolm Andrew and Ronald Waldron (eds), *The Poems of the Pearl-Manuscript* (London, 1978), lines 800–2. *Carneles*: crenellated battlements.

9. Giorgio Vasari, *Lives of the Italian Painters*, quoted in Erwin P. Panofsky, *Meaning in the Visual Arts: Papers in and on Art History* (Garden City, N.Y., 1955), p. 176.

10. Maerlant is the subject of a biography by Fritz van Ostroom (*Maerlants Wereld*, Amsterdam, 1996), who, with Mary-Jo Arn, has provided me with a helpful introduction to the literary culture of medieval Flanders.

3

The Gothic Achievement

The Gothic Cathedral

The primary meaning of the term 'Gothic' has to do with a style of church-building which developed in northern France in the later twelfth century, spread quickly to the rest of western Europe, and dominated ecclesiastical architecture, and the grander forms of secular architecture, throughout the period covered by this book. It was an extraordinary phenomenon, matched only by the spread of steel-framed skyscrapers in the modern period: a new style of building set the economic, cultural and aesthetic priorities for two centuries, so that between 1150 and 1350 there were built, in France alone, 80 cathedrals and 500 large churches. It was to this style of building that the term 'Gothic' was first abusively applied in the Renaissance (as described in the introduction to Chapter One), and, in its modern use, 'Gothic', though it has been extended to apply to styles in sculpture and painting and other arts, and even used as a periodising epithet in itself, is principally understood to refer to architecture. The Gothic church is thus, both in historical reality and modern vernacular usage, the archetype of 'the Gothic', and the Gothic cathedral or larger Gothic church is the supreme embodiment of the spirit and ambition of the age called 'Gothic'.[1]

THE ORIGIN AND CHARACTER OF THE GOTHIC STYLE IN ARCHITECTURE

The new style was announced by Abbot Suger (1081–1151) in his work towards the rebuilding of his abbey-church of Saint-Denis (a few miles north of Paris), the choir of which was consecrated in 1144. He supervised the new building closely, and left a detailed record of his ideas and plans for what he called, with unusually deliberate self-consciousness, his *opus novum*, or *opus modernum*.[2] His aim was to create a vast stone vessel into which light could

flood through stained glass windows as a symbol of the Light which God brought
into the world through Christ, and to give to the whole a soaring upward thrust
which would symbolise man's aspiration towards God. It was the building
techniques that he employed to bring these purposes to fulfilment that marked
the emergence of the new style. Not all of them were, in a technical sense, new,
nor were any of them, at this stage, fully developed: it was their integration into
a harmonious building programme that was the significant new departure.

The three major structural characteristics of the new style are the pointed
arch, the rib-vault, and the flying buttress. All serve to increase the volume
and height of the enclosed vessel of the church and enable it to be filled with
light. The pointed arch is capable of bearing a heavier load than the rounded
arch characteristic of the older Romanesque style as it derived ultimately from
classical models. More important is the capacity of the pointed arch to permit
vaults to be built over four-sided or polygonal areas so that the apex (where
the arches cross) is the same height as the transverse arches and wall-arches. In
other words, different-sized spaces can be vaulted at the same height, where
with vaulting based on rounded arches there is a fixed relation between height
of arch and width. Majestic solidity, shadows and sudden shafts of sunlight, the
deep coolness so welcome in Romanesque churches in Spain and the south of
France, give way to space and light, and a perception of uninterrupted spatial
modulations (Plate II). Saint-Denis was the first church to have the ambulatory
and the connected radiating chapels vaulted at the same height (Fig. 9).

The rib-vault is associated with the pointed arch. Struts or ribs, made of
narrow moulded masonry blocks, concentrate the weight of stone at particular
points, where it can be absorbed in piers or buttresses. It is the rib-vault that
helps give to Gothic buildings their sense of excitement and tenseness, of
massiveness miraculously suspended, as opposed to the solidity of Romanesque. The effect is indeed so miraculous that there has been some debate as to
whether the diagonal ribs do actually support the vault, further prompted by
the visual evidence of churches that were damaged during the two World
Wars, where many were found with the ribs fallen and the vaults standing.
But the opposite also happens, particularly in buildings that have gradually
fallen into ruin. The answer is probably that the ribs were not 'mere' decoration (though they did serve a decorative function in covering the awkward
junction at the groin of the vault) but were needed for the construction and
early settlement of the vaults, especially the larger ones, where timber supports
took a long time to prepare with the hand-worked adze.

Buttressing is a technique for absorbing the lateral thrust of arches and
vaults (that is, their desire to push their vertical supports outwards) and dissip-
ating it outside the structure. It enables the walls between the buttresses to be
thinner and to accommodate more glass. Flying buttresses, first fully developed
at Notre Dame in Paris, are a means of achieving this purpose at higher and
higher level above the ground. As walls soared upwards, the upper levels of
triforium (often pierced to allow the insertion of windows) and clerestory
needed extra supports that would not obstruct the passage of light to the
windows below and that could rest upon the outer walls of ground-floor aisles

Figure 9: Saint-Denis, abbey-church, interior, from the south-west.

Saint-Denis saw the first development, under the patronage of Abbot Suger, of the new style of building later called 'Gothic'. Its new choir was consecrated in 1144, but little remains of the original building; when a new campaign of rebuilding began in 1231, the choir was raised to the same level as the nave, which was completed in 1281.

or chapels (Figs 10, 11). The flying buttress was the answer, and is in many ways the most striking external feature of large Gothic churches, as well as the means through which the wall-structure, viewed from inside, was pared to the bone, as if in defiance of gravity. There is a miraculous difference, in Gothic cathedrals, between the taut equilibrium of forces plainly visible in the forest of piers, arches and buttresses on the exterior (like modern 'space-frame' architecture) and the insubstantial soaring space of the interior, seemingly unsupported. The flying buttress was extravagantly developed as an architectural feature in its own right, with its own slender soaring pinnacles (such pinnacles had an original structural function in exerting compensatory vertical thrust) and canopied niches. The choir at Le Mans cathedral (begun 1217, completed 1254), with its seven-sided apse, double ambulatory, and thirteen deep radiating chapels, seems to hang upon its arches and buttresses, it has been said, like a giant spider suspended upon its legs (Fig. 12).[3]

There are other, non-structural elements introduced at Saint-Denis, none of them new in themselves, that were to become part of the stylistic repertory of Gothic: the rose-window; the sculpted tympana above the doorways; the carved figures in the archivolts; large sculpted figures set in the wall. Such features are of great importance in embodying in visual and symbolic form the doctrinal programme which it was the business of a Christian church to provide for its users. But it is the newly integrated structural elements that give the new style its special character. A classical building is complete, as a design, before it is begun, and when the building is finished there is nothing more to be done: it is centralised, symmetrical, 'closed'. A Gothic church may be finished, but it is never complete, for the nature of the structural elements is that they can be repeated or added to more or less indefinitely – not in a mechanically aggregative way, but often with a rich variety of inventiveness, verging on the playful and improvisatory, such as gives the Gothic style its characteristic subjective impression of mobility, excitement and restlessness. An old nave or choir can be thrown down and a grander structure, in a newer form of Gothic, erected; naves and choirs can have bays, aisles, chapels, transepts, porches, portals added; roofs can be raised, window-space extended.

No large Gothic church comes down to us as it was originally planned – very little, for instance, remains of Suger's original building at Saint-Denis – and most of them were the product of long and piecemeal building programmes. It was not unusual for a hundred years or more to separate the building of the choir from the building of the nave: the choir of the cathedral of Saint-Etienne at Auxerre was begun 1215–34,[4] but the nave not until 1309, and not completed until 1392–1401, when a rose-window was added in the north transept in the latest version of *rayonnant* style (*rayonnant*, 'light-radiating': like most such terms, it arises from emphasis on a particular componential feature within a style). At Canterbury, it was two centuries after the rebuilding of the choir in the late twelfth century before the Norman nave begun by Archbishop Lanfranc and completed in 1094 was rebuilt in the Perpendicular style by Henry Yevele, master-mason to Edward III and Richard II, and the Bell Harry Tower, the dominant external feature of the edifice,

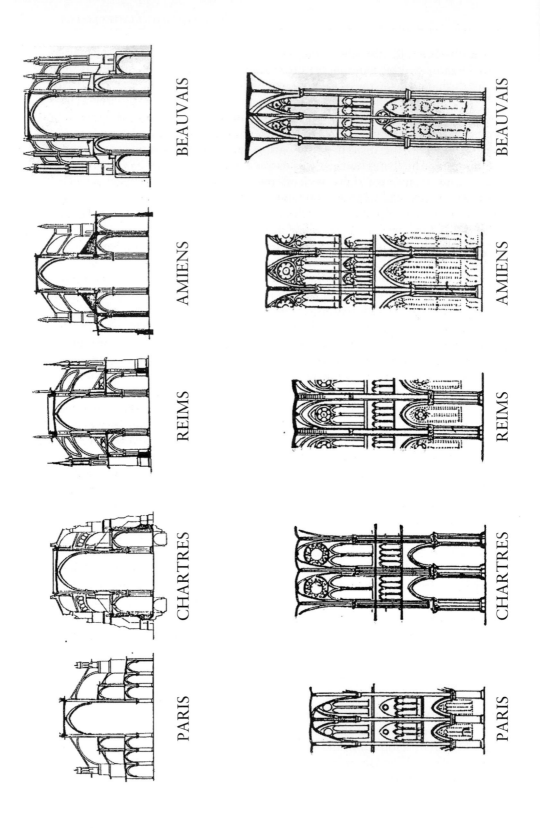

BEAUVAIS

AMIENS

REIMS

CHARTRES

PARIS

BEAUVAIS

AMIENS

REIMS

CHARTRES

PARIS

was not begun until 1493. There are other, more spectacular examples: Milan Cathedral, begun in 1387, had its choir and transepts by 1450 but had to wait for Napoleon for the completion of the west façade in 1809; Cologne Cathedral, begun in 1248, and the work much advanced in the fourteenth century, was only completed in 1842–80, when the 'temporary' partition dividing choir and unfinished nave was demolished in 1863 after 541 years, and the crane removed that had stood on the top of the south-west tower for three centuries. The progress of modern projects in Anglican Gothic has been likewise chequered, for similar financial and other reasons: Liverpool Cathedral was under construction from 1914 until 1978, when it was dedicated (it was consecrated in 1924), while the Cathedral of St John the Divine in New York City, which had its first cornerstone laid in 1892, and which will eventually be the biggest church in Christendom, is still not completed.

The infinitely aggregative possibilities of the large Gothic church, and the sprawling structures they can give rise to, are an offence against classically trained taste, but they were of enormous practical and spiritual benefit. That a church should be rebuilt, extended, left unfinished, added to, is not inappropriate to its larger purpose, since man's striving towards God is never complete. Sources of funding were not usually regular or reliable in the long term, and energetic patrons came and went, but the practice of piecemeal addition and renovation ensured that what money and means were available could be put to good and immediate use. Once a cathedral had been consecrated – and there was usually some haste to get at least the choir built for that purpose – it was no offence against God that it remained unfinished, as it would have been an offence against the goddess Athene Parthenos if her temple on the Acropolis in Athens had lacked a few pillars and pediments. For many years during the fourteenth century, as the enthusiasm of its royal patrons waxed and waned, Westminster Abbey lay with Henry III's magnificent choir unattached to the surviving western bays of the nave. A temporary porch was thrown over the rebuilding area, for a church must have some kind of roof if the rain is not to wash down on its altars, and the nave was brought to a final state under Henry V and eventually finished off in the reign of Henry VII (c.1507–9): but no one seems to have been ashamed, or talked of the building being an eyesore. God's work was being done in it, all the time. For patrons, too, those who financed church-building with their gifts, endowments and bequests, it was important only that the church should remain for ever on its site. It did not matter how it changed, so long as their share in its dedication

Figure 10: Cross-sections and elevations of the cathedrals of Paris, Chartres, Reims, Amiens and Beauvais.
   The cross-sections show clearly the essential function of flying buttresses, springing out from the roofs of the ground-floor aisles and chapels to support the upper levels of the triforium and clerestory without blocking out the light. The elevations show the inventiveness of the builders in varying the elements of the three-storey design, as well as the dramatic increases in the height of the whole structure.

Figure 11: Paris, Cathedral of Notre Dame, nave, north side.

Compare Figs 9 and 10. Building began at Notre Dame in 1163, and the choir was completed by 1182. The nave was completed by 1250, but immediately a new phase of building began with the extension of the transepts and the insertion of rose-windows. Rebuilding was to continue throughout the following centuries, as Paris grew in importance and influence, and much of the detail of the modern building is due to the restorations (1841–65) of Viollet-le-Duc.

was remembered. Fund-raising in the present day for the older Oxbridge colleges and the older American universities is easier, for something like the same reasons, than for more recently established institutions.

THE SPREAD OF THE GOTHIC STYLE IN ARCHITECTURE

Work began at Saint-Denis in 1137: the choir was complete by 1143, and consecrated in 1144 (the nave was not completed until 1281). The new style quickly caught on, and by the end of the twelfth century a rage for Gothic was spreading through the Ile de France, the area radiating out from Paris that formed the French royal domain, and into adjacent regions such as Champagne, Burgundy and Normandy. The Cathedral of Saint-Etienne in Sens had its new Gothic choir consecrated in 1164, and new choirs were built at Noyon (c.1150/55–1185) and Senlis (1155–91). A new cathedral was begun at Laon, a former capital (840–987) of the Carolingian kingdom of Francia, about 1160, and completed in 1230: it was the first complete cathedral to be built in the Gothic style, and proved extraordinarily influential. The west front is one of the great achievements of Gothic, with its magnificent rose-window, and western towers honeycombed with niches and deep-cloven arches (Fig. 13) – and unexpectedly crowned with oxen (commemorating a helpful beast who miraculously turned up to take the place of one who had fallen dead when dragging a wagon loaded with stone). The choir at Notre Dame in Paris was begun in 1163 and completed by 1182, and the nave by 1250, at which point the transepts were extended (1250–67) and rose-windows introduced with the radiating tracery of the new *style rayonnant* (Fig. 14). The central position of Notre Dame made it very influential, but also vulnerable to modernisation in the latest fashion: the Gothic high altar was replaced in the late seventeenth century with a white marble Pietà flanked by kneeling statues of Louis XIII and XIV, while at the Revolution a frieze of 28 statues of kings of Israel over the portals of the west front was torn down in revolutionary fervour (they were thought to be kings of France) and the festival of the 'Goddess Reason' held before the altar. Like many French cathedrals, the present building is the product of restoration (1841–65) at the hands of Viollet-le-Duc, who had his own idealised vision of the Gothic style.

The Cathedral of Notre Dame at Chartres, the masterpiece of French Gothic, was begun in 1194, and, sustained by a remarkable surge of energy and enthusiasm, was largely complete, as to its structure, by 1220; at Bourges, the choir, begun in 1195, was in use by 1232 and the cathedral completed by 1285; the choir at Soissons, begun 1197–98 under the influence of Chartres, was complete by about 1212. The early years of the thirteenth century saw new Gothic cathedrals begun or planned at Reims (1211), Auxerre (c.1215), Le Mans (1217), Amiens (1220), Beauvais (1227) and Dijon (the church of Notre Dame, begun c.1220–30). The new cathedral at Coutances, begun immediately after the great fire of 1218 and complete by 1250, is the masterpiece of Norman Gothic, a uniquely homogeneous structure, with soaring western towers and a striking octagonal lantern tower over the crossing. Like Bayeux ('Gothicised'

over a period of more than a century from 1165), it survived the fierce fighting of the battle of Normandy (1944) almost intact. Elsewhere, the archetypal design was amplified and extended, the west front was elaborated and developed (most notably at Amiens) (Fig. 15), walls soared upward – much in the form of vast stained-glass windows separated by buttressed pillar-like wall-sections – and the apex at the crossing reached higher and higher. At Laon it was 79 ft high (24 m), at Paris 110 ft (33.5 m), at Chartres 114 ft (34.75 m), at Reims 125 ft (39 m) and at Amiens 139 ft (nearly 42.5 m). The choir at Beauvais, over 157 ft high (nearly 48 m), was completed in 1263; in 1272 the vault collapsed; rebuilt, it collapsed again in 1284; it was rebuilt again, with heavier buttresses and narrower windows (spoiling some of the essential Gothic effect). No further attempt was made, in the Middle Ages, to improve on Amiens, except at Cologne, 141 ft (43 m), and Palma de Mallorca, 145 ft (44 m).

Meanwhile, new refinements in Gothic were being announced, again at Saint-Denis, where the upper sections of Abbot Suger's choir were being re-constructed from about 1231, while the nave and transepts were being built. Again it was the harmonious combination of pre-existing elements rather than mere innovation that characterised the new style: the piercing of the triforium, thus extending even further the window-space; the covering of the round piers with colonettes that respond to the numerous vault-ribs; and the insertion of rose-windows (first recorded at Laon somewhat earlier). This new 'Court Style', the harbinger of the more fully developed *style rayonnant*, was followed in the cathedral at Troyes, where work had resumed in 1228, and in the no longer surviving abbey-church of Saint-Nicaise in Reims, begun 1231; it reaches its climax in the Sainte-Chapelle attached to the royal palace in Paris, built 1241–48 as a monumental glass reliquary for the Crown of Thorns that Louis IX had bought from the Byzantine Emperor. *Rayonnant* was well established by 1250–60, especially under the influence of the new work in the transepts at Notre Dame in Paris, and is evidenced at Tours, completed about 1260, and Strassburg, completed 1277.

Gothic had spread quickly beyond the French royal domain, first to regions and countries that were politically and economically close to Paris, and prin-cipally to areas that were reasonably prosperous – though there was no iron economic law in this (Amiens, for instance, had its cathedral finished long before Cologne, which was a far wealthier city), and local enthusiasms and money-raising activities (fairs, markets, special processions of relics), and other circumstances, could play a large part. England was close to France in a special way, being in possession of large parts of it, and the new style very soon crossed the Channel, with the rebuilding of the choir at Canterbury

Figure 12: Le Mans Cathedral, choir with flying buttresses, aerial view from the east.

The choir at Le Mans was begun in 1217 and completed in 1254. With its seven-sided apse, double ambulatory, and thirteen deep radiating chapels, it needed a forest of flying buttresses, and seems to hang upon them, it has been said, like a giant spider suspended upon its legs.

Figure 13: Laon Cathedral, west front.

Laon, begun about 1160 and completed in 1230, was the first complete cathedral to be built in the Gothic style, and was to prove extremely influential. The west front, with its magnificent rose-window, deeply recessed doorways, and towers honeycombed with niches and arches, is one of the great achievements of Gothic. 'I have never seen such a tower', said Villard de Honnecourt, as he made his architectural tour of France soon after Laon was built.

begun under a French-trained architect, William of Sens, in 1175. New choirs were begun at Chichester (1187), Rochester (c.1190), Lincoln (St Hugh's choir, 1192) and Salisbury (1220), and a great surge of cathedral-building in England came after the magnificent rebuilding of the choir at Westminster Abbey by Henry III. A tendency towards thicker walls and less ambitious elevations meant that flying buttresses were less used in England, but other elements in the Gothic repertoire were correspondingly emphasised, as in the magnificent west front at Wells (c.1230–40), with its profusion of richly decorated arcades and statued niches, the finest ensemble of medieval sculpture in England, and the prototype of other western façades at Salisbury and Exeter.

Salisbury, begun in 1220, was completed by 1266, a building-programme to compare with Chartres, though the spire, which many viewers would consider the focus of a uniquely harmonious composition, was not completed until after 1320. Salisbury is in some ways the characteristic type of the English cathedral, with its square eastern end, long nave (good for processions) and boldly projecting transepts, and its setting in a tranquil close (like Exeter, Lincoln, Winchester, and other English cathedrals) rather than at the hub of a busy town, as often in France (Plate III). The unified building-plan means that it is less of a sprawl than some other English cathedrals, and less an example of the informal effect of mixed styles, but it is typically English in the comparative restraint of its decorative and sculptural programme. English cathedrals generally have less monumental sculpture than French cathedrals, more foliage-work on capitals, corbels and roof-bosses, and more fondness for genre-scenes in glass and misericords. There is often an impression of improvisation and idiosyncrasy: the scissor-arch at the crossing in Wells (Fig. 16), erected when the piers started to give way in 1320, may allude to the cross of St Andrew, to whom the cathedral is dedicated, but it is undoubtedly one of the most unexpected structures in all Gothic architecture. Sometimes, improvised solutions to building problems could produce magnificent results. When the Lady Chapel at Ely was begun in 1321, the piers supporting the central lantern and tower collapsed, and a huge space had to be vaulted. Timber was the only possibility – an English solution – but even so, massive oak timbers, 63 × 3 ft (20 × 1 m), had to be found and transported to the site, with roads improved and bridges strengthened along the way. The octagon and lantern, so unpremeditatedly arrived at, are Ely's glory.

At Westminster, rebuilding began in 1245 with the multangular east end, with ambulatory and five radiating chapels, very much on the model of French choirs and under the influence of the Court Style. A new decorative polychromatic effect was achieved by the use of dark Purbeck marble for the alternate engaged shafts of the piers and by the use of two-toned ornament in the spandrels. The chapter-house was completed in 1253 as a separate building: these dramatic free-standing structures are an impressive surviving feature of some other English cathedrals, such as Salisbury and York, that were non-monastic foundations but built on the model of abbey-churches. The rebuilding at Westminster was further influential at Lincoln, at Lichfield, and in the east end of Old St Paul's (c.1280–85), known now only from engravings made before the Great Fire of London in 1666, but probably much imitated in its day.

Figure 15: Amiens Cathedral, west front.

Compare Laon (Fig. 13). The new cathedral at Amiens was begun in 1220, the nave (unusually) completed first, about 1236, and the whole cathedral by 1269. The *flamboyant* tracery of the rose-window was installed in the sixteenth century and the whole west front restored by Viollet-le-Duc in the nineteenth century.

Figure 14: Paris, Cathedral of Notre Dame, general view from the south.

See also Fig. 11. The west towers soar to a height of 69 m (226 ft). The magnificent rose-window in the south transept, much restored, was part of the building campaign of 1250–67. The flèche was added during the restorations of Viollet-le-Duc (1841–65), which followed upon the romantic surge of interest in the decayed building inspired by Victor Hugo's *Notre Dame de Paris* (1831).

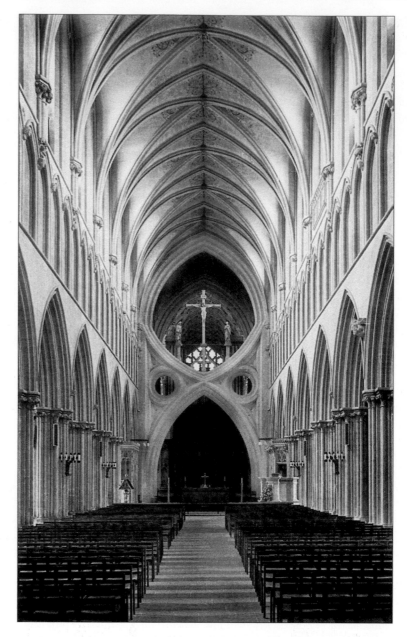

Figure 16: Wells Cathedral, scissor-arch, looking from the nave towards the crossing.
     Wells was begun before 1200 and most of the building completed in the
thirteenth century, including the nave (completed in 1239) and the splendid west
front. But the west piers of the tower crossing began to subside in 1320, and had
to be strengthened. The solution was found in the extraordinary scissor-arch that
was built (1338–48) to brace the piers, along with similar arches on the north
and south sides of the crossing.

A particular influence in the spread of Gothic through Europe was exerted by the Cistercian movement (recognised 1119), which needed new abbey-churches at just the moment when the new style was coming into vogue. Elements of the style, such as cross-ribbed vaulting, were early introduced in the chapter-house at Fontenay (c.1150) and the nave at Pontigny (1150–55) (Fig. 17), and a simplified Cistercian Gothic spearheaded change in England (Rievaulx, Fountains), Germany (Maulbronn, Heisterbach), Spain (the chapter-house at Las Huelgas, near Burgos, begun after 1225) and Italy (Sant'Andrea at Vercelli, in Piedmont, begun 1219) before the advent of the fully developed style.

The *camino francés*, the pilgrimage route to Santiago de Compostella, carried French Gothic into north-west Spain and the kingdoms of Castile and Aragon, and there are elements of Gothic already in the choir of San Vicente at Avila, begun c.1200, and in the cathedrals at Lérida and Cuenca soon after. A more developed Spanish Gothic was established by about 1230, and the pace of events was similar in eastern France and beyond the Rhine. There were new beginnings at Magdeburg and Limburg-an-der-Lahn about 1220, and more fully developed and idiosyncratic variations of Gothic at Trier (the Liebfrauenkirche, begun 1235) and Marburg-an-der-Lahn (the Elisabethkirche, also begun 1235, to house the shrine of St Elizabeth of Hungary, canonised in that year). But the decisive influence in Germany was Strassburg, where the Romanesque rebuilding of the cathedral after the fire of 1176 was abruptly switched to Gothic when a French-trained architect was appointed in 1225. He announced his arrival with the extraordinary Chartres-inspired Angels' Pillar, with figures of evangelists and angels arranged in ascending order around a free-standing pillar. The nave was built in 1240–75, and the towering western façade (with rose-window), virtuoso-work in malleable red Vosges sandstone, was completed in 1277. The single (north-west) tower was begun in 1275, and the 466 ft (151 m) spire, the highest masonry structure of the Middle Ages, completed in 1439. Strassburg inspired Freiburg-im-Breisgau, across the Rhine, begun in 1235 (not consecrated until 1510), and Cologne, begun in 1248. The waning of German Romanesque, whose massive state-ment of power had fitted well with imperial ambition, had been slow, but it came to an end with the ending of the Hohenstaufen dynasty in 1254 and the weakening of imperial power.

South-central and southern France, the feudatory duchies and counties of the King of France, saw a remarkable spurt of building in the 1260s and 1270s, as French hegemony was more fully asserted, with new Gothic cathedrals or choirs begun at Clermont-Ferrand (1262), Narbonne (1272), Toulouse (1272), Limoges (1273) and Rodez (1277). Even in Italy, where classically inspired styles were bound to exert more influence, the new style made its way, though chiefly where Dominican and Franciscan friars, who favoured airy preaching spaces, were the patrons. The church of San Francesco at Assisi was begun as early as 1226 (dedicated 1253), and was followed by San Francesco at Bologna (begun 1236, dedicated 1250). The first Gothic in Tuscany was the Dominican church of Santa Maria Novella in Florence, begun in 1246, and there are the

Figure 17: Pontigny, abbey-church.

    An example of the plainer style of Cistercian architecture. The Cistercian order of monks, founded in 1095 and profoundly influenced by St Bernard of Clairvaux (1090–1153), was early vowed to a new austerity of life. This included the rejection of unnecessary ornament and display in church buildings. The church at Pontigny, about 100 miles east-south-east of Paris, was begun about 1150, during the period of severest restraint.

beginnings of an Italian Gothic style in the characteristically wide rather than high nave of the Franciscan church of Santa Croce, also in Florence, begun in 1294.

In eastern Europe, Prague Cathedral was begun in 1248, consecrated in 1322, and when the nave was continued by Peter Parler after 1353 it became, with its open triforium and high wide clerestory, one of the most impressive Gothic cathedrals in Europe (Fig. 18). In the far north-west of Europe, the nave of Christ Church Cathedral in Dublin was built in the early thirteenth century, after the Anglo-Norman invasion of Ireland in 1172, in the 'Early English' Gothic style. In the north, Denmark has brick-built churches showing the influence of North German Gothic, including St Knud's (the former Greyfriars church) in Odense (begun 1301), St Peter's in Malmo (then part of Denmark) begun in about 1400, and the cathedral church of St Clement at Aarhus, founded in 1201 but much altered and enlarged in later Gothic centuries. In Sweden, too, it was foreign masons who were brought in for major building works, as for the Gothic choir of Linköping Cathedral, built by Master Gerlach of Cologne, and the cathedral at Uppsala (consecrated in 1435), originally designed on English models but much modified by the French architect who was contracted to complete it, Etienne de Bonneuil. Trondheim, made the seat of the archbishopric of Nidaros in 1151, with authority over the whole of Norway, has the finest Gothic church in Scandinavia, first founded in the eleventh century, and the transepts and chapter-house surviving from that period, but the nave and choir completely rebuilt in the English-influenced Gothic style in the thirteenth century. A succession of fires reduced the whole western end of the church to ruin, and restoration was not undertaken until 1869 (completed 1930). There is little of medieval Gothic in Finland, but some influence of painting and sculpture from Hanseatic connections, and at Turku (Åbo) a massive brick cathedral built in late Romanesque style in the thirteenth century with Gothic elements added later.

VARIETIES OF GOTHIC

There was an 'archetypal' Gothic, such as has been described above, but it underwent continual variation, amplification and elaboration at the hands of different architects, in different countries, and in different circumstances. Even the basic ground-plan can vary considerably. Chartres has what one might call the 'classic' design – cruciform, with projecting transepts, eastern apse and laterally projecting double-towered western façade – but at Paris and Bourges there were originally no projecting transepts (there are now), while Laon has a square eastern end and at Reims the transepts merge with the apsidal chapels to form a single eastern arc (Fig. 19). Square eastern ends were favoured in the version of Gothic known in England as 'Early English', as at Salisbury, where there is a 'cross of Lorraine' ground-plan, with double projecting transepts. Wall-elevations also vary: early cathedrals, at Sens, Laon and Paris, favoured a four-storeyed elevation, with a vaulted gallery (the tribune) between the ground-level arcade and the triforium. The vaulting of the tribune over the

Figure 18: Prague Cathedral, choir, from north-west.

The Cathedral of St Vitus in Prague was begun in 1248, one of the earliest penetrations of Gothic into eastern Europe, and consecrated in 1322. But the rebuilding undertaken by Matthew of Arras (1344–52) and, following him, by Peter Parler, under the patronage of Charles IV of Bohemia, produced a virtually new cathedral, with lofty arcades and a vast clerestory.

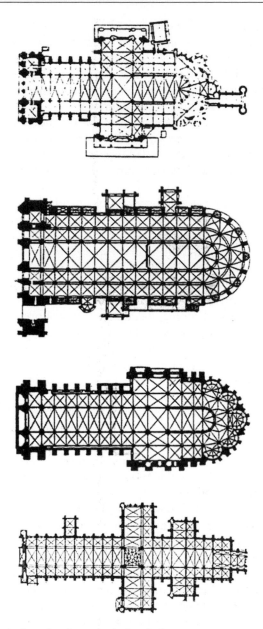

Figure 19: Ground-plans for the cathedrals of Chartres, Bourges, Reims and Salisbury.
   Chartres (begun 1194) was built on a cruciform plan with three-aisled projecting transepts and a long choir with double ambulatory and choir chapels of alternating size. Bourges (begun 1195) originally had no transepts or ambulatory chapels; the latter were added later in the thirteenth century. Reims (begun 1211) has three-aisled transepts and a choir with ambulatory and chapels. Salisbury (begun 1220), by contrast with the French cathedrals, has a square east end and deeply projecting double transepts.

side-aisles was used as a way of strengthening the total structure and support-ing the roof. But the more sophisticated development of the flying buttress meant that the tribune, which necessarily obstructed the passage of light, could be dispensed with, and four stages reduced to three. The tribune was abandoned at Chartres and Bourges, and a three-storey structure (arcade, triforium, clerestory) became usual (see Fig. 10).

French Gothic was everywhere by 1250–1300, but with many regional variations. England had its version of the more elaborately decorated and traceried French *rayonnant* style, called, appropriately, the 'Decorated' style, dominant about 1290–1340. Its beginnings are traditionally associated with the 'Eleanor Crosses' built by Edward I along the route taken by the funeral cortège of Queen Eleanor on its journey from Lincolnshire, where she died in 1290, to London. Twelve were built, and three remain, characterised by floral decoration, crocketed gables, delicately ornamented finials, and arches in the defiantly functionless ogee (double S-curve) style. The same decorative features appear almost simultaneously in larger edifices such as the choir at Exeter, begun in 1280–90 and continued in this style, and the chapter-house at York, completed in 1290. There followed the choirs at Lichfield and Wells (1320–63), and the Lady Chapel at Ely (begun 1321), a supreme example of the Decorated style, with nodding ogees and the widest single-span stone vault in English Gothic (the chapter-house roof at York, which is bigger, is made of wood). The two-storeyed cloister at Norwich, begun in 1297, gave particularly free scope for decorative exuberance in its traceries and roof-bosses, and there was elsewhere, around 1300, a fashion for highly naturalistic foliage carving, as in the Angel Choir at Lincoln, in the presbytery at Exeter, and above all in the chapter-house and its vestibule at Southwell, where leaves of oak, maple, vine, may, rose, hop and fig are distinctly recognisable.

Lincoln is perhaps the supreme example of the beauty of Gothic accretion. When rebuilding in the Gothic style began under Bishop Hugh after the earth-quake of 1185, the magnificent west façade and towers, which had escaped damage, were left untouched, and work concentrated at the east end. St Hugh's Choir is full of English idiosyncrasy, with asymmetrical vaulting (apparently purely decorative) and staggered double arcading of the choir aisles, the one arcade leap-frogging the next so as to give a combined sense of interrupted depth and onward drive. The nave was barely finished and the west front incorporated before building began again at the east end to accommodate the throngs of pilgrims to St Hugh's tomb. The polygonal east end was rebuilt square-ended, in the more favoured English style, to make space for the Angel Choir (1256–80) – so called from the angels carved outstretched in the spandrels of the triforium – one of the great triumphs of English Decorated Gothic. The central tower meanwhile had collapsed and been rebuilt (1238–55): it was increased in height 50 years later, and a spire added in the late fourteenth century, which was destroyed in a gale in 1584.

'Perpendicular', in the time-hallowed chronology of English church archi-tecture, followed 'Decorated': it is the name given to a specifically English form of Gothic, characterised by regularly rectilinear wall-panelling and window-tracery. It is presumed to have derived from a minor variant in French Gothic, and to have been introduced into England by a 'Court School' of architects in London in the 1330s, whether in the chapter-house at Old St Paul's, designed in 1332 by William Ramsey, the King's Mason, or at St Stephen's Chapel, the royal chapel at Westminster, where work restarted in the 1330s in a renewed English attempt to vie with the Sainte-Chapelle in Paris (St Stephen's Chapel was destroyed in the great Westminster fire of 1834, and is known only from descriptions, engravings and surviving fragments). Whatever the sequence of events in London, the style was soon in the west, and the first major surviving example is the choir and south transept at Gloucester abbey-church, rebuilt as a shrine for the murdered Edward II in the years immediately after 1330. The abbot's decision to house the body, when it turned up at the abbey in the difficult time after the murder in 1327, was an inspired act of charity, for Edward III paid for a splendid tomb and monument, bristling with pinnacles (1331), and offerings at the tomb provided funds for the rebuilding of the south transept and east end, with rectilinear panelling imposed on the Norman walls (Fig. 20). A massive window was opened at the east end (72 × 38 ft, 22 × 12 m, the largest window in England) with clear glass incorporating the heraldic shields of Edward III, the Black Prince and other nobility, making it an early kind of war memorial, commemorating the victory at Crécy in 1346. Fan-vaulting, another characteristically English development, also made its first full appearance at Gloucester (Fig. 21). This multiplication of rib-vaults was later to reach its climax in the spider's-web canopies of King's College Chapel in Cambridge, begun in 1446 by Henry VI, and the Chapel of Henry VII (completed 1519) in Westminster Abbey.

The new rectilinear style was soon in evidence in the choirs at St Augustine's in Bristol (now Bristol Cathedral), completed in 1341, at Winchester, and in the east end of York Minster, begun in an intensive campaign between 1361 and 1373. Perpendicular long continued to dominate English church-architecture and, with the building of the great cathedrals more or less completed, was the characteristic style of the newly built or enlarged parish churches that sprang up in villages and towns throughout the prosperous south and east of the country in the late fourteenth and early fifteenth centuries. The grand parish churches in Newark, in the seaport-towns of Hull (Holy Trinity), King's Lynn (St Nicholas) and Bristol (St Mary Redcliffe), and in the wool towns of East Anglia (Lavenham and Long Melford) and the Cotswolds (Chipping Campden), are cathedrals in all but name. There was some resistance in England to the more extravagant *style flamboyant* ('burning with flames') of late French Gothic, though it appears in some window-tracery. This late French style, which took hold when major building works resumed after the Hundred Years War, has other characteristic features than the window-tracery from which it derives its name, including the ornamentalisation of previously structural elements such as rib-vaults and pier-colonettes. The great monuments of the period are Saint-Maclou at Rouen, begun 1436, and the choir of the abbey-church at Mont-Saint-Michel, begun in 1446, the climax to a tide of monastic building that had risen over four centuries upon the island.

Figure 20: Gloucester Cathedral, choir wall panelling.
   Gloucester is the first major surviving example of English Perpendicular,
evidenced in the regular rectilinear screenwork and panelling (1337–67).
The work at Gloucester derived perhaps from a design by William Ramsey,
the King's Mason, who was the architect at St Stephen's Chapel
(now destroyed) in Westminster Palace in the 1330s.

Figure 21: Gloucester Cathedral, fan-vaulting in the choir.
    This elaborate form of rib-vaulting, ornamental rather than structural, took particular hold in England, and made its first appearance at Gloucester in the fourteenth century.

Other variations on Gothic, manifested in the large abbey-churches and priory-churches, were the result of the preferences of the religious orders for whom they were built. The Cistercian order of monks, who professed a special simplicity of life and observance (as has been described in Chapter Two), early adopted an austere version of the Gothic style (as at Fontenay and Pontigny) with lower arcades, clean precise masonry-work, non-figurative decoration restricted to foliate and other simple motifs, and neutral grisaille glass instead of sapphire and ruby – though more licence was allowed in non-church buildings such as the chapter-house and refectory. It was this simpler Cistercian style that took particular hold in Germany, first in a piecemeal way at Heisterbach (1202–37), and Maulbronn (1201–55), and then more fully at Altenberg, begun soon after 1255 on the model of the Cistercian Royaumont in France (consecrated 1236), and consecrated in 1287 (the whole church completed in 1379). Doberan, begun in 1294–99 (choir finished 1329, the whole church completed 1368), exemplifies a particular north German regional form of Cistercian Gothic. Like many German churches, it was built of brick, which required a more cautious articulation of structural elements. Another local German variation, not to do with the Cistercians, was in south Germany, where the single-tower western façade of Strassburg inspired a number of imitations. The spire of the west tower at Freiburg-im-Breisgau, built *c*.1275–*c*.1350, with its filigree of pierced stonework, is one of the most extraordinary stylistic digressions in Gothic architecture (Fig. 22). The tower and spire at Ulm were equally ambitious, and part of a burgher-inspired movement to assert the independence and prosperity of their new 'free town', but the design of Ulrich von Enstingen was not finally realised until the nineteenth century, when Ulm could finally boast the highest stone spire ever built.

The friars, and especially the friars of the Dominican Order, or Order of Preachers, had their own different priorities: for them a high wide hall-space was needed for large-scale preaching, and the Gothic nave, with high aisles, was ideal. Many such churches were built throughout Europe in the thirteenth century, as the order expanded its operations. In Germany, the new choir at Regensburg, begun in 1248, was typical in creating a large open unencumbered space, with choir and nave united. The church of the Franciscans (Greyfriars) in Newgate Street in London, begun in 1306 and completed in 1337 (following the church of the Dominicans, or Blackfriars, begun in 1276), was the largest building in the city after Old St Paul's. It survived the Reformation, renamed Christ's Church, only to be destroyed in the Great Fire of 1666. The masterpiece of Dominican architecture in France is the church of the Jacobins in Toulouse, begun in 1230–35 and much enlarged in 1275–92, with central piers dividing two vast naves and supporting the lofty roof with 'palm-tree' rib-vaulting.

In Italy, it was the Dominicans, and also the Franciscans, as we have seen, who had the greatest influence in introducing Gothic, but otherwise it was difficult for the style to make headway against prevailing architectural traditions, and there is little that could be called 'Italian Gothic'. The abundance of marble meant much veneering and inlaying, and zebra-striped piers most un-Gothic in appearance, while the weather, especially further south, dictated

Figure 22: Freiburg-im-Breisgau Cathedral, tower.

Like Strassburg, Freiburg has a single tower at the west end (by contrast with the two-towered west façades of England and France). It was completed about 1350. On a square base stands a pierced octagonal belfry surmounted by an extraordinary openwork spire of stone. The ascent of the inside stair of the spire is like climbing into outer space.

murals in preference to windows. As late as 1263, when a miracle of the host (some drops of blood fell from the wafer and stained the corporal-cloth) necessitated an even bigger rebuilding programme at Orvieto Cathedral than had been planned, it was a basilica-like style that was chosen, on the model of Santa Maria Maggiore in Rome. But by 1300 the influence of Gothic could not be resisted, and the choir and apse were continued in soaring Gothic style, with fine stained glass and Gothic choir-stalls. The magnificent west façade, designed but not completed by Lorenzo Maitani and his school (1309–30), with polychromatic carved, marble-inlaid and painted decoration covering the whole flat wall-space, is the great glory of Orvieto.

At Siena, the prosperity of the city in the fourteenth century (it outshone Florence for a time) led to ambitious plans on the part of the commune in 1339 for a further Gothic renovation of the thirteenth-century Romanesque basilica, including a vast new south transept which would become the nave in a re-orientated cathedral. But the Black Death, economic decline, and structural problems with Gothic that always confused Italian masons led to the abandonment of the *Nuovo Domo*, which still stands half-finished, and to the concentration of work on the consolidation and ornamentation of the old building and the completion of the magnificent western façade. Meanwhile, the new cathedral at Florence (begun 1294), despite Giotto's campanile (completed in 1357, after his death) in full-flowering Gothic style, has none of the verticality or spatial fluency of northern Gothic, and the classicising tendency was confirmed when Brunelleschi's dome was placed upon it in 1434. Further north, in the late fourteenth century, there were the megalomaniac projects at Milan (begun 1387) and Bologna (San Petronio, begun 1390), vast ambitions not fulfilled until centuries later. In Venice, there were the great mendicant churches of SS Giovanni e Paolo, called San Zanipolo (Dominican), and Santa Maria Gloriosa dei Frari (Franciscan), both begun in the thirteenth century and surviving as evidence of the influence of the Gothic style (they are the largest churches in Venice). There are also Gothic elements ('Islamicised Gothic') in the lagoon façade (1301–1423) of the Doge's Palace, but the Gothic style had no profound influence on Venetian architecture and much of what there was of Gothic Venice was swept away in the frenzy of building in the Renaissance style in the late fifteenth and sixteenth centuries as the city reached and then declined from its peak of prosperity.

Spain, unlike Italy, proved receptive to Gothic, despite the presence of a strong Romanesque tradition and of Moslem (*mudejar*) influences (the Moslem Moors were finally pushed into the southern enclave of Granada after the Christian recapture of Seville in 1248). A distinctive Spanish Gothic began to emerge at Burgos (begun 1221) and at Toledo (begun 1227), already exemplifying the dark tones and heavy textures characteristic of the Spanish style, though in both cathedrals the Gothic effect is swamped by Renaissance additions. The beautiful cathedral at León, begun in 1255, is an exception to the developing trend, having something of the grace of the *style rayonnant*, and also the pleasing integrity of a building completed in a single campaign (by 1303, except for the towers) (Fig. 23). Later Spanish Gothic shows a particular

Figure 23: León Cathedral, choir, from the west.

Begun in 1255 and completed in a single building campaign by 1303 (except for the towers), Leon, with its high wide clerestory and fine thirteenth-century glass (skilfully restored 1859–1901), is like a French cathedral transplanted into Spain. The *trascoro* (choir-screen) in the foreground is of the Renaissance.

fondness for star-vaults, as in the chapter-house at Burgos (1316–54) and the monastery-church at Guadalupe, begun about 1340.

Catalonia, in the north-east, had close ties with southern France, and the influence of Narbonne (1272) was felt in the cathedrals of Girona (begun 1312) and Barcelona (begun 1317). Both were long left unfinished: when work finally resumed on the nave at Girona in 1416, it was built so much higher than the choir that three rose-windows had to be inserted in the nave-wall above the choir-roof. Equally ambitious were Santa Maria del Mar at Barcelona (completed 1383) and the Cathedral of Palma de Mallorca (choir completed 1327), where the nave, nearly as high as Beauvais, towers over the sea-wall on the south side, supported by a double-ranked palisade of flying buttresses on massive deep piers (Fig. 24).

New cathedrals were begun about 1400 in north-west Spain at Oviedo and at Pamplona, where the fine early fourteenth-century two-storeyed cloister, with elaborately traceried arcades, has been fortunately preserved, but all are eclipsed by Seville. There a decision was made in 1401 to demolish all of the old mosque except the tower called La Giralda (the cathedral had been housed within the mosque until then, as it continued to be, and still is, at Córdoba). Advisers were called in, and building went on until 1519, the result being a vast eclectic praying-palace, representing every refinement of Gothic known to Europe, though the sense of horizontal rather than vertical space, and the obstruction of the view by interior chapel and choir, make an extremely un-Gothic impression.

Gothic came early to Portugal in the Cistercian church at Alcobaça, consecrated in 1223, but the masterpiece of Portuguese Gothic is the Dominican three-nave hall-church of Santa Maria de Vitoria at Batalha, begun in 1388 as a royal edifice and burial-site for King John I and the new Aviz dynasty, marking the emergence of Portuguese sovereignty after the battle of Aljubarrota in 1385.

There were also, in addition to these broader kinds of variation in Gothic, an infinite number of particular circumstances that could influence particular buildings. At Canterbury, for instance, it was thought a good idea that an extra chapel should be built to project at the east end in order to house the crown of Becket's skull, the church's most precious relic: it was called the Corona ('crown') Chapel. The immense choir to the east of the octagon at Aachen was begun in 1335 as another vast glass sanctuary, like Sainte-Chapelle, where pilgrims could come to pay homage to the relics of Charlemagne. At

Figure 24: Palma Cathedral, Mallorca, nave exterior, from the south sea-facing side.
The cathedral at Palma was begun in 1230, immediately after the seizure of Mallorca from the Moors by King James of Aragon in 1229. Building went on until 1601: the south doorway, known as the *Mirador*, dates from the fifteenth century. The dramatically deep and tall buttresses supporting the flying buttresses, alternating with pairs of buttresses of lesser height, give the impression of a military palisade, guarding the cathedral from sea-attack.

Albi, in the south of France, a new cathedral was begun by Bishop Bernard de Castanet in 1277, with a delicate Gothic cloister but a huge high nave, with wide vaults. The main roof is supported from the outer walls of the high side-chapels, so that there are no flying buttresses, and the effect, with the colossal western tower, is of a massive fortress. The bishop was, so to speak, 'making a statement' about the need to fortify the church against the threat of Catharism (which the Albigensian crusade of 1209–31 had attempted to extirpate) and providing space within it where there could be great preachings against heresy (Fig. 25).

THE BUILDING AND FINANCING OF CATHEDRALS

A cathedral was built by a building-lodge, an association of stonemasons under the direction of a master-mason, who acted as architect (under the direction of a patron such as a bishop), construction engineer, site supervisor and senior works foreman (Fig. 26). The role of the master-mason would vary according to the energy and interest displayed and the influence exerted by the bishop or dean and chapter or cathedral canon or other member of the clergy who gave him his instructions. The master-mason was paid three or four times as much as an ordinary mason, and was hired for longer periods, or even for life. In fact, to call him any kind of 'foreman' is misleading. He appears in illustrations elegantly dressed, and was often granted unusual privileges: Pedro Balaquer was given 50 florins from the fabric fund at Valencia Cathedral in 1414 so that he could visit Lérida, Narbonne and other cities and see how the best towers and campaniles were built. The master-mason gave the masons their forms or templates to work from (which meant that he controlled the details of style), while lesser foremen made tools and checked the work of the journeymen. The mason who worked with freestone (fine-grained stone capable of being freely worked) was a 'freemason', and the origin of masons' lodges was in the need for a companionable living environment for these skilled workers, who were often on the move or employed for months away from home. The shaping and carving of the masonry blocks was done in worksheds during the winter, ready for putting in place during the summer. It was a slow business, but the masons did their work well, and when trouble came and towers collapsed it was usually due to the foundations, consisting of rubble in deep trenches, being asked by later builders to bear more than their intended weight. There were other problems with foundations that were impossible to foresee: the 25,000-ton tower at the crossing in York Minster was supported on four piers carrying nearly four times the weight permitted

Figure 25: Albi, Cathedral of Sainte-Cécile, general view from the south.
Albi was begun in 1277, and the decision of Bishop Bernard de Castanet to have the main roof supported from the outer walls of the high side-chapels, with narrow windows and no flying buttresses, is what gives his cathedral, as he intended, the appearance of a great fortress against heresy. There is little that is Gothic about it. The three upper storeys of the keep-like tower were added in the nineteenth century.

Figure 26: New York, Pierpont Morgan Library MS 638, fol. 3r. Old Testament miniatures. Construction workers building the Tower of Babel (Genesis 11). French, 1250–60.

In the foreground a mason chisels away while another checks a right angle with his square. Two labourers carry stone in a hand-barrow, a third mounts a ladder with a basket containing mortar. On the tower a gloved stone-setter works with a trowel, and another steadies a basket of stone being hoisted on a treadmill-operated pulley. The Almighty surveys progress from a cloud above. The book from which these miniatures survive was given by the Pope in 1608 to Shah Abbas of Persia, and the miniatures glossed then in Persian (see also Fig. 45).

in modern building practice, but it only started to give trouble when the water-table dropped and caused wooden piling to be exposed which had been previously water-logged, and which proceeded to crumble as it dried. The work to remedy this, begun in 1971, was on a scale that the original builders would have appreciated.

The role of the master-mason is not much documented for the earlier period, but Gervase, a monk of Canterbury, has left an eye-witness record[5] of the arrival of William of Sens at Canterbury to begin the rebuilding of the cathedral after the disastrous fire of 1174. The murder of Thomas Becket on the steps of the altar in 1170, his immediate canonisation (1173), and the spectacular penitence of Henry II had brought in a flood of offerings, and a new shrine was urgently needed for the reception of the saint's relics. William first had to persuade the monks that the whole thing had to be rebuilt from the ground (he did not quite succeed), and then proceeded to design machines for loading and unloading the boats that brought the stone from Caen in Normandy (it was far easier to carry heavy loads by sea than by land, and Caen stone was a fine easy-to-work creamish sandstone) and for transporting it to the site. He also made the models for carving the stone, and supervised the building as it progressed from pillars to arches to vaults to triforium to clerestory. In 1180 he fell from the great arch at the crossing, an accident that was variously attributed to diabolical envy and to divine punishment for pride, but he continued to oversee the work from his bed with the help of a clever monk who transmitted his instructions (and made himself very unpopular with the masons). Soon another William, an Englishman, took over. Gervase, in his account of the rebuilding, shows himself much aware of the newness of the new style – the piers that are 12 ft taller than the old ones (but the same thickness), the stone vaults that replace the ceilings of painted wood, the use of the chisel instead of the stone-axe for the decorative sculpted work.

It is unusual to find a name given thus to the 'architect' of a great cathedral. We are likely to hear more of the patrons who gave them their commissions and instructions: Abbot Suger, though he explicitly gave all the credit for planning and bringing about the new work to the Divine Artificer, made sure that there was a written record of his pious modesty in doing so, and also had his name recorded in several Latin inscriptions around the church. But the names of the men who actually supervised the building operations do not get into the usual records, even though they probably had no more desire to remain anonymous than did Suger. A few names of early master-masons are known from unusual forms of record, mostly now lost. Hugues Libergier, architect of the church of St Nicaise in Reims, begun in 1231 and destroyed in the French Revolution, is portrayed on a grave-slab in Reims Cathedral in a fine gown holding a model of his church. Also in Reims Cathedral, up until the eighteenth century, there was a labyrinth pattern in the floor of the nave commemorating the four men who built it, the 'maistres des ouvrages' who supervised the work over a period of nearly 80 years to 1290; the labyrinth lasted until 1778, when one of the canons paid to have it removed because of the commotion caused by children and 'idle people' following the maze. There was a similar labyrinth in Amiens Cathedral. At Strassburg there was formerly an inscription over the gigantic western façade recording that it was begun in 1277 by Master Erwin von Steinbach. In England, the first record of the appointment of a 'king's mason', as work on Westminster Abbey got under way, is in the Close Rolls for 1256, where a Master John is so designated. As time went by, more such documentation tended to be generated, and more to survive, so that more master-masons come to be known by name – Peter

Parler (*c*.1330–99) at Prague, Ulrich von Enstingen (1359–1414) at Ulm, and Henry Yevele (d. 1400) at Canterbury and Westminster.

An extraordinary survival from the thirteenth century is the notebook of Villard de Honnecourt, a sketchbook such as any master-mason would keep, with clear and precise working drawings of ground-plans, elevations, timber structures, machinery, mouldings, and designs for statues. The album, as it now survives in the Bibliothèque Nationale in Paris, consists of 33 vellum pages of unequal size stitched together in a heavy well-worn leather cover. The drawings are on both sides of the page, and the fact that some of them appear upside-down shows clearly that they were pages that he carried around as a kind of sketchbook and that got stitched together afterwards, at which point he added explanatory notes. There is something of Leonardo about it, and it includes much apart from architectural drawings – lifting devices, a 'cross-bow that cannot miss', perpetual motion machines, a water-powered sawmill, and sketches of men and animals. Villard visited and made drawings at Amiens, Paris, Beauvais, Chartres and Laon ('I have never seen such a tower!' he exclaims, appreciative of the drama of stylistic innovation), as well as sketches of everything at Reims, the architectural last word of his day. There is evidence in the album, too, that Villard de Honnecourt knew of the theories of mathematical and musical proportion that were believed to govern the harmony of architecture: some of his designs show attention, for instance, to the ratio 5:8, which is the notation of an important interval in music and also very close to the Golden Section in mathematics (0.618:1, that is, A is to B as B is to A+B). Similar analogies can be elicited from some original cathedral plans. But much of it stayed at a theoretical level, and when, at the architectural 'seminar' called in 1387 to advise on the building of Milan Cathedral, it was suggested that a particular building problem should be solved by an appeal to mathematical theory, the advice was fortunately not acted on.

Cathedrals and large churches cost a great deal of money to build: it has been estimated that, in western countries during the thirteenth and fourteenth centuries, roughly the same large proportion of the Gross National Product was spent on cathedral-building as is now spent on the terminal care of people in hospitals. Financial and other support came from a variety of sources: from gifts, offerings and bequests; from wealthy individual patrons, including bishops and members of the cathedral clergy; from endowments; from lands and estates, especially in the case of abbey-churches; and from the local community. Forty-five of the windows at Chartres are associated with the city's trades, whose workmen also contributed to the building of the cathedral by giving their work free; at Bourges, the crafts likewise advertise their skills in stained glass (as they were later to do in dramatic form in the guild-plays of northern England); at Freiburg, the design of the 'tailors' window' shows a great pair of scissors.

Many different motives came together in the impetus towards the building of a new cathedral. There was of course the work of God to be done, the regular performance, day in and day out, of the divine office, and in a great cathedral the *Opus Dei* became a particularly spectacular act of veneration.

There were also saints and shrines and relics to be housed; larger and larger processions to be accommodated; civic, episcopal and ducal pride to be satisfied. The complexities of circumstance can best be understood from a few specific examples.

The Abbey of Saint-Denis, where Abbot Suger gave the first impetus to Gothic, was not an ordinary abbey: it housed the relics of the patron-saint of France and the tombs of many French kings. It was in many respects the 'royal abbey' (Westminster was a later imitation), very wealthy and of great political importance. Abbot Suger, though of humble birth, was an ambitious and important political figure, adviser to two French kings and Regent of France during the Second Crusade (1147–49). He had a vision of the destiny of France, and for him the rebuilding and aggrandising of his abbey was a way of strengthening the throne of France as well as venerating God and St Denis. The rapid spread of Gothic through the French royal domain was in part due to Suger's brilliantly successful propaganda in identifying the new architecture with the developing power of the French royal house of Capet. He was a skilful diplomat, too, and remained on good terms with St Bernard, the other dominating figure in the twelfth-century French church, despite fundamental differences in their view of the monastic life.

Suger was an impresario of the faith: the attention he lavished on the outfitting of his new church with sculpture and stained glass, plate and vestments, candelabra and altar-panels, was for him part of the expression of that faith. In demonstrating thus that the homage of devotion was paid through magnificence of outward ornament as well as through prayer and less ostentatious offices, he offered a rationale for Gothic decorative art (as against the austerities of St Bernard and the Cistercians) and an assertion of the continuing strength of Benedictine monasticism. He had also read or heard of the writings of the Pseudo-Dionysius, the fifth-century theologian of Light and of the mystical *via negativa*, whom he was happy to identify with the Dionysius known to Paul and with St Denis, the Apostle of Gaul. He found in them the mystical identification of God with ineffable Light that was to inspire his passion for fenestration. Light and radiance were for him, as they were for St John the Evangelist and later for theologians like Grosseteste and Aquinas, the experience of the divine. It was God's light that shone in the darkness and broke down the gates of hell, and that illumined men's souls with truth: it was what led to God, and it was God. Brilliant reflective ornamental surfaces (gems, precious metals, gold leaf in manuscript miniatures), as well as translucent materials like stained glass, were the agency through which this sense of the divine was transmitted.

Abbot Suger's ambitions for Saint-Denis did not die with him. Faced with competition from the Cistercian house of Royaumont founded by Louis IX and his mother in 1228, where members of the Capetian royal house (though not yet any sovereigns) were increasingly finding their last resting-places, and from the old coronation-church at Reims, which was being magnificently rebuilt, the abbey inaugurated a campaign of rebuilding in 1231. An important element was the abbey's success in persuading Saint-Louis to permit the construction of 'retrospective' effigial tombs for the sixteen early

Frankish and Carolingian kings whose bones, it was said, lay in the crypts of Saint-Denis.

At Chartres the cathedral had a famous image of the Virgin, the *Virgo paritura* ('Virgin about to bring forth'), and a famous relic of the *sancta camisia* worn by the Virgin at the birth of Christ. These made Chartres an important place of pilgrimage. The whole cathedral, except for the western towers and narthex, burnt down in 1194 (such disasters were not rare, given the use of candles and torches for lighting), but the two relics were preserved intact, having been carried down by clerics to the ancient subterranean crypt. It was decided that the Virgin was asking for a new church. There was some real sense of a divine mission; there was also a real economic incentive, since the relics brought in pilgrims, and it was pilgrims who helped make the fairs at Chartres specially prosperous (the main fairs were held to coincide with the four principal feasts of the Virgin). Offerings poured in (including a handsome gift from Richard I, then at war in France with Philip Augustus), rebuilding started immediately, and by 1220 the main structure, astonishingly, was complete; all sculpture and glass was in position for the dedication in 1260. The speed with which the building was carried on was all the more remarkable in view of the structural complications consequent upon the decision to retain the great pre-1020 crypt and the twelfth-century west end. Architects often had fearsome problems to surmount in building over Carolingian or even Roman foundations: visitors to York Minster can see in the undercroft how the foundations of the medieval church had to be built at a diagonal upon the foundation-walls of the Roman legionary fortress in order to maintain the east–west orientation of the church.

A different combination of circumstances brought the Gothic cathedral at Amiens into existence. In 1206 the cathedral acquired a portion of the skull of John the Baptist after the sack of Constantinople by the Crusaders (the acquisition of such relics is not appropriately to be thought of as a purpose of the Crusades, more a consequence or coincident circumstance). In 1218 the Romanesque church was destroyed by fire, and Bishop Evrard de Fouilloy began the rebuilding campaign in 1220. Usually the choir of a church would be built first, so that the church could be consecrated and services held there (often under a temporary wooden roof); this did not happen at Amiens because of complications introduced by pre-existing structures, and building began with the nave. But it was completed by 1236 and the whole building, despite lack of funds and another fire in 1258, by 1269.

Enthusiasm had a speedy reward at Amiens, though not so speedy at Palma. The Balearic Islands were recaptured from the Moors in 1229, and Palma after a siege of four months. Work began at once on a cathedral on the site of the mosque, but funds ran short and by the end of the thirteenth century, in a striking anticipation of modern fund-raising techniques, donors were being offered a coat of arms on a roof-boss for a stipulated contribution. The choir was finished by 1264, but the nave went on through the next two centuries. When it was at last finished, this vast nave, 62 ft (19 m) wide and 145 ft (45 m) high, with aisles rising to 98 ft (30 m) – as high as any English nave – had the lowest ratio of support to enclosed volume in all Gothic architecture. The nave was in the end so much higher than the choir that its east wall was opened (as at Girona) with a great oculus 38 ft (12 m) in diameter.

The history of York Minster is particularly instructive in illustrating some of the human factors, as well as economic realities, that lie behind a long programme of church building. The enlargement of the church began with the building of the new south and north transepts during the archepiscopate of Walter Gray (1215–55), who was both generous and energetic and also enormously wealthy, and had the added advantage of being in office for a long time and therefore able to recover from the colossal expenses of going to Rome for his pallium. Work on the chapter-house and nave progressed during the latter part of the century and into the fourteenth century, receiving unexpected support from the contributions of those passing through York on their way to and from the Scottish wars (the shrine of St John of Beverley, nearby, profited in the same way, his banner having been found particularly effective in battle). The west window was paid for by Archbishop William de Melton (1317–40), who otherwise spent most of his money endowing his brother's family; and, though we should not underestimate the part played by the residentiary canons in prompting and encouraging, it was left again to the individual initiative of another archbishop, John Thoresby (1352–73), to push ahead with the now sorely needed new choir. He put this in hand at a chapter session in 1361, paid £2,600 toward it himself, and even got the cathedral clergy to accept a levy on their earnings to help pay for it. Archbishop Scrope (1398–1405) contributed in an unusual way, for the offerings at his shrine, after he had been summarily executed as a rebel by Henry IV's forces, were diplomatically diverted to the fabric fund and the less contentious St William by the cathedral clergy. Archbishop Henry Bowet (1407–23) managed to get local aristocrats and ecclesiastics to contribute to the completion of the glazing of the windows in the new east end. Not much came from the burghers of York, though this may have been as much because they were excluded as because they were reluctant to contribute: this had a spectacular effect on the York parish churches.

In Milan, things were different. Gian Galeazzo Visconti, who became duke in 1385, was a vicious tyrant, but he was prepared to spend a large amount of money proclaiming his pride in his new ducal state. He determined on a new cathedral, led a funding drive among the wealthy men and trades of the city, no doubt finding ways of offering them special encouragement to contribute, and hired experts from France and Germany to advise on construction. Their uneasy collaboration with the Italian masons, more used to working in marble, produced an extraordinary building, the second largest Gothic church in Europe (126,000 sq.ft, or 11705 sq.m, in ground area, second only to Seville), a wide-flung nave with small high clerestory windows, giving the appearance of a vast and gloomy forest. Outside and above, there is a wilderness of statue-crowned pinnacles (2,245 statues in all, it has been estimated), of which very few, it must be said, are likely to be old. It is a truth we must come to terms with, even with the noblest medieval cathedrals, that very little of the original carved and sculpted stonework will have survived. Anyone who has watched the progress of a major modern restoration of a big city cathedral will have seen the effects of erosion, even on restored stonework only a century old, as pathetic worn and faceless figures are brought down. Saddest of all is the situation at Lincoln: the seventeen surviving panels of the famous sculpted frieze on the twelfth-century west front were removed in 1983 for restoration, and it now seems unlikely that all or any of the originals will ever be returned to their position on the wall.

THE USE OF CATHEDRALS

Once built, a great church or cathedral would have many uses other than the performance of the divine office, some of them surprising to the expectations of puritanically irreligious modern people. Within the church there would be an accumulation of chapels and oratories for private devotions, and later of Easter sepulchres, chantry chapels (there were 74 chantries in St Paul's in London in the fourteenth century) and tombs. Outside the church, in a big city, there would be accretions of lean-to shops, market-stalls, booths, anchorholds, clinging like barnacles to an ark.[6] The city cathedral was in many ways the focus of the city's public life. The nave would have no chairs or pews, and the open space was used for civic and university meetings, and everyday business was often conducted there. Lawyers and businessmen would arrange to have meetings there, pilgrims would eat and sleep there on arrival, and wine merchants had stalls in the nave at Chartres. From prohibitions issued, it is clear that people also went into the nave to meet their lovers, play ball-games, exercise their dogs, and throw missiles at the birds flying about. Ordinary people rarely got to worship there, except on great occasions, when a whole city might be accommodated in its cathedral, but they could go into the nave to gawp and wonder at the stained glass, as we see Chaucer's Canterbury pilgrims doing in a poem, *The Tale of Beryn*, written by one of his admirers after his death, showing the pilgrims arriving at Becket's shrine in Canterbury Cathedral. The poem makes it clear that a cathedral nave was as full then of souvenir-sellers as it is now, and as full of people disagreeing about the interpretation of the stained glass.[7] Public use of the nave in these ways was facilitated by the increasing use of elaborate stone-carved rood-screens to separate the nave from the choir, where the cathedral clergy would officiate and into which they alone would be permitted to penetrate (ambulatories around the choir allowed public access to the side-chapels). In this way the clergy would constitute themselves more and more as an elite within the Christian community of the church.

The nave of a medieval cathedral would also have a very different appearance from what it usually has now. For one thing, it would not be frowned upon by a huge pipe-organ of the kind that was being fashionably installed everywhere in the eighteenth century, often to the detriment of the church's appearance, as at Notre Dame in Paris, where the organ obscures the western rose-window, or at Coutances, where the whole west end is monstrously disfigured. There would also be much more decoration and colouring of the walls and interior stonework, as can still be glimpsed in some churches: the coloured interior of the Sainte-Chapelle in Paris, though modern, probably gives a good impression of what it once looked like. Bare stone was not much admired; everything that could be painted was painted, including stone statuary that it would later be thought vulgar to cover with paint. The tomb of Edmund Crouchback (d. 1296), the brother of Edward I, in Westminster Abbey, looked very different when all its crestings and pinnacles were gilded, its sculpted figures of 'weepers' painted, and its canopy inlaid with stained glass set in tinfoil. *La Vierge Dorée*, the elegant Madonna at the portal of the south transept at Amiens, is so called from the gilding of the statue, only traces of which survive. Painted and decorated stonework had a better chance of surviving in countries unaffected by the puritanical cleansings of the Reformation and the iconoclasm of later periods (the Civil War in England, the Revolution in France): many traces of colouring remain, for instance, in the darker interiors of Spanish churches, as on the animated sculpture of the Death of the Virgin, in high relief, on the inner portal leading to the cloister at Pamplona.

STAINED GLASS

For a modern observer, a Gothic cathedral is an object of awe and admiration. For its medieval user, it was a spatial expression of God's nature as Light, and the product of a desire to achieve a harmony of proportion which would share in the geometry of the divine. It was also a place of edification and instruction, an embodiment of the elements of the faith and a vehicle for communicating and teaching them, and here it is that representational glass, painting and sculpture come into their own.

The primary inspiration of Gothic architecture was the desire of creating vast high enclosed spaces into which light could flood through large stained-glass windows. Where the twelfth- and thirteenth-century glass survives more or less intact, as at French cathedrals like Chartres (Plate IV) and Bourges, or at the Sainte-Chapelle, it is the single most overwhelming experience of being inside the cathedral and the single most unforgettable memory. Windows of this kind and on this scale had only just become technically feasible: the new ability to make thinner the lead strips that enclosed the segments of coloured glass meant that a wider range of designs became possible, including, for the first time, figurative designs; at the same time, since the thinner lead strips made for weakness in large expanses of glass, the window had to be strengthened and made rigid with iron bars anchored in the stone at regular intervals. In this way, tall windows acquired their characteristic storeyed structure, with free and mobile designs, often in round medallions, enclosed within strict rectangular compartments. New freedoms of design within the compartments and medallions were matched by the new needs and opportunities for the emphatic reordering of narrative that were introduced by the multistorey structuring of these large windows.

The special bejewelled effect of this early glass comes from the depth and intensity of its reds and blues (the range of colours is not large), but also from accidents of manufacture: the thickness and imperfection of the glass caused bubbles and flaws that shot light in unexpected directions, while the practice of laminating glass, that is, covering a layer of clear glass with a layer of red glass (which on its own would have been almost opaque), produced dazzling refractive effects. Later advances in glass-manufacture made more complex compositions possible, and more delicate figure-drawing, but the effect is less powerful.

The visual impact of the glass in a great French cathedral is so overpowering that it takes a while before the observer settles to read what it represents, and of course some of the glass is so far away and high up that it was never able to be viewed at all, except by the occasional cathedral official or workman, before the introduction of modern binoculars. But the stories told and the symbolism represented are an essential part of the programme of Christian doctrine which the church embodied for the instruction of the people. St Gregory had explained the principle: 'For what writing supplies to him that can read, that does a picture to him that is unlearned and can only look'. The images in the glass are reminders of the plan of salvation, of the life of Christ in which that plan was made manifest, of the biblical stories from the Old Testament in which Christ's life was prefigured, and of the lives of the saints, including especially the church's dedicatee, which witnessed to the power of the faith. In the west window there would often be a representation of the Last Judgement, as a fearful warning to the sinners who entered at that door, while the east window would customarily focus upon the Crucifixion and its attendant circumstances, as a message of hope. Rose-windows in the transepts or west wall were generally of abstract design. Along the aisles the windows contained banks of stories to be read as sequences of episodes, like an illustrated bible, or else monumental figures of patriarchs, apostles or saints. Often the windows presented episodes from the Old and New Testaments in parallel, emphasising the typological fulfilment of the Old Law in the New, of the lives of the patriarchs and prophets in the life of Christ. The cleansing Flood was made fully meaningful in Christ's Baptism, the feast of Melchizedeck in the Last Supper and in the establishment of the feast of the Eucharist, and Abraham's sacrifice of his only son in God's own like sacrifice. At Chartres, in a variation on this kind of typological representation, the four evangelists are shown sitting on the shoulders of the four major prophets (Fig. 27).

Glass is more uncertain of survival than any other part of a church's structure, and the preservation of the glass at Chartres and Bourges, as at Auxerre and Troyes, is a miracle. At Chartres, where the windows are like a translucent part of the wall rather than openings in it, nearly 25,000 sq.ft (2,700 sq.m) of glass remain, nearly all from 1215–40, some of it financed by donations raised from the local tradespeople, some by royal gift, like the rose of the north transept, but most from taxation of the bishop's tenants in the wheatlands around Chartres. Some of the windows contain representations

Figure 27: Chartres Cathedral, window in south transept, detail of Mark on the shoulders of Daniel. *c.*1230.

Stained glass windows often incorporated, for the purposes of doctrinal instruction, typological scenes showing the prefiguration in Old Testament episodes of the life of Christ and the time of Grace. Sometimes the paired scenes were in opposite banks of windows, sometimes within the same window, as here at Chartres, where the fulfilment of the Old Testament prophecies in the New Testament is symbolised by showing the four evangelists sitting on the shoulders of the four major prophets (Isaiah, Jeremiah, Ezekiel and Daniel).

of trades and their patron-saints – goldsmiths, masons, butchers, carpenters, bakers, tanners – but they seem to be there as images of idealised corporate donation to the building of the cathedral rather than evidence of organised donation by tradespeople (there were no trade-guilds in Chartres until *c*.1260).

Stained glass is also the great glory of the Gothic cathedral of León, in Spain, and a remarkable amount of the late thirteenth-century glass survives: the building almost collapsed in the nineteenth century, because of the extremely pared-down wall-structure, but the windows were skilfully preserved and restored during the major rebuilding work of 1859–1901. Elsewhere, changes of taste dictated the replacement of much early stained glass by grisaille or clear glass, as at Notre Dame in Paris: the fashion was for more light rather than an effect of refracted submarine radiance. Often only odd windows survive, or even scraps and fragments of old glass grouped by modern re-storers in abstract patterns. Only occasional examples of glass survive from the court school workshops of Vienna and Prague, but there is a very elegant and accomplished Nativity (*c*.1315) from the former monastery of Königsfelden in Prague, and a fine Annunciation and Presentation (*c*.1355) from the church of Strassengel in Austria now in the Victoria and Albert Museum in London.

England was a particularly perilous place for glass. It was an easy target for Reformation iconoclasts, and what they passed over was generally smashed by Commonwealth soldiers in the seventeenth century. There were also unfortunate accidents: at Cirencester the glass, having survived earlier dangers, deteriorated sadly through neglect in the eighteenth century and at the end of the century what was left was collected by an antiquary and packed away in crates for future use. The glass was forgotten, the crates disappeared. Later, one crate was recovered at the bottom of a railway embankment and the remnants of the glass installed in two small windows in the still beautiful Perpendicular church. Enough glass remains at cathedrals like Canterbury, and in odd parts of other cathedrals, such as Lincoln and Wells, to show the quality of what there was (Fig. 28), but the odds against survival were high. Glass in small churches, which was less publicly offensive, had a better chance of surviving these disasters, but nearly all of it was swept away in Victorian restorations.

An exception has to be made for York, where the intervention of Sir Thomas Fairfax, the commander of the Commonwealth army, saved the glass of the Minster and other city churches from routine destruction by Round-head soldiers when the city was captured after the siege of 1644. Half the surviving English medieval stained glass is said to be in the city of York, some of it in small parish churches such as All Saints, North Street, where there are windows displaying the Seven Works of Mercy and the Fifteen Last Signs before Doomsday, but most of it in the Minster. Some of the finest glass in the Minster is early: the 'Five Sisters' (*c*.1250), five slender lancets 53 ft (16.3 m) high and 5 ft (1.6 m) wide in the north transept, contain the finest ensemble of grisaille in Europe, though much darkened through age and coarsened in restoration. The west window, with its exuberant curvilinear tracery above

Figure 28: Canterbury Cathedral, window in Corona Chapel, return of the messengers from the promised land, laden with grapes. Early thirteenth century.

Moses sends scouts to spy out the land of Canaan: 'And they came to the Valley of Eshcol, and cut down from there a branch with a single cluster of grapes, and they carried it on a pole between two of them' (Numbers 13:23). The promised land of Canaan was interpreted typologically as a figure of the Christian heaven, and the grape-harvest as the gathering of all souls for the Last Judgement and general resurrection (Joel 3:13).

majestic standing figures of saints and apostles, was inserted in 1339 after the rebuilding of the nave, and the aisle windows of the nave were filled at the same time (*c.*1310–*c.*1350) with glass in Decorated style with borders containing inventive genre detail, much like the borders of contemporary illuminated manuscripts. The best-known is the Pilgrimage window in the north nave aisle, with borders showing the fable of the cock and the fox, a funeral conducted by monkeys, and a monkey-physician inspecting a urine-flask (Fig. 29). The east window, the great glory of York Minster, was made in 1405–08 by John Thornton, a professional glass-painter who had established

Figure 29: York Minster, Pilgrimage Window, north nave aisle, monkey-physician inspecting urine-flask. *c.*1320–30.

This window is like a page from an East Anglian psalter, with scenes of St Peter and of Calvary in the central and upper lights bordered with humorous and grotesque scenes. Much of the lower border, like a bas-de-page, is taken up with *babewyerie*, or 'monkey-business', including a monkey funeral. The scene of the monkey-physician has an element of satire (physicians were easy targets – though uroscopy was a perfectly respectable form of diagnosis) but is chiefly for humorous effect.

his reputation working in Coventry. The window is the size of a tennis-court, 76 × 32 ft (23.4 × 10 m), with 117 main panels in its regular rectilinear tracery (thirteen rows of nine), each a yard (nearly a metre) square, showing scenes of the Old Testament, of the Revelation of St John, and of northern English saints and bishops. The glass is of a consistently high standard, and well-preserved, but the new form of manufacture, with careful and detailed designs painted onto white glass in yellow stain, with solid blue or ruby glass for background, produces a less dramatic effect than the old.

PAINTING AND SCULPTURE

Glass was the medium through which the message of the faith was transmitted to those inside the church. It was supplemented by mural painting, the subjects of which were similar to those of glass, and more easily able, because of the greater simplicity of design, to be used as visual aids by a preacher. Most churches had wall-paintings on whatever wall-spaces were available – the Last Judgement painted over the chancel-arch would be a particularly impressive feature – but many such paintings have been lost or are only just being recovered from under later plaster or paint. In large northern churches glass reigned supreme and there was little space left for figurative wall-painting; such painting was the humbler and less expensive medium, and tends to survive now and therefore to be associated with the smaller parish churches. Cycles of scenes illustrative of the lives of Christ and the Virgin, with simple reminders of the main events of Annunciation, Nativity, Passion, Resurrection and Assumption, survive from fourteenth-century churches at Croughton in Northamptonshire and at Chalgrove in Oxfordshire. Denmark is particularly rich in churches with cycles of wall-paintings, perhaps because restoration has generally been more recent and therefore more careful of the past. They come from the thirteenth, fourteenth and fifteenth centuries and are in simple styles but often startlingly direct and expressive. Those at Keldby and Fanefjord on the island of Møn have become famous, but there are many treasures too on Zealand, particularly Vester Broby and Førslev and, in the north-west of the island, Tuse, Mørkøv Kirkeby, and Skamstrup.

In Italy, with a long tradition of mural decoration and wall-mosaic, and practical reasons for restricting rather than increasing the admission of outside light, wall-painting is the medium of choice. Most of the painting of Giotto was in the form of church-murals, as of the life of St Francis in the upper church of San Francesco at Assisi (1296–1304), or of the lives of the Virgin and Christ in the Scrovegni family chapel (the Arena Chapel) at Padua (1304–06). Most of the great Italian painters of the Gothic period – Cimabue, Simone Martini, Masaccio, Fra Angelico, Benozzo Gozzoli – made their reputations or tried their hands as fresco-artists, and it remained an important medium. But free-standing altarpieces and other panel-paintings had always been part of the visual furniture of churches. Duccio di Buoninsegna was commissioned in 1308 to do a great Madonna in Majesty, or *Maestà* (Fig. 30), for the central altar of the cathedral at Siena, and later, the lyricism and refinement of International Gothic was first announced in the panel-painting of the Annunciation that Simone Martini did for the chapel of Sant'Ansano in Siena Cathedral (now in the Uffizi Gallery in Florence) in 1333 (Plate V). Another prototype of the style is the gorgeously decorated altarpiece made for the Bohemian monastery of Vyšší Brod or Hohenfurth (*c.*1350–*c.*1360),

a cycle of panel-paintings now in the National Gallery at Prague (Fig. 31). The paintings show Florentine influence in the heavy modelling of the darkened faces – an example of the Italian connections encouraged by Charles IV of Bohemia – though there is an elegance and delicacy too that comes from miniature painting.

Altarpieces became increasingly important, as dedicated panel-paintings, during the late fourteenth century. Increasingly, and especially from the time of the Dijon altarpiece of Melchior Broederlam (1399) (Fig. 32), they take the form of folding altarpieces, shrines with carved figures and paintings, with two, three or many different sections and wings (diptychs, triptychs, polyptychs). They can contain a comprehensive programme of images, some carved, some painted, such as used to occupy a whole cathedral façade. They are designed to be seen from close up, and therefore encourage and cater for a more personal kind of devotion, as if the observer were the sole person present in a theatre of images. Nowadays, the wings of these altarpieces are mostly left open, but in the Middle Ages they were usually opened only on feast-days. The exterior surfaces would have simple scenes, such as single figures of saints, often done in grisaille as *trompe-l'oeil* paintings in imitation of sculpture; often the outer scene is of the Annunciation, as if to act as a prelude to the story told within. Later in the century these altarpieces began to tower upwards to dizzying heights, as well as sprawl sideways: that at St Mary's, Cracow (1477–89), is over 42 ft high (13 m) and 35 ft wide (11 m).

Folding altarpieces became a main type of artistic commission in the fifteenth century, particularly in the Low Countries and Germany. A fine example in the International Style is that of Konrad von Soest at Bad Wildungen (1404), with delightfully courtly scenes of the Annunciation, the Nativity, the Adoration of the Magi and the Presentation in the Temple. Subsequently, these altarpieces accommodate all the perspectival advances and experiments of fifteenth-century Netherlandish and German painters. There are examples by the Van Eyck brothers in Ghent (1432), by Stephan Lochner in Cologne (*c.*1435), by Hans Multscher in Wurzach (1437), and by Konrad Witz in Geneva (1444), and of course, at a much later date, the Grünewald altarpiece at Isenheim (1511–16).

On the outside of the church, it was statuary and relief sculpture that communicated the stories and symbols of the faith. Again it was Abbot Suger who seized on the doctrinal argument that might be conveyed in stone. The sculptured tympanum depicting Christ in Majesty, presiding over the Last Judgement, was a favourite subject for Romanesque west front tympana, as at

Figure 30: Duccio di Buoninsegna, Maestà (Virgin and Child in Majesty, surrounded by angels and saints). Altarpiece, central panel 14 × 7 ft (430 × 215 cm). Siena, Museo dell'Opera Metropolitana.

Commissioned in 1308 for the main altar of Siena Cathedral, completed in 1311 and escorted with great pomp on 9 June from the artist's studio to the Cathedral. Duccio's painting still shows the dominance of the grand, formal, neo-Byzantine style, as it was about to be superseded in Siena by the 'International Gothic' of Simone Martini.

Figure 31: Vyšší Brod (Hohenfurth), abbey-church, panel from altarpiece, 96 × 86 cm. Christ on the Mount of Olives. Now in the National Gallery, Prague. *c.*1350.

There is expressivity in the face of Christ, darkly modelled in a manner that recalls the Florentine painting that was becoming known in Prague through the influence of Charles IV of Bohemia. The landscape background is done in dramatically formalised fashion, with conventional 'broken terrace' structures for the hillsides and decoratively stylised trees. Yet, counterpointed against this, in a manner characteristic of the International Style, there is the exquisite naturalism of the leaves of the trees and the birds perched so improbably upon them.

Figure 32: Melchior Broederlam, wing of an altarpiece with carved and gilded figures, 168 × 126 cm, commissioned by Philip, Duke of Burgundy, in 1394 for the Chartreuse de Champnol and installed in 1399. Now in Dijon Museum.

The Annunciation and Visitation are on the back of one wing (seen when the altarpiece was closed), and the Presentation and the Flight into Egypt are on the back of the other. The sculptural solidity of the figures, the atmospheric background of the outdoor scenes, and the sense of actuality are new Netherlandish features, though the dizzy perspective belongs very much to the International Style.

Beaulieu-sur-Dordogne. It was Suger who brought order to the design, arranging angels, apostles and the risen dead in an intelligible composition and excluding irrelevances. Soon such tympana were everywhere. A Christ in Majesty, arrayed in order among evangelist beasts and evangelist scribes, is the first Gothic sculpture in Spain, in the tympanum in the south transept at Burgos.

Suger also introduced entrance-way columnar statues, in the form of the kings of Israel that stand in the jambs of the west portal at Saint-Denis (later much mutilated and now much restored), as if ushering the entrant through the Old Law into the church of the Heavenly Jerusalem and the New Law of grace. The lessons are multiplied at Strassburg, where the superseding of the Old Law by the New, perhaps a more urgently triumphant theme in a city with a large Jewish colony, is represented in the beautiful carved figures of the Church and the Synagogue, blindfolded, at the south portal. Elsewhere in the same portal statues of the Wise and Foolish Virgins represent the Elect and the Damned, and the Tempter seductively holds out an apple, unaware that his bare back is being gnawed by adders and toads (symbolising the death of the soul through sin). The image of Frau Welt (Lady World) at Worms Cathedral has toads, serpents and worms clinging onto and burrowing into and out of the flesh on her back: she is devoured by sin from within and without.

Strassburg was of course influenced by Chartres, which has the finest surviving collection of statuary, thousands of figures, many of them original. The sculptures of *c*.1150 in the western *Portail Royal* are stylised in their long-bodied expressiveness, and integrated within the architectural surround, but those of *c*.1250 from the north and south portals are nearly free-standing, with space to live and breathe (Fig. 33). This high summer of Gothic was perhaps anticipated, if anywhere, in the extraordinary enamelwork altarpiece in Klosterneuberg, near Vienna, made by Nicholas of Verdun in 1181, and in the same artist's relief figures in silver-gilt on the shrine of the Three Kings in Cologne (completed by his workshop about 1230) and on the shrine of the Virgin at Tournai (1205). The inspiration for his vividly lifelike representations of human figures and for his expressive drapery probably came from classical sources, perhaps through Byzantine intermediaries: it is well illustrated in the figure of the Baptist in the Tournai shrine, where the physical effort of raising the pitcher of baptismal water above Christ's head can almost be felt by the observer (Fig. 34).

Not just figures and drapery, but the carving of heads and faces too acquired a new flexibility, as if responsive (in an idealising way) to what the artist saw around him and not just to what he 'knew' was appropriate to the composition. The head of a king, perhaps once on the west façade of Notre Dame in Paris (*c*.1225) and now in the Metropolitan Museum of Art in New York, has a powerful regal individuality (despite the lack of nose) that suggests to some that it may have something in it of Philippe-Auguste, King of France. Particular attention was paid to women's heads, as in the poignantly symbolic blindfolded Synagogue at Strassburg (*c*.1225), and to the representation of the Virgin as a woman of simple and appealing youthful human beauty, as in the Visitation scene on the west façade at Reims (*c*. 1230–35) (Fig. 35), where the intimations

Plate I: Chantilly, Musée Condé MS 65 (*Très Riches Heures du Duc de Berry*), fol. 9v. September, from the Calendar sequence. French, 1411–16. *See note p. xvii.*

Plate II: Bourges Cathedral, interior, from the west. *See note p. xvii.*

Plate III: Salisbury Cathedral, general view from the north-west. *See note pp. xvii–xviii.*

Plate IV: Chartres Cathedral, rose-window and other windows in the north transept. *c*.1230.
See note p. xviii.

Plate V: Simone Martini, Annunciation, altarpiece. Commissioned for Siena Cathedral, and now in the Uffizi Gallery in Florence. 1333.
See note p. xviii.

Plate VI: Orvieto, Museo dell'Opera del Duomo. Reliquary of the Sacred Corporal by Ugolino di Vieri and assistants. Enamel on silver-gilt. 1337–38. *See note p. xviii.*

Plate VIII: Paris, Musée Jacquemart-André MS 2 (the Boucicaut Hours), fol. 65v.
The Visitation. 1405–8. *See note p. xix.*

Figure 33: Chartres Cathedral, portal of north porch, sculpted figures, *c*.1250.

These figures (from left to right, Melchizedek, Abraham, Moses, Samuel, David) represent the second phase of monumental figure-sculpture at Chartres. They have assumed a natural stance and are almost free-standing. Abraham is shown with his hand poised to strike the fatal blow; both he and the bound Isaac look serenely up towards heaven. All these figures are typologically significant: Melchizedek 'brought out bread and wine' before Abraham (Genesis 14:18) and this was taken as a prefiguration of the eucharist; Isaac was a prefiguration of Christ, as was the brazen serpent that Moses holds (Numbers 21:9), and the sacrificial lamb that Samuel prepares for the burnt offering (1 Samuel 7:9); the spear that David holds (from 1 Samuel 26:11) prefigures the spear that pierced Christ's side.

Figure 34: Nicholas of Verdun, Baptism of Christ, from the Shrine of the Virgin, now in the Cathedral Treasury, Tournai. Silver and copper with enamel filigree. 1205.
The flowing draperies and the vivid impression of effort in the Baptist's raised arm are striking innovations in early Gothic sculpture.

Figure 35: Reims Cathedral, west front. The Visitation. *c.*1230–35.

The Virgin is presented as a beautiful young woman, with perhaps some memory of classical statuary such as was plentiful among the Graeco-Roman remains in the area. St Elizabeth is portrayed with unexpected realism as an old woman: the point of the story is that she was thought too old to conceive (Luke 1:7) but nevertheless, by miracle, she is now six months pregnant with the child who is to be St John the Baptist.

of classical portraiture in the figure of the Virgin may have to do with a visible classical legacy in the Graeco-Roman remains that were plentiful in the area. In these figures, drapery is treated in a new fashion: gathered to a single point, it falls dramatically in a fan of folds, as in the *Vierge Dorée* at Amiens (*c*.1255–60), focusing the composition upon the Christ-child held in the Virgin's arms.

Scenes such as this, of the standing Virgin with Child, were the most frequent subject of both monumental sculpture and smaller statuettes in softer stones and precious metals, endless variations on a single simple theme. In some examples, the Virgin holds the child well up, as if 'presenting' him to the devout observer, as in the widely imitated Madonna in the north transept of Notre Dame in Paris (*c*.1250). Many later examples show the child held more comfortably and exchanging an affectionate gaze with his mother, as in the *Vierge Dorée*, or playing with her veil, as in the Virgin and Child in the abbey-church at Fontenay (*c*.1290–1300), or touching her face, as in the exquisite and very well-preserved Madonna and Child in silver-gilt given by Jeanne d'Evreux, Queen of France, to Saint-Denis in 1339 (see Fig. 6).

The new sculptural styles spread quickly across the Rhine and are found in the 1230s in figures and sculpted reliefs in the cathedrals of Bamberg and Naumburg (Fig. 36), and in the remarkable sandstone relief of St Martin dividing his cloak now in the parish church at Bassenheim. The standing Madonnas were also much favoured in eastern regions of Germany, done in limestone and painted in white, blue and gold as free-standing devotional images. Workshops for the production of such images were set up in centres like Prague and Vienna, and a fine example survives from Krumau in southern Bohemia (*c*.1400), now in the Kunsthistorisches Museum in Vienna. Later, these images acquired a more histrionic expressiveness, for instance in the work of Hans Multscher, active at Ulm in 1427–67, and others.

Italy, in sculpture as in architecture, was less receptive to the Gothic, though there are evidences of French influences in the panel-figures in relief of the goldsmith Andrea di Jacopo d'Ognabene in Pistoia Cathedral (1316), or in the Madonna and Child of Giovanni Pisano in Pisa (1299) or in his pulpit at Pistoia (1301), or in the dramatic figures in French-style quatrefoils created by Andrea Pisano for the bronze doors of the Baptistery at Florence (*c*.1335). But the influence of classical sculpture is always stronger, intensifying the solidity of the figures and working against the spiritualisation of the human to which Gothic aspires.

Free-standing figures like these embody their significance in themselves. There were also elaborate sculptural programmes, both figures and scenes, such as those developed in the magnificent Gothic west front façades at Amiens, Wells, Siena, and later at Rouen, during the English occupation (1413–49), though nowhere with quite the glamour of the Gothicised marble sculpted reliefs at Orvieto – the birth of Eve, the creation of the animals, the Last Judgement (Fig. 37). At Bourges most of the free-standing sculpture was destroyed by fanatical Calvinist forces in 1562, but the magnificent Last Judgement in the tympanum of the central west portal comes down in an excellent state of preservation (Fig. 38). The vigour and sensuality of its portrayal of the figures

Figure 36: Naumburg Cathedral, statues in the west choir. *c.*1255–65.

The west choir at Naumburg (25 miles south-west of Leipzig) was started after the consecration of the nave in 1242, and in 1249 Bishop Dietrich issued an appeal for funds to help with the building and to honour the eleventh-century benefactors. The twelve figures of the *fundatores*, done with careful attention to details of faces, hands and clothing (though, of course, nothing to do with the original people), are a remarkable display of secular power in a church. The Margrave Ekkehard II and his wife Uta are vividly human before us, the former fiddling with his shield-strap, the latter pulling her ermine cloak around her neck to keep out the cold.

Figure 37: Orvieto Cathedral, west façade. Last Judgement. 1309–30.
   This façade was designed by the Sienese sculptor Lorenzo Maitani and continued according to his plans after 1330 by Andrea Pisano and others. Marble reliefs were carved on the four buttresses of the façade, and this scene of the damned being pushed into Hell by an angel and tormented by devils is on the extreme right buttress. The precise anatomical detail adds a new terror to the scene.

Figure 38: Bourges Cathedral, tympanum of central west portal. Last Judgement. *c.*1230–50.
   Christ sits in judgement, flanked by angels and kneeling intercessors. Below, St Michael holds the scales in which the sins of those who come to judgement are weighed: those who are saved move to the left (clad in the garments of their earthly estate, like the Franciscan friar and the king at the head of the procession, next to St Peter), where Abraham waits to take them into his bosom; those who are damned are seized by devils and forced into the mouth of Hell. Below, the dead climb from their graves in readiness to meet their Maker.

Figure 39: Rouen Cathedral, north transept, Portail des Libraires (Doorway of the Booksellers), detail of bas-reliefs on left of doorway. 1278.

On either side of the doorway (it owes its name to the fact that books were sold in the courtyard in front of it from the fifteenth century), below the tympanum (incomplete) and the rows of saints and angels in the archivolts, are three empty niches above square pillars set diagonally. On the faces of the pillars and the adjacent stonework are carved 154 quatrefoil reliefs, an extraordinary array of fantastic creatures and centaur-like hybrids, an encyclopaedia of the medieval imagination of the grotesque. In the upper medallions are scenes from Genesis (symbolising the establishment of order over chaos?).

of both the newly resurrected and the damned (the saved are clothed) make its survival in such circumstances surprising, but tympana took more effort to smash than free-standing statues, and more of them survive.

Sometimes, in such cases, it is hard to see precisely what form of doctrinal instruction is provided by the sculptures, and it seems that the craftsman may have been indulging his fancy. The *Portail des Libraires* (Booksellers' Door-way) in the north transept at Rouen (*c.*1278) has an extraordinary collection of bas-reliefs carved in quatrefoils – hybrids, sirens, centaurs (one of them wearing a cowl and showing two human feet in boots behind), a philosopher with a boar's head striking a pensive pose as he holds his snout, a physician with a fish's tail inspecting a urine-flask (Fig. 39), all very reminiscent, again, of the inhabitants of the borders of an illuminated manuscript-page. These are famous images, and have provoked much discussion, periodically stimulated by feverishly overheated descriptions such as that in Sext of the First Day in Umberto Eco's *The Name of the Rose* (1980), the impressionable Adso's first sight of the great abbey doorway with its monsters and hybrids. Are these comical and grotesque figures the product of free-ranging fantasy and invention, or are they symbolic of creative profusion, a kind of divine surplus, or programme of encyclopaedic instruction in the things of this world and the next? Or are these creatures chosen because their supple and versatile limbs are so easily twisted to fill a given space? It has been claimed that each figure and scene has a specific meaning in relation to a particular iconographic pro-gramme such as would have been familiar to an educated observer. Some do, of course, and others may do, and others can be made to have such a meaning. Any bagpipe will be a reminder of the 'old dance' of sensuality set against the new law of Christ; any representation of an animal performing a human task will be a reminder of the 'animal' inclination of human nature; any hybrid or grotesque will be an embodiment of the potential unnaturalness or monstrous-ness of the unredeemed nature that rejects grace.

The same kinds of meaning can be forced upon the genre-scenes of apparently low or secular life that often appear in the carving of capitals, roof-bosses, bench-ends and misericords. Is the Lincoln misericord of a knight pierced with an arrow and falling from his horse symbolic of the 'Fall of Pride', and something suitable therefore to be under the rump of a fat cleric? (Fig. 40). A capital at Wells has four vignettes carved on its four sides: two thieves are stealing grapes from a vine (Fig. 41); they are chased by a farm-hand with a pitchfork; he catches one of them and twists his ear; he thrashes him with the pitchfork. Is such lively work explained, or justified, or excused, by its obvious exemplary meaning? Or is that meaning superfluous?

In some cases, it is true, whatever lesson was meant to be conveyed could not be read, only apprehended to be present. High in the transepts and angel choir of Norwich Cathedral, and seen only by cleaners and repairers before modern days of binoculars and floodlighting, are roof-bosses carved with infinite delicacy, lines and dots, for instance, representing the writing in books held in the hands of the figures, and the hawthorn berries precisely carved down to their black tips. Such roof-bosses, it might be noted, are a

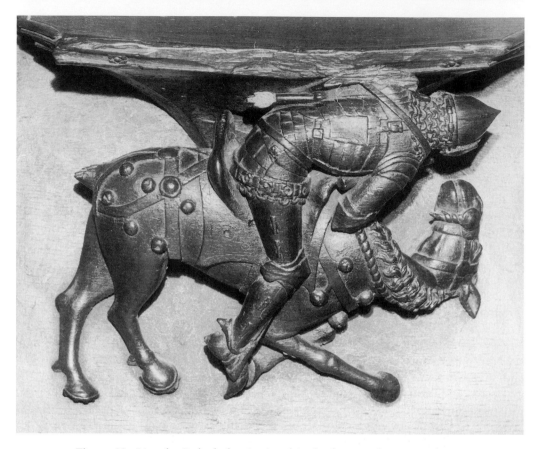

Figure 40: Lincoln Cathedral, misericord in the fourteenth-century choir.
A wounded knight falls from his horse.

Such carvings are often taken to have a symbolic meaning, here 'the fall of Pride'. But the detail of the knight's armour and the horse's trappings is what is extraordinary: such carvings, because of their position, had a good chance of surviving and remaining unworn.

disproportionately important source of knowledge about medieval carving in England, surviving in unusual quantity because they were generally out of reach of depredators at the time of the Reformation and Commonwealth. Their remoteness may have encouraged a certain indulgence of fantasy and irrelevance on the part of the carvers, though generally speaking they are no more fanciful than other objects such as misericords, hidden but not invisible. Sometimes we may be dealing with the natural ebullience of the craftsman, sometimes with the constraints placed upon the craftsman by the medium, and the near-impossibility of doing anything that does not look, on the whole, fantastic.

Figure 41: Wells Cathedral, crossing capital, with 'vine thieves'. *c.*1220.

    This is the first scene in a narrative sequence around the four sides of the capital. It shows one of the thieves caught in the act, sly, alert, tense, angry. The thieves are caught and thrashed by a farmhand round the corner. The swiftness and appropriateness of the punishment make this seem a genre scene of local misbehaviour rather than a lesson against sinfulness.

CHURCH DECORATION, FURNITURE AND EQUIPMENT

Everywhere that a church offered a space or a surface for teaching through images, the opportunity was taken. Water-spouts from the roof-gutters were done in the form of gargoyles – grotesque and diabolical creatures, there perhaps to symbolise their ejection from the church and their subjection to God's will. The symbolism may be more spiteful: at Freiburg-im-Breisgau, a water-spout in the form of an athletically doubled-up figure points its anus in

Figure 42: Freiburg-im-Breisgau Cathedral, gargoyle.
    The figure, for all its apparent discomfort, still performs its function as a water-spout.

the general direction, it is said, of the nearby archdeacon's house (Fig. 42). Doors were wooden functional objects in most churches, but Andrea Pisano incorporated a whole programme of instructive pictures in the panels of the bronze south doors of the Baptistery at Florence (1330–36), while the north and east doors by Lorenzo Ghiberti (1403–52) were pronounced by Michelangelo to be fit for the 'Gates of Paradise'. Even non-figurative interior decorative work may readily be construed to have had a doctrinal function, as bearing witness to the precision and beauty of God's creation. No doubt stone-carvers took delight in the minutely accurate representation of foliage on capitals at Southwell, Exeter, Lincoln and York, but there was nothing purely aesthetic in such an impulse. Decoration of this kind could still be seen as an act of craftsmanly dedication in the service of God. The intricate wood-carving on the choir-stalls at Cologne (*c.*1320), the largest ensemble of such work in Germany, is thus intrinsically different in inspiration and function from the even more intricate wood-carving of a Grinling Gibbons.

All this is to reckon, too, without the furniture and apparatus that were not part of a church's structure but that were no less capable of carrying doctrinal significance. The precious service-books and massive lectern-bibles had covers done in silver-gilt and ornamented with gems and enamel-work, with figures and scenes sometimes carrying a whole programme of images such as might be found in a church portal or doorway. Pulpits, lecterns, fonts and font-covers were carved with biblical and other scenes, as were the silver ewers, chalices and other vessels used in the celebration of the Eucharist. Displayed now in glass cases in a cathedral treasury, or in a museum somewhere else, they have become *objets d'art*, but in the Middle Ages they were holy objects in themselves and were brought out on special occasions to be a witness to the presence of the divine. The story of Belshazzar's desecration of the holy vessels was always available in the Book of Daniel (chapter 5) as a fearful warning, typologically, of the respect due to them. The lurid and powerful account of Belshazzar's feast in the late fourteenth-century English alliterative poem of *Cleanness* gives a vivid description of the kind of ornament lavished on such vessels in the late Gothic period (no doubt expensively embellished in the way that poets have) – gold basins enamelled with azure, covered goblets made like castles, with projecting horizontal courses, their covers formed with turrets with pinnacles and carved with branches and leaves with blooms of pearls and precious stones, and candlesticks with bases like the trunk of a tree, springing out in branches above with birds perched amongst them.[8]

The most lavish figurative decoration was reserved for the reliquary in which was kept the church's own precious relic, whether of the Passion or some other event of Christ's or the Virgin's life or of the saint to whom the church was dedicated, perhaps their hair, lips, teeth, fingers, limbs. This was the spiritual centre of the cathedral, the nuclear core of the power-house. At Pamplona, now in the cathedral treasury, there is a silver reliquary of the Holy Sepulchre, dated 1258 and said to have been the gift of Louis IX of France. It is made in the form of an open shrine, with the three Maries at the tomb, and an angel pointing to the stone from the Sepulchre which is the actual relic and lies under the glass lid of the tomb. Below are tiny figures of the guards, asleep, with minute jug, mugs and dice. At Orvieto there is the reliquary of the sacred corporal-cloth, stained with blood during a performance of the Eucharist. One of the great triumphs of the goldsmith's art, made in 1337–38 by Ugolino di Vieri from Siena, it is 400 pounds (181 kg) of gilt and polychrome solid silver, with coloured plaques illustrating the meeting between the pope and the bishop sent to fetch the relic (Plate VI).

The very vestments of the priest were a lesson in the scriptures. The different garments each had their own symbolic significance, and the mantle or cope which went over all was a favourite site for figurative embroidery-work. English embroiderers were the most famous in western Europe during the years 1250 to 1350, and *opus anglicanum* found its way all over Europe. The work was expensive and time-consuming, and much of it was done by women, as we may judge from the mention of Mabel of Bury St Edmunds, who executed two large commissions for Henry III in 1239–43. A complex piece of embroidery-work – an altar-frontal, a cope, or a chasuble – could take years to complete and would cost the equivalent of fifteen years' wages for one of the stitchers. The papacy was much in the market for these expensive pieces, and a Vatican inventory of 1295 lists over a hundred items of *opus anglicanum*. The museum at Pienza has a historiated cope made in England in 1315–50 and given to the cathedral at Pienza by Pope Pius II, with 27 large panels showing the lives of Mary and the virgin martyrs St Margaret and St Catherine, and smaller panels in the interstices showing the inhabitants of the Tree of Jesse and the apostles with their creed. Work of such exquisite and expensive craftsmanship was likely to have spent most of its time in the treasure-chest and to have been brought out only on great feast-days.

There were many scenes of death in medieval churches, some of them doctrinal portrayals in glass of Christ's triumph over Death, some of them deaths of saints by martyrdom that were similarly auguries of resurrection. Tombs were comparatively rare in churches in the twelfth and thirteenth centuries, and were mostly those of kings or high-ranking nobles, or of bishops and abbots in the churches they had served. The tomb of Edmund Crouchback, brother of Edward I, in Westminster Abbey is a magnificent example (Fig. 43). But as cathedrals and great churches became more central to the public life of the community they were increasingly filled with the tombs of those rich enough to pay for an expensive burial and to guarantee appropriate endowments. In the fourteenth century there developed the practice of building chantry chapels within the church to house a tomb and provide a space in which one or more priests could say masses in perpetuity for the soul of the donor. On the continent these were incorporated in the existing structure of the church, but in England they were often built prominently along the aisles of the church.

Figure 43: Westminster Abbey, tomb of Edmund Crouchback (d. 1296). Edmund, Earl of Lancaster (1245–96), was the second son of Henry III and a lieutenant in his brother Edward I's wars. His nickname may be derived from his enthusiasm for crusading (where he wore a cross or *crouch* on his back) or, more likely, from his crooked back. His tomb is in the Sanctuary, next to that of Edward I. In the Middle Ages the tomb looked much more colourful: the crestings and pinnacles were gilded, the sculpted figures of 'weepers' were painted, and the canopy was inlaid with stained glass set in tinfoil.

Figure 44: Winchester Cathedral, nave, chantry chapel (1394–1403) of William of Wykeham.

Chantry chapels began to invade the aisles of England's churches from the mid-fourteenth century. Rich people paid for masses for their souls to be said there in perpetuity. William of Wykeham (1324–1404), Bishop of Winchester and Chancellor of England, had his chantry set up in the south aisle of the nave of Winchester Cathedral at the place where he had been accustomed to pray as a boy before an altar dedicated to the Virgin. Like Wykeham's new buildings at Winchester College and at New College, Oxford, the chantry chapel is a superb example of the Perpendicular style.

The Percy tomb (*c*.1342–45) in Beverley Minster, one of the most lavish masterpieces of the high Decorated style, is a chantry, and the opportunity that these structures gave for architectural virtuosity is similarly displayed in the Perpendicular tracery and panelling of the chantry chapel (1394–1403) of William of Wykeham (d. 1404) in the nave of Winchester Cathedral (Fig. 44).

As time went by, tombs proliferated, especially in the great new churches of the friars, who enjoyed the use of the burial fees. In England, marble gave way to the more easily worked alabaster for the tomb-effigy, and alabaster statuettes began to fill every niche in the tomb-shrine. From the late fourteenth century, as alabaster figures and retables began to be exported, incised brass slabs, which had been among the triumphs of English art-work in the Decorated style (like the brass of Sir Hugh Hastings at Elsing, in Norfolk: he was a veteran of Crécy, and the 'weepers' are a company of his brothers-in-arms, including Edward III), began to be imported from Flanders, and every knight and lady came to be commemorated with a brass in the parish church (some of them very splendid, like those in St Margaret's, King's Lynn). Spain, Denmark and Poland all imported Flemish brasses.

There were many other reminders of mortality in medieval churches. The Last Judgement was frequently portrayed in the tympanum over the west door, or in the west window, or over the chancel-arch, often in such a graphic form as to instil terror of death in the onlooker rather than hope, in those disposed to be hopeful, at the faithful fulfilment of the divine promise, as it was expressed in two verses of the Athanasian Creed: 'They that have done good shall go into life everlasting; and they that have done evil into everlasting fire'. The extended programmes of mural decoration in fourteenth-century churches gave opportunity for a wider range of scenes of death, more graphic and more personal, and these, along with the newly fashionable cadaver-tombs, give a special character to the fifteenth-century contemplation of death.

Gothic Illuminated Manuscripts

A recurrent theme in the foregoing account of the Gothic cathedral has been destruction, decay and change. The cathedrals are the great surviving witnesses of the Gothic inspiration, but they do not survive unchanged. Many of them have their original grand structure more or less intact, even if with additions and modifications, and retain their authentic power to stagger the senses of the observer, but in the exterior detail of stonework and carving and in the interior decoration and furnishing much will have been changed, eroded, removed, restored, replaced, lost. A doubt, a shadow, hangs over the observer: is this or that feature, so much to be admired, 'authentic', or is it the product of an ideal imagining by a later restorer of a style that never was? No doubt there are reassuring answers to be given in some cases, but scholars of illuminated manuscripts have always been pleased to point to the different nature of the artefacts with which they deal. Though the vast majority of the manuscripts that were produced in the Middle Ages have disappeared, and though some that survived to modern times have had pictures cut out, or have been disassembled and sold off page by page, or have been destroyed or severely damaged by the accident of flood, fire or explosion, yet for the most part those that do survive have been carefully preserved, and remain perfectly as they were when first made and painted. The materials of their manufacture – parchment, ink, pigment, gold leaf – are very durable, and they have such a pristine presence, even today, that the observer may be tempted to think of them as overleaping the constraints of their history and their material form.

The history of the illuminated manuscript-book is part of the history of the book, and the history of medieval book production begins in the monasteries, which maintained a virtual monopoly of all aspects of book production in western Europe until the twelfth century. The most famous examples of their work are the great Hiberno-English gospel-books of the seventh and eighth centuries, such as the Lindisfarne Gospels and the Book of Kells, in which the very making of the book is an act of worship before the Word, and the Carolingian and Ottonian bibles and gospel-books of the ninth, tenth and eleventh centuries. The twelfth century saw the production of great lectern-bibles in England, such as the Bury Bible and the Winchester Bible, but the great innovation in France, from about 1200, was the production of smaller-size single-volume bibles, arranged and ordered in books and chapters for convenience of reading, study and reference in much the manner of a modern bible (prior to this, the bible had been mostly available in single books or groups of books such as the Gospels and Epistles): so many of these were produced in the thirteenth century that they supplied most of the demand until the fifteenth. There was also an explosion of biblical commentary and exposition, and of production of glossed books of the bible. Biblical and theological scholars now needed to be able to find their way around biblical commentaries and theological treatises – to be able to look things up and do research – and a whole apparatus of text-formatting (*ordinatio*) developed to enable them to do so: rubrication, numbering of chapters and paragraphs, decorated initials and pictures as punctuation markers and text-finding signals, explicits and incipits, running heads, page numbers, and eventually alphabetically organised indices and concordances. Books were now things to be studied, tools to be used, rather than representations of the presence of the Word.

Though monastic scriptoria continued to be active throughout the Middle Ages, particularly in the production of service-books and of theological and devotional writings in Latin, professional scribes, illuminators and binders began to cut into their monopoly in the twelfth century. The beginning of a commercial book-trade is commonly associated with the growth of the universities, in Paris, Bologna and Oxford, in the twelfth and thirteenth centuries. The demand of teachers and students for texts, commentaries and reference-books led to a professionalisation of the book-trade, in which 'stationers' (*stationarii*) would act as entrepreneurs. They would have copies of authorised or 'set books' copied by professional scribes and then loan out corrected exemplars piecemeal in quires (*pecia*, 'pieces') to students for them to copy or have them copied out on their own behalf and so build up their own collection of the medieval equivalent of photocopies. But of course the new book-trade was responsive also to demand for books from non-university sources, and stationers worked with ateliers of commercial artists as well as with scribes in the production of religious books for aristocratic patrons and buyers and also, increasingly, of secular books. Many of these were illustrated manuscripts of the prose cycles of Arthurian romance, especially *Lancelot*, but manuscripts of the verse-romances of Chrétien de Troyes begin to appear in the early thirteenth century, large books, in two- or three-column format, some with illustrations: about 45 survive. Later, authors themselves, such as Petrarch and Boccaccio in Italy, Machaut, Froissart, Deschamps and Christine de Pizan in France, would begin to play a part in the commissioning of manuscripts of their own writings, and a whole new range of secular texts would be written down and illustrated.

However, it is amongst the psalters, apocalypses and books of hours produced for wealthy customers in the professional and court workshops of Paris and London in the thirteenth century, and subsequently there and in other centres, that the great masterpieces of the Gothic illuminated manuscript-book are to be found.

ILLUMINATED BOOKS IN THIRTEENTH-CENTURY FRANCE

Psalters were the kind of book principally favoured by secular patrons at first: the psalms were commonly read as a form of pious and devotional exercise by lay-people, and they lent themselves well to illustration, both of their own content and of their typologically generated allusions. Anticipations of the Gothic psalter can be found in the Ingeborg Psalter (Chantilly, Musée Condé MS 1695), made in north-eastern France about 1195, with some suggestions of Gothic intimacy in the composition of its scenes, but it was Paris and the Parisian court of Louis IX in the mid-thirteenth century that saw the first flowering of Gothic illuminated manuscripts. It was here that new methods of production were first brought in by the bookmakers clustered on the rue Ermebourg de Brie (now called rue de la Boutebrie), and it was here that new aristocratic patrons began buying books as private owners, and supporting the beginnings of new subjects. Much of the new inspiration came from the cathedrals and their stained glass. The Psalter of Blanche of Castile (1187–1252), mother of Louis IX (Paris, Bibliothèque de l'Arsenal MS 1186, *c*.1230), concentrates illustration, like many psalters, in a series of full-page miniatures relating to Fall and Redemption preceding the text of the Psalms. Each page consists of two interlocked medallions, Romanesque in the rigidity of the figures, but suggestive of the new stained-glass windows in their composition and in the brilliant saturation of their colouring, dominated by blues and reds.

A later phase of the same style can be seen in the *Bibles Moralisées* of the mid-thirteenth century, three of which survive, all associated with Louis IX. These massive books are not 'illustrated bibles' but compilations of thousands of pictures with accompanying texts selected from the bible and from commentaries of an allegorically explanatory kind, such as the elaborate new *Postillae in Bibliam* of the Dominican Hugh of St Cher (d. 1252). Text and commentary run down in columns beside the medallions, usually eight per page. The effect is even more strikingly that of a tall stained-glass window, with the spandrels decorated in mosaic or diaper patterns as in such windows, and reflective light-effects created by the raised convex surface of the gold leaf.

The most magnificent of these bibles, the Bible of Saint-Louis, was made in 1226–34 in Paris and given by Louis IX to Alfonso X of Castile, and is now in the Treasury of the cathedral at Toledo. It contains thousands of illustrative medallions.

But the 'stained-glass style' was already being superseded in a manuscript that now survives as a collection of Old Testament illustrations that perhaps once formed part of a psalter, 1250–60 (now mostly in New York, Morgan Library MS M.638). It had moved to Italy by the fourteenth century, and marginal inscriptions in Persian were added to explain the Christian subjects to Shah Abbas of Persia, to whom it was sent by Cardinal Maciejowski as part of a papal mission organised by Pope Clement VIII in 1608 (it is also known as the Maciejowski Bible, or Psalter, and the Shah Abbas Bible). It shows great animation in the figures and a concern to integrate them in their relation to each other in the now rectangular picture-space. Also – an innovation perhaps derived from contemporary English manuscripts – the figures spill over into the margins (a decisive break with pictorial conventions derived from stained glass), as on fol. 23v (Fig. 45), where a siege-scene illustrating 1 Samuel 13 shows an archer on a battlemented tower above the picture-frame shooting down at the besiegers within it while a figure suspended in mid-air in the left margin seems unprepared to release a massive stone from a catapult and to be in danger himself of being projected over the walls of the town. The new style and its English influences are also present in the Psalter of St Louis (BN MS lat.10525, *c*.1256). Smaller, designed for private use, it has 78 full-page miniatures on Old Testament subjects preceding the psalm-text, with finely drawn figures, supple and unmonumental, more elegantly decorative architectural frames and borders, and more subtle and varied colouring (Fig. 46). The canopies, with their arches, gables, pinnacles and rose-windows, are clearly modelled on those of the Sainte-Chapelle, built in 1243–46. They seem to frame the scene rather than provide a background for it, so that the figures exist in rather than merely occupy the picture-space.

English drolleries (pictures with odd and fanciful subjects) had quickly made their way into France and appear for instance in the Picardy Psalter of *c*.1290 (BN MS lat.10435), where the borders house a variety of crouching rabbits and angry dogs, and the musicians, dancers and lovers of the bas-de-page (lower margin) often have inscriptions in the Picard dialect identifying

---

Figure 45: New York, Pierpont Morgan Library MS 638, fol. 23v. Old Testament miniatures. *c*.1250–60.

See also Fig. 26. This manuscript is strikingly representative of an early attempt to give greater solidity to the figures in miniatures, to integrate them within the picture-space, and at the same time to draw attention to the 'artefactual' nature of the scene by allowing figures to overpass the frame. In the upper scene is the battle of Saul against the Philistines (1 Samuel 13–14) portrayed as a medieval siege; in the lower scene Samuel anoints Saul (1 Samuel 10:1) and makes a sacrificial offering (1 Samuel 7:9).

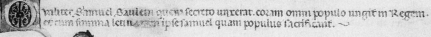

uultcr Samuel Saulem quem secreto unxerat. coram omni populo ungit in Regem.
et cum summa letitia ipse samuel quam populus sacrificant.

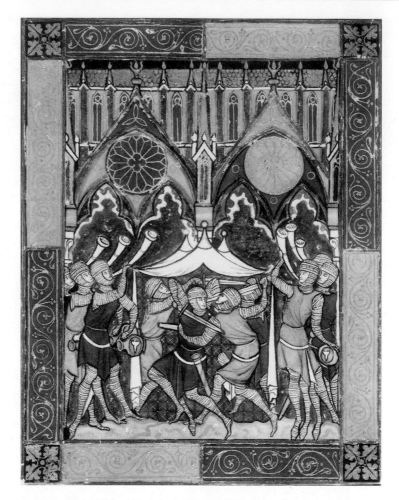

Figure 46: Paris, BN MS lat.10525 (the St Louis Psalter), fol. 52r. Old Testament battle-scene. *c.*1250–60.

This little psalter, designed for private use, has 78 full-page miniatures on Old Testament subjects preceding the psalter-text. They show something of the sculptural solidity of the Morgan MS (Fig. 45) and considerable influence, in the pinnacled canopies, from the new Gothic architecture of the Sainte-Chapelle.

them with friends of the manuscript's owner – a glimpse of one of the unexpected pleasures to be obtained from having such a book in one's possession. In the miniatures of manuscripts of the same period there are also signs of the increasing tenderness of human feeling associated with Gothic. The Crucifixion in the Psalter and Hours of Yolande of Soissons (New York, Morgan Library MS M.729, *c.*1275, fol. 345v) takes place on a cross of metallic bars blossoming as the Tree of Life, with the Pelican of Piety sitting in a nest on the top of the Cross feeding her young. It is all set against a burnished gold background. But Christ himself droops, poignantly, the left knee crossed over the right, the feet nailed with one nail in the new and more painful style. This manuscript is closely associated with the atelier of the Parisian Maître Honoré, one of the few names that have come down to us from this earlier period. He is reliably credited with the Breviary of Philippe le Bel (BN MS lat.1023, dated 1296), in which formal diapered backgrounds and traditional iconography combine with lively and expressive figure-drawing and the more sophisticated sense of figures in space that comes from the overlapping of figures within the scene and the overpassing of the lower frame by their feet.

OUTSIDE FRANCE

German manuscript illumination of the period shows little evidence of or reaction to these developments in Paris. It continued to be dominated by Ottonian and Romanesque models, apart from a few signs of greater express-ive freedom in thirteenth-century manuscripts of *Parzival* and *Tristan* and other secular works. A psalter from south Germany of *c.*1260–70 (Zurich, Zentral-bibliothek Cod.Rh.167) has artificially restless drapery and stereotyped human figures, and even a manuscript as late as the Manesse Codex (Heidelberg, Universitätsbibliothek Cod.pal.germ.848), the masterpiece of German chivalric court culture, made in south Germany near Lake Constance about 1315–30, draws on older German traditions and shows little influence of French Gothic. In 137 full-page miniatures it shows Minnesinger ('singers of love') in scenes of hawking and hunting, jousting, sport and general dalliance, framed in col-oured bands, with coats of arms and badges above. It is a kind of pictorial album of the aristocracy.

Flemish artists generally followed Parisian and northern French traditions, though there is an unusual rent-book, the *rentier* of Audenarde (Brussels, Bibliothèque Royale MS 1175), made in 1291–1302, which has pen-drawings of farming scenes and activities in the spaces between the entries, as if antic-ipating the taste for genre-realism which was to become a feature of Flemish margins in the fourteenth century. An example is a bible of *c.*1330–40 (Brussels, Bibliothèque Royale MS 9157) which has a menagerie of animals in its borders and a regular animal ballet of rabbits, hares and dogs in the bas-de-pages.

In Italy, the outstanding centre of manuscript production in the thirteenth century was Bologna, with its great university. The manuscripts were mostly legal texts and choir-books, massive volumes illustrated with small historiated initials and borders with foliage and stems incorporating motifs from the classical decorative repertory. Sometimes, the space for illustration in the law-books was left blank and was supplied in the local styles when the books were exported to Paris or Oxford.

In Spain, there was some continuation of the magnificent tradition of Romanesque Apocalypse illustration of the 'Beatus' manuscripts, but the most striking survivals of the period are the richly illustrated manuscripts commis-sioned by Alfonso X, King of Castile 1252–84 (described in Chapter Two), which were painted by artists brought in from Seville.

ENGLISH ILLUMINATION IN THE THIRTEENTH CENTURY

In England,[9] there was a strong native tradition of book-illustration in the 'tinted outline' style kept alive by Matthew Paris, monk and historian of St Alban's, active 1236–59. A beautiful example of his work is the tender Virgin and Child in the *Historia Anglorum* (BL MS Royal 14.C.vii, dated 1259, fol. 6r), with Matthew Paris on his knees below, his praying hands among the words of the inscription celebrating the kiss exchanged by the Virgin and Child.

But Henry III was a sedulous imitator of Louis IX, whom he visited in Paris in 1254 and 1262, and in London there was an immediate response to the new French style, and a 'court school' of manuscript painters at Westminster began to produce a remarkable series of illuminated manuscripts. A *Life of Edward the Confessor* (CUL MS Ee.3.59), made about 1255–60 for Eleanor of Castile, wife of Prince Edward (later Edward I), is a key-work in the process of adaptation, but the full development of the style is announced in the Douce Apocalypse (Bodl. MS Douce 180), made for Edward and Eleanor about 1270. Apocalypse manuscripts were popular with aristocratic patrons in England at this time, perhaps because of a surge of interest in prophecy associated with the prediction of Joachim of Fiore that the world would end in 1260, perhaps also because the Apocalypse of St John (called the Book of Revelation in the English version of the bible) was a wonderfully exciting text to read (it was often translated into French in these manuscripts) and illustrate. A number of magnificent Apocalypses had been produced in the 1250s and 1260s, including the Morgan Apocalypse (New York, Morgan Library MS M.524), the Dyson Perrins Apocalypse (California, Getty Museum MS Ludwig III.1 [83.MC.72]), the great Trinity Apocalypse (Cambridge, Trinity College MS R.16.2), the most sumptuous of all thirteenth-century English manuscripts, and the Lambeth Apocalypse (London, Lambeth Palace Library MS 209), made for the Countess of Winchester in the fashionable mixture of tinted drawings and full paintings. But it is in the Douce Apocalypse, with its reminiscences of the Painted Chamber at Westminster, its sinuous flowing draperies and unstiffened figures, that the French influence is most successfully absorbed (Fig. 47). The development is well illustrated in a comparison with a picture of the Coronation of Edward the Confessor, in the English tinted outline style, in one of Matthew Paris's historical manuscripts of only a few years before (Fig. 48).

Psalters, however, were still the kind of illustrated manuscripts most frequently in demand in England (what bibles were needed were probably supplied from Paris, which had the organisation for these very large books), and it was here that a more independently English style began to be fashioned. Psalters were usually prefixed by a series of full-page miniatures ('miniature' does not originally mean 'small'; it comes from *miniare*, 'to paint with red pigment [*minium*]') illustrating the principal scenes of Christ's life, often arranged typologically with Old Testament scenes, and this gave the illustrators opportunity for ambitious figural and dramatic work as well as for initials and

Figure 47: Oxford, Bodl. MS Douce 180 (the Douce Apocalypse), p. 72. *c.*1270.

This is one of the great Apocalypse manuscripts made for aristocratic patrons in England in the late thirteenth century, with text and gloss in French as well as Latin. Some of the miniatures in the manuscript, like this one, are left uncoloured, as tinted drawings. The poses of the figures are expressive (perhaps over-expressive) and their garments flowing and easy, in a style that absorbs the latest French influences. The text is Revelation (Vulgate Latin Apocalypsis) 17:6. An angel shows St John the Whore of Babylon drunk (evidently) with the blood of saints.

borders. Scenes of the Nativity, of the Last Judgement and above all of the Crucifixion acquired a new emotionality, matching that which was contemporaneously being developed in Franciscan devotion to the humanity of Christ: Christ's body slumps more agonisingly, the Virgin swoons violently instead of inclining her head in grief, the tormentors gesticulate in demented fashion. The formal poses of the Crucifixion in the Amesbury Psalter (Oxford, All Souls College MS 6, fol. 5r), *c.*1250, can be compared with the complex drama of emotion in the Huth Psalter (BL MS Add.38116, fol. 11v), *c.*1285 (see Figs 2 and 3). In the Rutland Psalter (BL MS Add.62925), made *c.*1260 for the Earl of Lincoln, and the Oscott Psalter (BL MS Add.5000), made *c.*1265–70, possibly in Oxford, a more characteristically idiosyncratic kind of Englishness

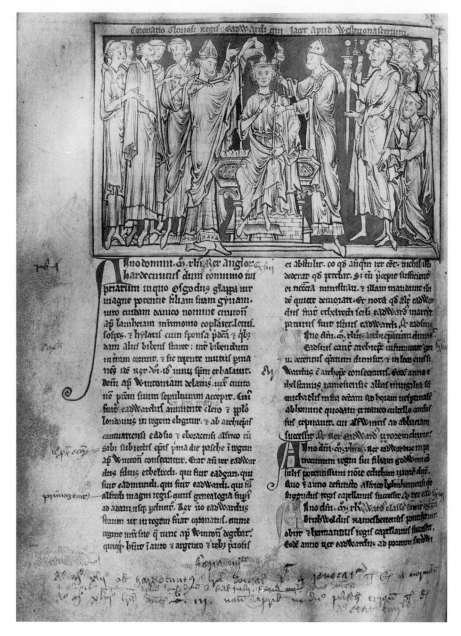

Figure 48: Matthew Paris, *Flores historiarum*. Manchester, Chetham Library MS 6712, fol. 115v. The Coronation of Edward the Confessor. *c.*1250.

Matthew Paris (d. 1259) was a monk of St Alban's and the greatest of the Anglo-Latin historians. He was himself also an artist, though the tinted drawings of the ten coronation-scenes that accompany his *Flores* (a digest of world history up to 1250) are by others. The comparative stiffness of the figures and drapery has not yet yielded to the sinuosity of the new French Court Style.

began to be asserted, with grotesques, animals and genre-figures – wrestlers, musicians, acrobats, jugglers, apes, centaurs, harpies, dogs, birds, a peacock, a scold on a ducking-stool, hybrid monsters in fantasy combat – crowding the margins for the first time, apparently gratuitously.

The Alphonso Psalter (BL MS Add.24686), formerly called the Tenison Psalter, is the masterpiece of the Westminster court workshop style, with painting of an elegance, richness of detail and vigour of figure-modelling that must owe a debt to an accomplished tradition of panel-painting now completely lost (except for the battered Westminster Abbey retable). It was begun in 1284 to honour the marriage of Alphonso, son of Edward I and his Spanish queen Eleanor, to Margaret, the daughter of the Count of Holland, but Alphonso died in the same year, and the manuscript was not finished for another 20 years. The Windmill Psalter (New York, Morgan Library MS M.102), *c.*1300, has a similar refinement. It is so called from the meticulously drawn windmill that appears on fol. 2r, for no reason but the pleasure of drawing it, in the background of the large E which is the second letter of the first word of Psalm 1 (*Beatus*), the first folio having been taken up with the initial B; the rest of the opening text (. . . *atus qui non abiit*) appears on a scroll borne by a flying angel beside the E; in the lower part of the page, again for no apparent reason but the love of beauty, a large pheasant stands peacefully.

Many will think the Queen Mary Psalter (BL MS Royal 2.B.vii), *c.*1310–20, the finest of these courtly manuscripts. An Old Testament narrative cycle of exquisite framed tinted drawings, generally two per page, with Anglo-Norman explanatory verses, is followed by four full-page miniatures, the calendar, and then the psalter, with miniatures and initials, and little scenes of courtly life and pastimes in the bas-de-pages (Fig. 49). These are delicate and quizzical, and often run page after page in little narrative sequences, like the one of the ladies chasing and snaring rabbits: they have none of the grotesqueness and occasional grossness of the later East Anglian psalters, and are some of the most familiarly delicious images in English medieval art. The grace, clarity and restraint of the drawing in this manuscript is wholly English and though these are qualities that are often associated with French influence it is hard to find them in contemporary French painting, and indeed the work of Master Honoré, a generation earlier, may itself owe something to English models. Not all good things came from France.

THE EAST ANGLIAN PSALTERS

There followed now an extraordinary efflorescence of uniquely and unmistakably English manuscript painting in the psalters of the next 30 years from East Anglia and other eastern provincial centres. Travelling workshops of artists could now take up commissions, often in collaboration with monastic scribes, for ambitious local magnates and country landowners and for local ecclesiastics. Early examples are the Tickhill Psalter (New York Public Library MS Spenser 26), which was made at Worksop, in Nottinghamshire, 1303–14, and

sût î înîquîtatibz: non est quî fa
cîat bonum

Deus de cœlo pspexît super filîos ho
mînû: ut uîdeat sî est întelligens

has a lavishness in its brilliantly executed naturalistic marginalia of flowers, leaves, animals and hybrids that is matched only by the Peterborough Psalter in Brussels (Bibliothèque Royale MSS 9961–2). This was executed 1299–1318 for Geoffrey of Crowland, Abbot of Peterborough, who gave it to the papal nuncio in England, from whom it passed to Pope John XXII and thence as a gift to Philip VI and Charles V of France and so to Philip the Good, Duke of Burgundy, whose territories included Brussels, where it stayed. The three artists involved in the illustration of the manuscript show a mastery of minutely exquisite detail but also an inclination to the bolder designs of the mature East Anglian style (Plate VII). The boldness is fully exemplified in the Gorleston Psalter (BL MS Add.49622) of *c*.1310–20, made for a Suffolk patron, where one begins to see some of the vigour of the East Anglian grotesques beside evidence of a range of other influences: a page has been inserted (now fol. 7) with a delicate copy of a Sienese Crucifixion panel, with thoroughly sophisticated modelling and drapery – a vivid example of the international trade in artistic skills. A certain Italianate sophistication of figure-modelling has been seen also in the Douai Psalter (Douai, Bibliothèque Municipale MS 171), which was made for a Suffolk patron in 1322–25 and was praised by scholars as incomparable in beauty and perfectness of preservation before it was shattered beyond recognition in the First World War, and in the St Omer Psalter (BL MS Yates Thompson 14 and MS Add.39810), made *c*.1325–30 for the St Omer family of Mulbarton in Norfolk. The St Omer Psalter has, amongst many, one of the most extraordinary *Beatus* pages. A panelled border with medallions is enfolded and linked by a complex network of interlaced cords, from every part of which grow curling tendrils and delicate sprays of oak, holly, ivy, daisy, maidenhair fern. In the crevices are a peacock, a man drinking from a wide-lipped goblet, a boy leaping over and spearing a unicorn, a raven pecking at a dead horse, two men straining at a rope attached to the Ark (being built in one of the roundels), other men working with axe and auger, mounting a ladder, and felling an oak, a wild man of the woods, a porcupine, a stag, a bear, two men mounted pick-a-back wrestling, a female dancer, rams butting, a swine, a horse grazing, birds, rabbits, squirrels, a swan, a heron, a hawk striking a duck, a caterpillar, a fly, a butterfly (Fig. 50).

The 'classic' East Anglian psalters are the Ormesby and Luttrell psalters. The former (Bodl. MS Douce 366) was given to Norwich priory by a monk,

Figure 49: London, BL MS Royal 2.B.VII (the Queen Mary Psalter), fol. 151r. Jesus teaching in the Temple; lady-falconer hunting. *c*.1310–20.

This beautiful manuscript contains an extensive sequence of New Testament scenes at the psalter divisions. They are framed tinted drawings, all done by one artist, and give always an impression of elegance, serenity and restraint. The unframed bas-de-page scenes are an independent little continuous narrative of aristocratic life and recreation. The text on this page is Psalm 53:1–2, the second verse beginning, 'God looks down upon the sons of men to see if there are any that are wise', to which the main miniature, displaying the prodigious wisdom of the child Jesus (Luke 2:46), may make reference.

Robert of Ormesby, probably one of the scribes, in the 1320s and had probably been in the priory workshop for 40 years. Several hands are involved, some not at all elegant, but the major artist is a genius, especially for his grotesques and wonderful figures and beasts in rich heavy borders. The 'dixit dominus' page is one of the best-known pages of English illumination (Fig. 51). At the top, an owl seated backwards on a rabbit is pursued by a monkey wearing falconer's gloves and seated on a greyhound; at the bottom, two naked men seated respectively on a lion and a bear fight fisticuffs; on the left, a half-naked man with upper and lower parts of his body facing in opposite directions blows on a trumpet from which a pennant flaps. The Luttrell Psalter (BL MS Add.42130) was made *c*.1325–35 in the Lincoln area for Sir Geoffrey Luttrell. A famous framed miniature (fol. 202v) shows him on horseback in chivalric pose receiving his sword and shield from his wife and daughter-in-law, while the marginal illustrations of farm and other estate work are images of his power and of the ordered hierarchy of which he is head. These vignettes have become particularly well-known because of their use by modern publishers' graphic designers to give vivid 'scenes of everyday life' for books on medieval social history. The same artist is responsible for the fantastic huge hybrids that inhabit the borders, vivid, unreal, 'nightmarish', 'decadent', as they have been called, decidedly un-French, but done with high technical skill, and some unforgettable physiognomical idiosyncrasies – dark deep-set eyes, puckered lips, fuzzy hair, all as if painted by someone slightly deranged, an early Van Gogh. Every page is a stimulus to visual exploration, in puzzling out for instance how the formal borders grow out of the hybrids and animals, such as it is difficult to imagine as ever having been a pious exercise (Fig. 52).

Such marginal illustration returns us again to the question of meaning and intention that was debated earlier in relation to church decoration and sculpture and that will return again. What are these strange and monstrous and often obscene pictures doing in the margins of books intended for pious reading? Interpreters have seen them as a kind of doodling or creative overflow, done for fun, or as the liberating expression of unconscious impulses repressed by religion, or as a form of subversive commentary on the main picture or text, or (in an opposed but closely related reading) as allegorically coded negative exempla, demonstrating the distractions of the flesh and the need to transcend them in the spirit of the main text. No doubt a single explanation for all apparently digressive marginal illustration is going to be hard to find, but something should be allowed to the sophistication and self-consciousness of

Figure 50: London, BL MSS Yates Thompson 14 and Add.39810 (the St Omer Psalter), fol. 7r. *Beatus* page. *c*.1325–30.

One of the most profuse of *Beatus* pages (see Colour Plate VII), with narrative medallions set upon a panelled border, and tendrils and sprays springing out in every direction and supporting a host of figures and animals and activities. In the initial B, David is in the first medallion of a Tree of Jesse that culminates at the top in the infant Christ.

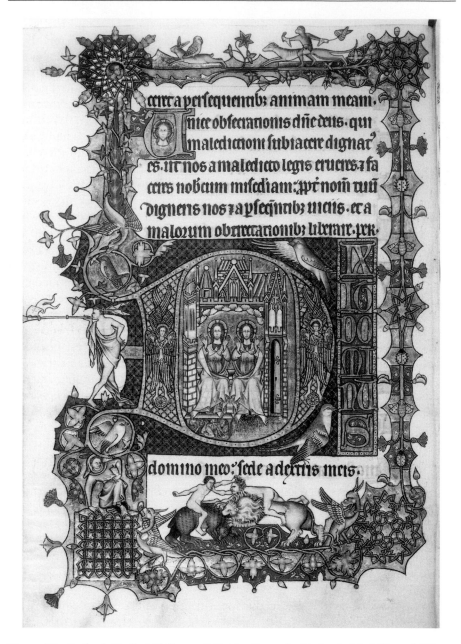

Figure 51: Oxford, Bodl. MS Douce 366 (the Ormesby Psalter), fol. 147v. *c.*1320.
    This famous page, with its extraordinary variety of border designs and motifs, is dominated by the opening D of Psalm 110, 'The Lord says to my lord' (*Dixit Dominus*, Vulgate Psalm 109). The initial miniature shows God the Father and God the Son with enemies underfoot, in allusion to the warlike theme of the Psalm. The scenes of grotesque combat at top and bottom and the trumpeter on the left (summoning to battle?) may have associations with the same theme.

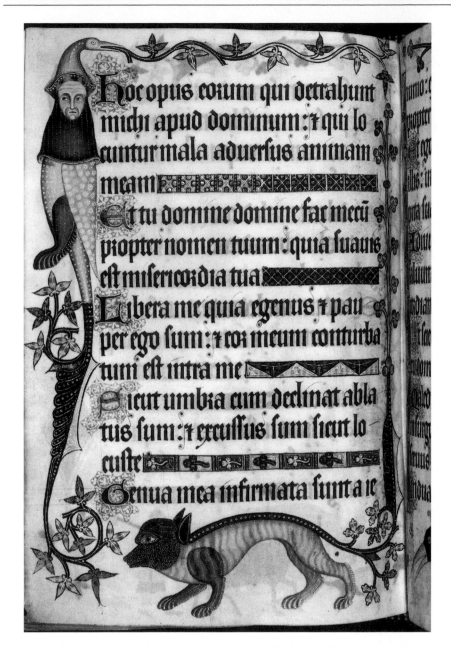

Figure 52: London, BL MS Add.42130 (the Luttrell Psalter), fol. 201v. Border decoration. *c.*1325–35.

One of the 400 decorative borders in this extraordinary manuscript, famous for its heavy lines, nightmarish invention and very high technical skill: the face, with its emphatic moulding and contouring, is unforgettable. One looks for its significance: are the words of the Psalm-text on this page a clue? 'I am gone like a shadow at evening . . .' (Psalm 109:23, Vulgate psalm 108:23, *Sicut umbra . . .*).

these artists, and the possibility that marginal illustration may exist not in a subversive, parodic or didactic relationship with the main picture or text, but rather as a complement to it, defining reverence through irreverence and the rational through the oppositional presence of the irrational.[10]

On one page of the Rutland Psalter (fol. 14r), the tail of the letter 'p' in *conspectu* ('sight' in 'the ungodly . . . do not set thee before them in their sight', Psalm 86:14) is extended into the bas-de-page and becomes the arrow that a negroid archer is shooting into the anus of a doubled-up fish-man (who appears to be enjoying the experience). The half-playful suggestion of other things that the ungodly may have in their 'sight' is made to grow directly out of the letter of the text. In a book of hours in the Walters Art Gallery in Baltimore (MS 102, fol. 56v), a contorted crucifix-type figure with a goose-head is perched in the bas-de-page. Is this a play on the text above, 'Thou hast anointed my head with oil' (Psalm 23:5), where the Latin for 'with oil' (*in oleo*) could be mis-taken for the French 'with a goose'? Words slip and slide, the illustrator seems to say to the text-writer.

Another illustrator, in a missal made at Amiens, portrays the scribe in the bas-de-page surrounded by monkeys mockingly 'apeing' his activities (The Hague, Koninklijke Bibliotheek MS D.40, fol. 124r). In the Ormesby Psalter, the text of Psalm 102:4, 'My heart is smitten' (*Percussus sum*), perhaps prompts a particularly rich bas-de-page (fol. 131r). A young man, likewise 'smitten', offers a ring to a lady who clasps the usual furry animal (in this case a squirrel) to her breast; meanwhile a phallic sword sticks out at an alarming angle from a hole in his gown and a gryllus (face set upon and between two legs) looks on lasciviously. Below, in the margin of the margin, a fat cat greedily eyes a mouse which is also half-poking out of its hole (Fig. 53). If the first scene is a mocking commentary on the text, the second is a mocking commentary on the comment-ary. Scenes like this, or of the lover shitting turds and then bringing the turds in a basin to his lady as a love-offering (in a book of hours, Cambridge, Trinity College MS B.11.22, fol. 73r), or of a nun kneeling in worship before a man with exposed anus bending and shitting before her (in the Alexander-romance in Bodl. MS Bodley 264, fol. 56r), are to be taken in the same spirit that fabliau is to be taken in relation to romance. The two forms are part of the same world of seeing, the obverse and the reverse of the same processing of experi-ence. The grossness of the one does not deny but rather defines the other.

Nothing in subsequent fourteenth-century English painting approached the energy and inventiveness of the extraordinary series of East Anglian psalters, and nothing much matched their sophistication until the great Carmelite Missal of the 1390s, which inaugurated a phase of English Gothic that will be discussed later. Italian influences were still at work, and the foreshortened upturned faces of the Genesis Picture-Book (BL MS Egerton 1894), c.1360, have been seen as evidence of a 'Giottesque episode' in English art;[11] the imitations, if they are that, are awkward and full of effort. The most import-ant manuscripts of the period are a group made in the 1360s and 1370s for the Bohun family, especially for Humphrey, Earl of Hereford (d. 1373), and his daughters Eleanor and Mary, the former of whom married Thomas of

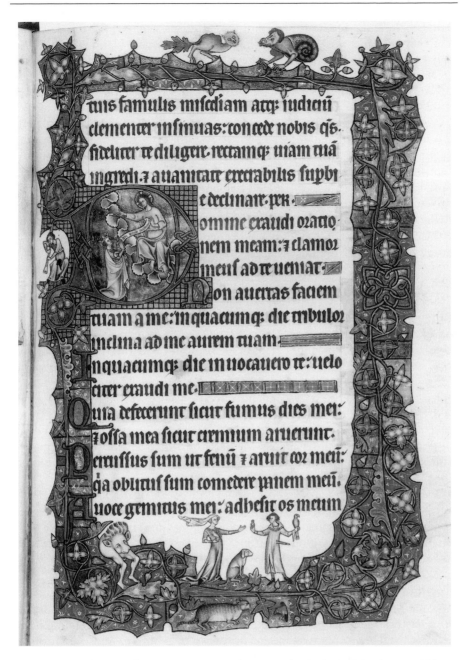

Figure 53: Oxford, Bodl. MS Douce 366 (the Ormesby Psalter), fol. 131r. *c*.1320.
Another example (cf. Fig. 51) of Ormesby's relentlessly inventive border
decoration. The cat-and-mouse scene in the bottom border and the combat of
snail-backed and leaf-tailed hybrids at the top may mimic the ambiguous
betrothal in the bas-de-page. The initial D (*Domine, exaudi orationem meam*,
'O Lord, hear my prayer', Psalm 102) shows King David praying to Christ.

Woodstock, Duke of Gloucester, and the latter his nephew, the future Henry IV. They include the Vienna Psalter (Österreichische National-bibliothek Cod.1826), the Exeter College Psalter (Oxford, Exeter College MS 47), the Egerton Psalter (BL MS Egerton 3277), the Oxford Psalter and Hours (Bodl. MS Auct.D.4.4) and the Fitzwilliam Psalter (Cambridge, Fitzwilliam Museum MS 38–1950). The manuscripts show exceptional command of biblical narrative and typology, and the illustration has fine detail, much gold leaf, and sporadically bold Italianate perspectival and illusionistic effects. A nucleus or 'school' of artists seems to have been involved, familiar with Italian and Flemish painting, perhaps working at one of the Bohun castles. They show a special fondness for slender metallic bar-borders with delicate sprays springing out and for forests of spires in the architectural canopy above the upper border. There is prolific marginal decoration, some of it irreverent, but, for all of the accomplishment and mannered refinement, something of the inventive energy of the earlier psalters seems to have gone.

FRENCH AND FLEMISH BOOKS OF HOURS

Psalters were the dominant form of illustrated book in England up to the end of the fourteenth century, but in France they had long been overtaken in popularity by books of hours. The book of hours was the favourite prayer-book of lay-people, and enabled them to follow, in private, the church's programme of daily devotion at the seven canonical hours. Until the thirteenth century it was attached as an appendix to the psalter (the only prayer-book used by the laity), but it detached itself and became extremely popular as an independent book, whether as a *de luxe* status symbol for the rich or, eventually, as an affordable little luxury in the form that Flemish shops began to produce in large quantities in the fifteenth century for sale 'on spec'. Literally thousands survive.

Derived originally from a short service in honour of the Virgin (the Little Office of Our Lady) composed in the ninth century, the book of hours centred on devotion to the Virgin and on the events of her life. The content could vary and be amplified, but the basic pattern was fixed. At the beginning was the Calendar, necessary to show the days on which particular devotions were to be performed, and accompanied by pictures of the 'Labours of the Months' (described in the account of the Duke of Berry's *Très Riches Heures* in Chapter Two, above). Then followed Gospel sequences describing the events of Christ's life, sometimes with pictures of the Evangelists and of the events leading up to the Passion. Then came two special prayers to the Virgin, and the Hours of the Virgin, the centrepiece of the book (and why it is called a 'book of hours'), with prayers, hymns, psalms and devotions for the seven canonical hours (eight originally, but Matins and Lauds were usually combined), adapted to the life of the Virgin and illustrated accordingly, usually thus: Matins (Annunciation), Lauds (Visitation), Prime (Nativity), Tierce (Annunciation to the Shepherds), Sext (Adoration of the Magi), None (Presentation in the Temple), Vespers (Flight into Egypt, or Massacre of the Innocents) and Compline

(Coronation of the Virgin). Finally, there came the Seven Penitential Psalms, with pictures of David, or David and Bathsheba; the Office of the Dead (not the Requiem Mass, but prayers said over the coffin), with a Last Judgement, or vigil, or dying man; and the Suffrages (Memorials) of Saints, with opportunity for any number of pictures of saints.

Basic illustration consisted of initials, miniatures and simple borders. The initial could be decorated or historiated (telling a story or *ystoire*); the border could be a rectangular frame with foliage or figures, or later a tail-like extension of the initial into the margin developing into vine-leaf or ivy-leaf tendrils round all of the page (*vinet*) or part of it (*demi-vinet*). Then the vinets started to throw shoots outward which act as platforms or trapezes for drolleries and grotesques, while miniatures expand so as to fill the whole page and are provided with their own architectural frames or with picture-frames as if they were easel-paintings that happened to be in a book, or with windows or door-frames as if one were looking through the page into space. The making of a *de luxe* book of hours was a complex operation: the vellum had to be gathered, ruled, written, passed to the rubricator for red lettering, to the *miniator* or limner for initials and borders, and to the artist for illustration. The artist did a drawing in the space left by the scribe, applied gold leaf with adhesive and burnished it, and then did the colouring. The pages then went to the binder.

Books of hours are the finest examples of Gothic illumination, and many were made for show, like the famous series done for the Duke of Berry. No doubt they provided opportunities for enjoyment, distraction, puzzlement and delight that would pass many an idle hour. But they were used too, and Henry V, and Isabel, the formidable queen of Charles VI, and Philip the Good, Duke of Burgundy, are all chronicled at their devotions with the 'Little Hours'. Henry VI recited the Little Office every day, as did Catherine of Aragon and Sir Thomas More. There is much evidence of use in the surviving books, which are often black from fingering and kissing. Books of hours were often given as wedding presents to a bride, and mentioned in wills as precious heirlooms. There were many ways in which they could be adapted for personal use, as for instance with special prayers against the tooth-ache (to St Apollonia, who was martyred by having her teeth pulled out one by one), against plague, against bed-bugs.

There are books of hours surviving from before 1300 but they came into their own in the early fourteenth century, and particularly in the productions of the Parisian workshops and their most famous master, Jean Pucelle. Pucelle worked on the Breviary of Jeanne de Belleville (BN MSS lat.10483–4) and the Bible of Robert de Billyng (BN MS lat.11935), but the tiny Hours of Jeanne d'Evreux (93 × 60 mm), now in the Cloisters Museum in New York, is his masterpiece. Commissioned in 1324 by Charles le Bel (Charles IV) for his bride, it contains 23 delicate miniatures in grisaille against coloured backgrounds, with drôleries in the margins. Grisaille, or painting *de blanc et de noir*, as it was called, was Pucelle's favourite technique, perhaps because it makes possible some more advanced experiments in the three-dimensional modelling of the figures. Pucelle creates space for his scenes and integrates his miniatures and related marginal figures in a skilful and witty way: in the Annunciation scene (the most important picture in a book of hours, always given to the workshop master), the Virgin is in a room from which the front wall has been removed, while Gabriel kneels in an adjoining space like a small anteroom. An angel outside the picture supports its lower right corner and opens the door which allows us to see the scene inside (fol. 16r) (Fig. 54): the picture seems to be trying to detach itself from the plane of the parchment. The French artist is influenced by Italian art in these innovations, indirectly by Giotto's monochrome Vices and Virtues in the Arena (Scrovegni) Chapel in Padua (c.1305) and directly by Sienese painting like the Maestà, or Madonna in Majesty (Virgin and Child enthroned with Saints), of Duccio (1308–15).

The connection of the marginal drôleries with the main picture is not always easy to make out – why, for instance, should there be two oddly-dressed knights mounted on rams tilting at a barrel-shaped quintain in the bas-de-page of the Betrayal in the Garden (fol. 15v)? But an attempt has been made, by Madeline Caviness,[12] to suggest that the imagery of the drôleries has a consistent theme and purpose of its own. There is a particular profusion of hairy monsters, phallic images, rabbits (commonly taken to signify female sexuality, because of the pun in French on *conin*, 'rabbit', and *con*, 'cunt') and other small furry animals, male grotesques with genital masks ('cock-horses'), bagpipes (iconographically associated with testicles, it is said), and other images, often suggestively juxtaposed. The argument is not for a riot of licence and aphrodisiac display but for a deliberate coding of fear and disgust at rampant male sexuality, through which the king can give warning to his fourteen-year-old bride of the dangers of lasciviousness. The mock-joust with the barrel, for instance, shows rampant males attempting penetration of a uterus-shaped barrel: *aforer le tonel* ('breach the barrel') is a euphemism for *foutre* ('fuck') in the fabliaux. On the same opening, the scene of female horseplay below the Annunciation is the 'playing around' or 'monkey-business' that the young bride must now eschew, and the angel of the Annunciation has a foot treading down a little woman-headed beast to make the same point. This seems more playful than some of the other pages, and perhaps Caviness's clinical description of the book, derived from a severely feminist reading, as a 'psychological clitoridectomy' could be modified. But there is no doubt that Charles, whose first wife had been imprisoned after the discovery of an adulterous liaison (as had the wives of his two brothers), had a reason for attempting to secure the marital chastity of his

---

Figure 54: Jean Pucelle, Hours of Jeanne d'Evreux (New York, The Cloisters, Metropolitan Museum of Art), fols 15v–16r. The Taking in the Garden; (bas-de-page) tilting at a barrel. The Annunciation; (bas-de-page) blindman's buff. c.1325.
The miniatures in this tiny book of hours are in grisaille (grey-shaded drawing). In his figure-moulding, sense of space and picture-organization, Pucelle was much influenced by contemporary Italian painting, and the Annunciation here owes much to the corresponding image in Duccio's *Maestà* (see Fig. 30). The text on the right is the opening of the prayer, 'O Lord, open thou my lips' (*Domine, labia mea aperies*); Jeanne d'Evreux herself kneels within the opening D of *Domine*.

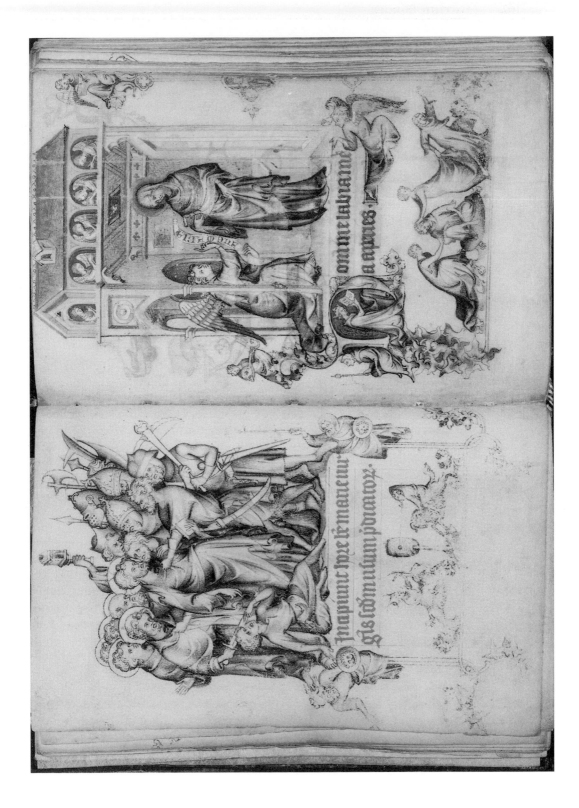

new queen, especially as the last hope of a legitimate male heir to the Capetian line rested with her (the hope was not fulfilled; she bore only daughters).

A slightly later book of hours, the Hours of St Omer (BL MS Add.36684), made in about 1350 in northern France for Marguerite de Beaujeu, the wife of the Grand Panetier (Butler) of France, is similarly packed with drôleries, though not apparently with any similarly didactic intent. Here apes and monkeys (*babewynnerie*, as they were called) are everywhere, including one who is holding up the platform on which Marguerite kneels to join in the Adoration of the Magi (fol. 46v). Architectural canopies to the miniatures are reminiscent of the almost-contemporary Bohun manuscripts in England, and the ivy-leaf borders are a cheerful riot: a monkey is tangled in the leaves, a dog is biting or licking the neck of another monkey who is chewing at an ivy-leaf, another dog is on its hind legs trying to get a closer look at a creature with red legs and no neck, while another bizarre creature is apparently leaning out from an ivy branch to be sick into a kind of ear-trumpet held by a strangely ordinary-looking helpful person (fols 47r, 59v).

THE BOOKS OF HOURS OF JOHN, DUKE OF BERRY, AND THE MARSHAL BOUCICAUT

The most famous series of books of hours are those commissioned by John, Duke of Berry (1340–1416), the greatest patron of the Middle Ages, son of King John II (reigned 1350–64) and brother of Charles V (1364–80). He would perhaps be surprised that he is best remembered for his illuminated manuscripts (almost a third of the 300 he commissioned survive) and not for his castles (disappeared or in ruins) and *joyaux*, or precious objects (nearly all lost). There are six manuscripts that have come to be most celebrated: their familiar names derive from inventories made in the duke's own lifetime. The *Très Belles Heures de Notre Dame* (BN MS nouv.acq.lat.3093) was begun in 1382, and has a beautifully expressive Nativity (p. 42) by the Master of the *Parement de Narbonne* (so called from his major work, an altar frontal now in the Louvre), but the second part of the manuscript was not finished and was later split off and completed as the Hours of Turin, in the style of Jan van Eyck, and the Hours of Milan. The *Petites Heures* (BN MS lat.18014) was made in about 1388 and has many additional prayers that make it into a kind of little devotional library; it seems to have been the duke's favourite, and the one that he generally carried around with him. It has the famous scene of John the Baptist in the Wilderness (fol. 208r), done by the Passion Master, with the Baptist surrounded by animals – lions, monkeys, birds, snails – all exquisitely drawn, listening to the good news as to a Gospel Orpheus (Fig. 55). The *Très Belles Heures*, or Brussels Hours (Bibliothèque Royale MSS 11060–61), painted by Jacquemart de Hesdin *c*.1402–09, is where we begin to see the developing personal ostentation of ducal presence, for instance in the inclusion of the duke with St Andrew and St John the Baptist in prayer before the Virgin (p. 14), the border being decorated with quatrefoils bearing the duke's arms, badges and cipher. The *Grandes Heures* (BN MS lat.919), completed in 1409, a truly

Figure 55: Paris, BN MS lat.18014 (Jacquemart de Hesdin and school, *Les Petites Heures de Jean de Berry*), fol. 208r. St John in the Wilderness. *c.*1388.

The Baptist is shown at the entrance to a cave in a broken-terrace hillside surrounded by exquisitely drawn birds (a hoopoe, a woodpecker or jay, a finch) and monkeys and other animals. A special office in honour of St John, the Duke of Berry's patron-saint, is incorporated in the *Petites Heures*, and the miniature accompanies a brief prayer for the hour of terce (*Deus in adiutorium meum intende*) drawn from the opening of Vulgate Psalm 69 (Psalm 70, 'O God, be pleased to help me'). The duke's coat of arms appears in the initial D.

immense book (435 × 325 mm), which has lost its seventeen full-page mini-atures, is even more ostentatious. On fol. 96r the duke is received by St Peter at the gate of heaven, the saint seizing him by the left hand as if to take him into custody. With his free hand the duke fingers a sapphire pendant surrounded by six petal-pearls, as if reluctant to leave it behind or perhaps contemplating the possibility of offering it as a goodwill gift. The *Belles Heures*, made in 1408–10 and now in the Cloisters Museum in New York, has a magnificent Annunci-ation by Pol de Limbourg, while the *Très Riches Heures* (Chantilly, Musée Condé MS 65), the most magnificent of the duke's manuscripts (far bigger than any normal book of hours), was made in 1411–16 by the three Limbourg brothers, who all died in 1416, the same year as the duke, leaving the illustra-tion unfinished (it was completed by Jean Colombe in about 1485–90).

The predecessors of the Limbourgs were by no means lacking in a desire for experimentation and innovativeness, but the *Très Riches Heures* marks a new plateau of achievement (see Plate I). Knowledgeable in and able to quote from the latest refinements in Italian perspectival panel-painting, the Limbourgs were still devoted primarily to dazzling ornamentation. The Calendar pictures are the area of freest experimentation, as in the January feasting-scene, where the tapestry behind the seated figures sweeps the eye into an illimitably deep landscape, so that the open space and the tapestry space blur into each other. The architectural detail of the Louvre in October is famously meticulous, and the foreground scene is optically highly sophisticated, with reflections in the water, shadows, and recession in space marked by regular diminution in scale and the taming of colour-tones without tilting of the plane of the picture or use of middle ground/background 'screens' or *coulisses* to achieve 'depth'. The integration of the figures into the landscape in the scenes of rustic haymaking and reaping and sowing is charmingly persuasive, but the wit of the detail is condescendingly patrician, and the courtly scenes subordinate landscape and compositional coherence to the fashionably dressed larger-than-life foreground figures.

The religious pictures are under greater pressure to be conventional, but they have their extraordinary moments, as in the virtuoso night-scenes of Gethsemane and of the eclipse at the death of Christ, and the suggestions of great depths of space in the Fall of the Angels. Preciousness always lurks, deliciously in the circled Fall and Expulsion from Paradise, like an historiated initial without the initial, and in the Map of Rome, with its monuments and tourist sites neatly arranged on a flat featureless disk suspended in space like a flying saucer. The commitment of these painters to a humanly defined sense of space is very sporadic and partial.

Something similar may be said of the illustrations in the Boucicaut Hours (Paris, Musée Jacquemart-André MS 2). This manuscript was made in about 1405–08 by an unknown artist ('the Boucicaut Master') of outstanding genius for the Marshal Jean de Boucicaut, a chivalric hero of the time who fought with the Teutonic Knights against the 'heathen' in Prussia (like Chaucer's Knight and the young Henry, Earl of Derby, later to be crowned as Henry IV), who was on the crusade that ended in disaster at Nicopolis in 1396, and who was taken prisoner at Agincourt and died in England in 1421. Viewers of the Boucicaut Hours have been overwhelmed by what Panofsky calls 'the natural-istic surge of his style',[13] and by the brilliance of his innovations in aerial perspective, the technique whereby things in the distance are portrayed as they are seen to be and not as they are known to be – an irregular spot of green is a tree, some wavy strokes a meadow. But there is a limitation imposed on the desire for an authentic sense of space, not by lack of technical sophistication but by a recognition of what is appropriate in a scene designed to act as a stimulus to devotion, and of the distance necessary to be maintained between the apprehension of the real and the representation of the real in such a scene.

Meiss points out, for instance, that the Boucicaut Master, whilst creating figures of saints that seem ready to step off the page into life, always encloses them in emphatic frames, or in doorways with an arch and a sill, as if both to protect the spatial illusion of depth and also to delimit it and draw attention to its artificiality.[14] We seem to be looking at the scene through a natural opening in the page but are also constantly aware that we are not. A fore-ground landscape-ridge with vegetation is sometimes used with the same effect, and also the representation within the scene of lookers-on, as in the Martyrdom of St Pancras (fol. 29v). In the first case, the impression of a real scene, so powerfully suggested by the location of the observer, is immediately contradicted by the out-of-scale tiny trees growing on the foreground ridge; in the second, the impression of reality given to the scene by the presence of others who are looking at it is dissipated when we recall the difference between those others and ourselves. A further ambiguity about naturalism is present in the skies, which often fade out at the horizon in accordance with true aerial perspective, or have clouds, but are always dark blue above, flat and formal, often made even more artificial by the presence of stars (even though it is daytime) and of a metallic gold sun with solid gold rays (symbolic of divine presence). In other examples of deep composition such as the famous Visitation scene (fol. 65v) (Plate VIII), the far landscape is seen through these rays, which thus paradoxically enhance the effect of hazy luminosity and aerial perspective at the same time that they deny it. The irresistible naturalism of the pictures is always shifting and inconsistent, always some moves away from a systematic illusionism. Even when painters like the Limbourgs and the Boucicaut Master are at their most advanced – when the latter, for instance, in another book of hours (BL MS Add.16997), has an extensive authentic landscape behind the Crucifixion with two men walking in the country engaged in conversation about *something else* (fol. 153v) – their allegiance to the Inter-national Gothic style remains strong.

ITALY AND OTHER COUNTRIES

In most countries of western Europe, the demand for illuminated books, chiefly books of hours for private use and devotion, was satisfied by imports from the northern French and Flemish workshops, and to a lesser extent from Italy, and by imitation of their work. England had vigorous secular and religious workshops, but was an importer rather than an exporter of influences. Spain had a strong tradition of court-painting in the styles of France and Siena, exemplified in the altarpieces of Ferrer Bassa (d. 1348), court-painter to Pedro IV of Aragon, and of Luis Borrassá (d. 1424), pioneer of the International Style in Catalonia, but there was little in the way of indigenous secular workshops for the production of illuminated manuscripts. Alfonso X had to bring artists from Seville to illustrate his *Cantigas* and the later ubiquitous influence of French art is well illustrated in the case of Bernardo Martorell, who made his first reputation with an exact copy of the miniature of St George in the Boucicaut Hours. Jan van Eyck's visit to Spain in 1428 inaugurated a further era of Flemish influence.

In Bohemia, there was a flourishing of the International Gothic style during the reign of Wenceslas IV, King of Bohemia and Holy Roman Emperor (1378–1400), though mostly in the form of panel and mural painting. A remarkable witness to Florentine influence in illuminated book production is the *Liber Viaticus* (Prague, Landsmuseum MS XIII.A.12), a travel-book with copious heavily modelled illustrations, made in about 1354 for Johann von Neumarkt, chancellor of Charles IV, King of Bohemia and Emperor (1347–78), himself an energetic patron of the arts.

In Italy, manuscripts tended to follow models from mural and panel painting, though there is French influence in a copy of the *Speculum humanae salvationis* in the Biblioteca Corsiniana in Rome (MS 55.K.2, *c*.1335). The *Speculum* ('The Mirror of man's salvation'), compiled by Ludolph of Saxony (1324), is a systematised treatise of typology, with Old and New Testament scenes set parallel and explained, in effect a codification for general use of the theological work of the thirteenth-century masters, and enormously influential on later works of biblical exposition and doctrine like the *Biblia pauperum*. There are hundreds of manuscripts. The Corsini version is exceptional in having scenes from the life of St Francis added into the typology: the Nativity, for instance (fol. 9v), shows the Christ child coming to life in the saint's arms at the ritual of the blessing of the Christmas crib (*Presepio*).

More authentically Italian is the modelling in the frontispiece to a manuscript of Virgil's works with the commentary of Servius (Milan, Biblioteca Ambrosiana MS S.P.10/27) done by Simone Martini in the high Sienese style about 1340 (Fig. 56). The original manuscript was made for Petrarch in 1325, stolen in 1326, and recovered in 1338. Another painting in the style of Simone Martini, the scene of St George slaying the dragon in the bas-de-page of a manuscript of about 1320 (Vatican, Archivio Capitolare di San Pietro MS C.129, fol. 85r), is of a kind that could never appear in a French or northern manuscript.

Bologna was still the most important centre for manuscript production in Italy. Here too there is little influence from French, and the miniatures look like monumental murals that have been scaled down to fit the page. In Florence, the outstanding book-illustrator was Pacino da Bonaguida, primarily a panellist, contemporary with and influenced by Giotto. He brings the Giottesque into a Life of Christ (New York, Morgan Library MS M.643), the scene of

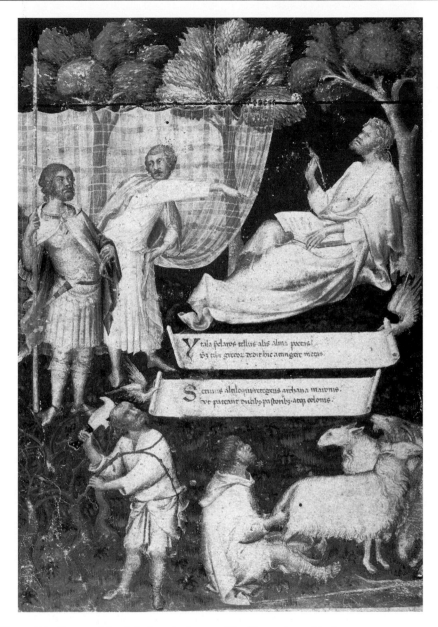

Figure 56: Simone Martini, frontispiece to Virgil's works, with the commentary of Servius. Milan, Biblioteca Ambrosiana MS S.P.10/27, fol. 1v. *c.*1340.

This is Petrarch's copy of Virgil with the gloss of Servius, written for him in Avignon about 1325, stolen in 1326, and recovered in 1338. The frontispiece was illuminated for Petrarch by Simone Martini, who settled in the papal court at Avignon in 1339. The figures, inspired by classical models, represent Servius 'unveiling' the secrets of Virgil. A soldier, rustic and shepherd look on: they stand for Virgil's three major poems, the *Aeneid*, the *Georgics* and the *Eclogues*.

Christ appearing to Mary Magdalene (fol. 27) being like a copy of Giotto's fresco of the subject in the Arena chapel in Padua. There were also many illustrated manuscripts made, in Giottesque and later styles, of Dante's *Divine Comedy*, the first in 1337 (over 600 manuscripts of Dante's poem survive from the fourteenth century alone). Florence, like other centres, continued to turn out the huge service-books that were used by singers. The monk Lorenzo Monaco did much decoration of such books, for instance Florence, Biblioteca Laurenziana, Corale 3 (*c*.1410).

The use of books of hours as an advertisement of the personal piety of their owner, and of the owner's personal physical appearance and importance in the world (something we see in the books made for John of Berry and René of Anjou), could hardly be more ostentatiously worked out than in the Hours of Gian Galeazzo Visconti, Duke of Milan (Florence, Biblioteca Nazionale MSS BR 397 and LF 22).[15] Seven years after the death of his father Galeazzo II in 1378, Gian Galeazzo seized the dukedom by having his uncle Bernabò murdered. He extended his rule over Verona, Pavia and other cites, began the building of a gigantic cathedral in Milan, and persuaded the Emperor Wenceslas in 1395 to raise Milan to a hereditary duchy of the Visconti family. He was about to turn his attention to Florence and Umbria when he died in 1402. The Hours were begun in about 1388–95 by Giovannino de'Grassi and his part of the work is one of the masterpieces of International Gothic. The lavish use of gold, silver and lapiz lazuli blue, all very expensive metallic paints, advertises the function of the work as a form of display for a small and privileged coterie – by contrast with the more community-oriented function of mural and monumental art in Florence and Siena. The duke himself appears frequently in the illustrations, not humbly kneeling, as patrons usually did, but participating in the scenes and often associated with the D of *Dominus*. In the picture of David giving his Blessing (fol. 115r), the duke appears in profile in a large medallion in the bottom border, looking very much as if he were sitting for his portrait and unconcerned about what was going on in the rest of the page. Belbello da Pavia, who completed the illustration of the book in 1428 with his usual hectic pinks and bulbous floral decoration, shows a fondness for violent Old Testament scenes but does not forget to insert the Visconti badge – a blue viper devouring a red child – at every opportunity, often in medallions surrounded by flame-and-sunburst effects to impart added glamour.

Earlier than this, and immediately upon the duke's death in 1402, there was produced a eulogy on the duke (BN MS lat.5888), with a picture by Michelino da Besozzo, chiefly known as a panel-painter, showing the Virgin and Child receiving the duke into heaven (fol. 8r) in a composition, if not a style, somewhat reminiscent of the Wilton Diptych.

ENGLAND: BOOKS OF HOURS AND OTHER ILLUMINATED MANUSCRIPTS

One of the earliest books of hours of English provenance is also one of the most beautiful, the Grey–Fitzpayn Hours (Cambridge, Fitzwilliam Museum

MS 242), made somewhere in the midlands around 1300–08. It is a large book, not a small private portable book, which indicates that the fashion for such books was new in England and psalters were still the model. It was a wedding present from Sir Richard de Grey, of Codnor Castle in Derbyshire, to his bride, Joan Fitzpayn, and she appears before Christ where he is shown giving his blessing in the initial D of fol. 29r, a page bordered with brightly coloured coats of arms and exquisitely drawn animals and birds in the English style. Similar scenes are to be found in the Taymouth Hours (BL Yates Thompson MS 13) of c.1325–40, owned by Joan, daughter of Edward II and queen of David II (son of Robert Bruce) of Scotland. Prayers are included in French for her benefit: one picture (fol. 7r) shows the princess kneeling in prayer before an altar where a priest is officiating, while at the bottom of the page St Jerome is portrayed writing out the prayer that she is saying. A remarkable series of hunting scenes involving ladies occupies the bas-de-pages of fols 68–84: they are shown chasing rabbits and brittling (cutting up) deer, and in one comical scene a lady shoots at a rabbit with a bolt-headed arrow, the rabbit meanwhile eyeing her nonchalantly (she's bound to miss, he thinks, even at this range). Attempts to read the rabbits as the little furry creatures of Venus, and to extract a didactic argument from their sexual suggestiveness, might seem far-fetched, but could be made, no doubt. Two other manuscripts of the same period, the Carew–Poyntz Hours (Cambridge, Fitzwilliam Museum MS 48) and the Smithfield Decretals, a law-book (BL MS Royal 10.E.iv), are done in the same eclectic and witty style.

Books of hours continued to bulk large in the production of illuminated manuscripts in England into the fifteenth century, but it is in liturgical books, made in monasteries and other religious houses, that some of the masterpieces of late medieval English painting appear. The most extraordinary is the reconstructed Carmelite Missal (BL MSS Add.29704–5), written and illuminated in the 1390s for a house of Carmelite friars. Between 1826 and 1833 the children of the Hanrott family, into whose hands the missal had fallen, were allowed to cut it up and paste the cuttings onto pink paper and make their own scrapbooks. In 1936, Margaret Rickert was given permission to remove the cuttings from the scrapbooks and attempt a reconstruction of the original. By 1938 she had completed one of the great works of restoration of modern times, sometimes working with pages of which only initials survived, or bits of text attached to decorative sprays, and in the process discovered one of the great painters of medieval England. Hand A, the main painter (several others are involved in the manuscript), has a sense of the human figure and of the dramatic scene extraordinarily sophisticated for its time, and maybe suggestive of a Flemish background or training.

Another manuscript made at a religious house, perhaps Glastonbury Abbey, is the magnificent Lovell Lectionary (BL MS Harley 7026) of c.1408, surviving only as a fragment. Visitors to the old British Museum became so used to seeing this manuscript open in its display-case at the famous picture of Lord Lovell, who paid for the book, receiving it from a monk of Sherborne Abbey (fol. 4v) (Fig. 57), that they perhaps forgot what an extraordinary picture it is.

Figure 57: London, BL MS Harley 7026 (the Lovell Lectionary), fol. 4v. Painting by John Siferwas. *c.*1408.

A monk in black (perhaps John Siferwas, whose name appears in the bottom border) presents a book to a finely dressed man (Lord Lovell), or possibly vice versa. The profound concentration of the painting on the faces of the participants and the dramatic moment of their intercourse is remarkable. A prayer for Lord Lovell (*Orate pro anima* . . .) is inscribed on a scroll around a slender columnette to the left; the cover of the book, turned awkwardly toward us by the monk, shows the Coronation of the Virgin.

There is nothing quite like the modelling of the face of the patron, as he appears half-length at a window, all the more striking because of the restraint and austerity of the picture's colouring and detail. Thomas Hoccleve obtained the services of an excellent miniaturist to do the portrait of Geoffrey Chaucer that he wanted inserted in the margin of a manuscript of his *Regiment of Princes* (BL MS Harley 4866, fol. 88r), beside his eulogy of Chaucer, and we

can believe that the painter did a good job in providing users of the manuscript with a lifelike portrait; but it is small and relies on hints and suggestions,
where Lord Lovell is put before us large and solid, as if we could reach out
and touch him.

This painter was so conscious of the merit of his achievement that he
signed himself 'frater Johan Siferwas', and he signs himself also as 'illuminator',
one of several, in the most magnificent illuminated book of the English fifteenth
century, the Sherborne Missal (Northumberland, Alnwick Castle, BL MS Loan
82), made for the Benedictine abbey of Sherborne, possibly at Glastonbury,
between 1396 and 1407. This enormous book (536 × 380 mm) contains
thousands of pictures, up to 20 or 30 per page, including the famous series of
precisely observed English birds in the margins. The historiated miniatures often
attempt scenes that had never been illustrated before and for which there is no
known source, the illustrators thus sharing in the excitement of innovation
with the painters who were doing pictures for the vernacular poems of Chaucer,
Gower, Hoccleve and Lydgate, and for vernacular texts like *Mandeville's Travels*.
Siferwas did some of the most important pictures, including the Entry into
Jerusalem (p. 169), Resurrection (p. 216) and Crucifixion (p. 380). They show
his skill with modelling and costume and his sense of the substantiality of the
human, but there is a stronger emphasis on surface decoration than in the
Lovell picture, a closer allegiance to the International Gothic style such as may
have been thought more appropriate to these sacred scenes.

More often, however, it was books of hours that were being produced,
usually for lay patrons or buyers, whether aristocratic, gentry, professional or
burgess, and most often commercially in workshops or in the house of a commissioning patron. Hermann Scheerre is an important figure in these first two
or three decades of the fifteenth century. Of Dutch or German origin, he came
to England about 1390 and by 1400 had set up as the master of a workshop. His
signature is found in a Book of Offices (BL MS Add.16998) of *c*.1405–10, and
the name Hermann in the Chichele Breviary (London, Lambeth Palace Library
MS 69) of *c*.1408–14. He also had a hand in Bodl. MS Latin liturg.f.2, in the
Neville Hours (Berkeley Castle MS) and in the Beaufort Hours (BL MS Royal
2.A.xviii), and his masterpiece is the sumptuous Bedford Hours and Psalter
(BL MS Add.42131) made for the Duke of Bedford about 1420–22 (Fig. 58).
This large and impressive manuscript was designed for display, probably on a
lectern, and not for private devotional use, and shows the way in which illuminated books were being used by the rival princes of France and England as
items of conspicuous consumption. Scheerre is a clever and versatile painter,
with a gift for vivid and expressive faces (he fills the borders of the Bedford
Hours with portrait-heads so lifelike that it has been thought it must be a
gallery of contemporaries), but it has been his misfortune to be deprived of
the credit for some of the greatest pictures in the manuscripts he supervised.
The beautiful Annunciation in the Beaufort Hours (fol. 23v) (Fig. 59) is now
usually ascribed to someone else, and another nebulous figure known only as
'Johannes' has taken over the best pictures in the Neville Hours, as well as the
illustration of the lavish Hours of Elizabeth the Queen (BL MS Add.50001),

c.1420–30. This manuscript, so called from having come into the possession of the queen of Henry VII in 1487, represents perhaps the last refinement of the International Style, subtle, elegant, brilliantly coloured, politely mediating the vivid anguish of the Crucifixion scene by throwing the whole drama up onto the planar surface of the picture.

ILLUSTRATION OF SECULAR TEXTS

'Johannes' also did part of the illustration of the travel-book of Marco Polo in Bodl. MS Bodley 264, *c*.1400–10 ('Johannes me fecit' is written on the robe of the great Khan). This was a Flemish manuscript of 1338–44, with a riot of pictures of scenes from the Alexander-romances, to which further material on the 'wonders of the East' has been added in England. Johannes did the famous scene of Marco Polo's departure from Venice (fol. 218r), with its exquisite cityscape of Venice. It is an example of the new kind of challenge that manuscript-painters were being faced with – pictures of scenes not illustrated before, and needing new kinds of flexibility and inventiveness on the part of the painters.

Some of the most important French manuscripts of the fourteenth and fifteenth centuries were the product of this new kind of commission. Of course, many kinds of illustrated manuscript, apart from books of hours, continued to be produced. Over 70 manuscripts, for instance, survive, mostly richly decorated, of the *Bible historiale*, the French version of the twelfth-century bible-history of Petrus Comestor, the *Historia scolastica*. The first copy is dated 1312; a famous one, now BL MS Royal I.A.xx, was captured with King John of France at Poitiers in 1356 and bought in England by the Earl of Salisbury. But in addition to these more traditional types of manuscript there were also many new ventures – illustrated copies of books on the Marvels of the East, of French translations of the Latin works of Boccaccio, of the histories of Livy, of the encyclopaedic *Tresor* written in French by Brunetto Latini, Dante's teacher, while he was in exile in France 1260–67 (the copy in the National Library of Russia in St Petersburg, *c*.1310–20, has 115 framed miniatures). A favourite text for illustration was the *Chroniques de France* (over 100 manuscripts survive), compiled at Saint-Denis, the great centre of royalist propaganda, in the mid-thirteenth century and translated into French in 1274. It

---

Figure 58: London, BL MS Add.42131 (the Bedford Hours and Psalter), fol. 73r. *c*.1420–22.

This magnificent manuscript has 298 small portrait-heads in the borders, a gallery of faces full of character (though not necessarily representing real persons). There are also eleven large historiated initials, including this illustration for Psalm 1 (*Beatus vir*) showing David anointed by Samuel, with Jesse looking on (and God too, in the roundel at upper left). The page has a Jesse-tree as its border, the portraits of the kings in the medallions being almost certainly, with their narrow strained faces, the work of Hermann Scheerre himself.

was a patriotic chronicle much favoured by the kings of France, who enjoyed having it updated to include themselves and giving copies to visiting dignitaries. There are also illustrated manuscripts of the works of contemporary writers – Machaut, Froissart, Christine de Pizan – often done at their own instructions. Two copies of Nicolas Oresme's translation into French from Latin of Aristotle's *Ethics*, *Politics* and *Economics*, with carefully designed illustration specially devised by Oresme, were commissioned in 1372 by Charles V.

England followed, not always modestly, in France's wake. Most striking is the frontispiece that was done *c*.1420 for a *de luxe* manuscript of Chaucer's *Troilus and Criseyde* (Cambridge, Corpus Christi College MS 61). It shows Chaucer, standing in a pulpit-like structure, reciting his poem to the richly costumed assembled court (of Richard II), while in the background is a scene of courtly procession and meeting, perhaps based on an incident from the poem. It is a picture that represents as a reality the poem's myth of its own delivery and address to a courtly audience ('But now to yow, ye loveres that ben here . . .', II.1751), and was clearly designed to promote the poem by emphasising its royal connections. The manuscript has 94 spaces left for miniatures to illustrate the story, but all are blank. Only one possible customer, it might seem, had the means and motive to commission such a manuscript and also died suddenly enough to throw the arrangements into such disarray, and that was Henry V.

The *Troilus* frontispiece represents a confluence of traditions, and despite its high quality and refinement one has the sense of having seen most of its elements in other forms before. Such uniformity is suggestive of the close community of the London workshops where most of these manuscripts were produced – a few tenements in Paternoster Row near St Paul's churchyard, with much interchange of illustrators and picture-models for different projects. Somewhat more idiosyncratic, and probably to be associated with provincial production for or by religious, are the manuscripts in the English 'tinted outline' style, including beautiful manuscripts of *The Privity of the Passion* (Cambridge, Trinity College MS B.10.12) and of *The Desert of Religion* (BL MS Cotton Faustina B.vi, Part II), both of around 1420. There is also a most

---

Figure 59: London, BL MS Royal 2.A.XVIII (the Beaufort Hours), fol. 23v. Annunciation, with patrons. *c*.1410.
This is one of thirteen full-page miniatures in a 22-page fragment of a prayer-book that was much later incorporated in a large Psalter and Hours made for Margaret Beauchamp, Duchess of Somerset, and her daughter, Margaret Beaufort, Countess of Richmond, mother of Henry VII. The artist responsible for this picture is unknown (the attribution to Scheerre is now generally rejected) but his face-portraits and his colouring make him one of the great masters of fifteenth-century English painting. Two unidentified donors kneel outside the frame; God looks on from above left in royal blue to associate him directly with the Virgin. The angel's salutation (*Ave Maria* . . .) is written on a curling scroll, Mary's reply (*Ecce ancilla* . . .) is written in the prayer-book before her; a cloth draped over her prayer-desk carries mottoes of unknown provenance.

exceptional survival in the Pepysian Sketch-Book (Cambridge, Magdalene College MS Pepys 1916), which is the model book of an artist training himself in the modelling of drapery and the human figure and in the portrayal of birds and animals. It is actually a series of originally separate bifolia now bound together, like the notebook of Villard de Honnecourt, and is thus a true 'sketchbook'.

THE INTRODUCTION OF PRINTING

Illuminated manuscripts had a century or more of history after 1450, and an Indian summer of splendour. But Johann Gutenberg's first experiments with printing with movable type were already being made in Strassburg around 1434 and were continued in Mainz after 1447. After a series of trial runs, he began setting his *Biblia latina* in 1452, and finished it in 1456. He chose the Latin bible because it was a book that was always in demand, and could therefore be confidently produced 'on spec' with a guaranteed return on the large capital investment involved in printing; also big lectern-bibles were coming back into fashion, and were one of the main products of the Netherlandish manuscript workshops. No one quite understood at the time the immense significance of what had been invented, but it makes another convenient date for the end of 'Gothic Europe'.

The Chivalric Love-Romance

The legacy of Gothic Europe is present for all to see in the surviving cathedrals and great churches. The illuminated manuscripts of the period are less widely accessible to the general public, but they have colonised modern culture in a multitude of ways, particularly through the use of Nativity miniatures and also medieval decorative images of all kinds in greetings cards. The chivalric love-romance, the third major manifestation and achievement of Gothic Europe, is everywhere even more palpably present in modern culture. Wherever pre-marital or non-marital sexual love between men and women is represented in fiction, drama, opera or film as the most important experience of life, wherever the love of a man for a woman *paramours* ('in the way of sexual love') is represented as the service of the highest ideal of existence ('love has made me a better man') – that is to say, in the whole tradition of romantic and Romantic poetry and drama and in the whole tradition of the novel of courtship (pretty well the dominant mode of the nineteenth-century novel) and its successors in the modern romantic novelette – the inheritance of medieval courtly romance is present. Through eight centuries, and until recent years, it was the dominant theme and troping device of western secular narrative, lyric and drama. It seemed to be 'the way things were', and the constructedness of this code of love, and particularly the manner in which it privileged the male experience of sexual desire at the same time as it figured him as the servant of the female, has only been fully analysed in recent years, primarily in the work of feminist critics.

LOVE

There are two main historical ingredients that go into the making of the medieval chivalric romance of love. The first is the revolution in the attitude to and representation of sensibility that began in the twelfth century and quickly gathered power – the growth of the idea that human emotion is not a disease of the will nor an enemy of the reason but an attribute to be valued for its potential to inspire nobility of behaviour. It was not a change of sensibility or a reformation of the human heart so much as a change in the cultural opportunities for the representation of sensibility. It was seized upon and encouraged in the new devotion of St Bernard and, later, of St Francis in the form of an emotional attachment to the person of Christ and the Virgin Mary. This affective devotion often used the idea of ordinary human love – sexual love, conjugal love, maternal love, filial love – as a preliminary image of what it meant to love God. Human love was not necessarily perceived as in opposition to the love of God, nor as a sinful weakness that had to be expunged, but as a seeing-in-the-glass-darkly.

More general was the beginning of the idea, in secular courtly culture, that sexual love was a high form of service. 'Courtly love' is an unhistorical term, invented (as *amour courtois*) by Gaston Paris in 1883 (for reasons that were important in the historical culture of his time) and fixed for ever in our consciousness of the Middle Ages in C.S. Lewis's brilliant and persuasive book, *The Allegory of Love* (1936). It was Lewis who codified 'courtly love' in terms of its dangerously memorable four elements – humility, courtesy, adultery, and the religion of love – and who summed up what the Middle Ages called *fine amour* ('fyn lovynge' in Chaucer) as the attachment of an exquisite refinement of ideal sentiment to the love of man and woman. But it would be dangerous to regard the cult of love, for all that it was the distinctive characteristic feature of medieval chivalric romance, as a single universal medieval phenomenon called 'courtly love': to do so would be to simplify a whole range of social and cultural practices which varied by region, by period, by class, by cultural inheritance and in the work of individual writers.

But though one would wish to problematise the term 'courtly love', it is clear that something did happen in the courts of twelfth-century France, first in the south, in Provence, and then in the north, in the way of a shift in attitudes to the cultural representation of sexual relationships. Something of the nature of the change can be deduced from comparison between the new writing of the twelfth century and the love-poetry of the Roman poet Ovid, especially the *Ars Amatoria*. For Ovid love is a form of war between men and women: for men it is a disease, an infatuation, a need, a game, a joke; for women it is a trap, a betrayal, a disaster. Something of the change can be discerned, too, if one tries, as C.S. Lewis put it, to imagine explaining medieval love-poetry to King Alfred or the author of *Beowulf*. The new element, and what distinguishes *fine amour* most clearly from other forms of human sexual love, is the belief in the value of sexual love as an intrinsically ennobling experience, the formal object of which is not the satisfaction of desire but the lover's 'progress and growth in virtue, merit and worth'.[16] It is the male lover that is referred to, of course, since femininity (of which the female person is a cipher) is already constituted as the essence of these qualities.

Ideas of this kind were cultivated in a rather slick way by the courtly Provençal poets of the early twelfth century, perhaps influenced by the sophisticated Moorish culture of southern Spain, with which Provence was in contact through Catalonia and the kingdom of Aragon. Arabic philosophers had developed Greek Platonic and neo-Platonic doctrines of love, which already associated love with progress to a higher spiritual being (with the difference that among the Greeks it was homosexual love that was idealised in this way), so as to offer a quasi-spiritualised goal for sexual passion. It was in the late twelfth-century courts of northern France, courts in which powerful ladies like Eleanor of Aquitaine and Marie de Champagne were creating a new environment for courtly behavioural display, that these high ideals of love first found full narrative expression (one would not imagine that it went much farther than that), above all in the poetry of Chrétien de Troyes. Chrétien's four love-romances – *Yvain*, *Cliges*, *Erec*, and *Lancelot* (*Le Chevalier de la Charrette*) – are the originals and masterpieces of the form, full of examples and expressions of the highest refinement of sentiment, but also suffused with wit, irony and self-reflexivity. Chrétien is confident in his appeal to the knowledgeableness of his courtly audience, always playing games with them and with the stories, developing fine points of love-sentiment, straining the logic of amorous argumentation. His poems delight in problems of conduct, especially the problem for the knight-lover of reconciling his chivalric obligations with the imperative of love: Chrétien's romances can be seen from one point of view as scripted examinations in amatory ethics, designed to elicit discussion among an assembled listening group.

According to Chrétien's story, he was commanded by Marie de Champagne to provide a lover for Arthur's queen Guenevere – since she could hardly be counted a fashionable lady of romance unless she had an adulterous liaison with someone – and Chrétien conjured Lancelot into existence. In the romance that bears his name he is put through a series of tests in order to show the omnipotence of love, the most extreme being that on occasion he must violate knighthood for Guenevere's sake and at her command – ride in a peasant-cart (whence the sub-title of the romance), attempt to lose in battle, fight all day with his back to his opponent so as not to take his eyes off his lady. He must rhapsodise over a comb he finds with strands of her hair in it, and reverence it as if it were the relic of a saint. One sees, in fact, both the demonstration and the ironic mockery of the extravagances of this all-consuming passion, and is reminded that medieval audiences loved the rhetoric of casuistry, wit and ingenuity, even when the targets were only exaggerated versions of cherished ideals. One can see, too, how Chrétien might have resorted to irony in order to deal with a certain wistful embarrassment that he might have felt, as a cleric, in glorifying adultery, even at a lady's command.

CHIVALRY

The other strand in the weaving of the chivalric love-romance is the high idealism of chivalry itself, something that was in existence before the twelfth century in French and German courts, but that was brought now to a new pitch of fervour. Romance is the literature of chivalry and exists to reflect, celebrate and confirm the chivalric values by which its primary consumers, the noble or knightly class, live or purport to live. It does not record their way of life, but how they would like to think of themselves and be thought of as living, without the contradictions and boredoms of real life. In life a knight would sometimes have behaved like a romance hero – spared a city at the request of noble ladies (as Edward III did at Calais in 1347), yielded up a brave adversary without ransom – and consciously so. But he would often too have acted according to the dictates of expediency – sacked a city that refused to surrender (as the Black Prince did at Limoges in 1370), killed the prisoners (as Henry V did at Agincourt in 1415). Romance purges life of impurities, and presents chivalry in extreme and heightened form.

The nature of romance may be seen clearly from a comparison with epic, which is the literature of the more warlike and male-centred society that dominated in western Europe until the twelfth century. Epic, saga and *chanson de geste* are the celebration of the values of this society, most of which have to do with fighting. The setting is historical or quasi-historical; the events and persons are assumed to be real as well as important. The central reality is not love or honour but death: loyalty to one's kin or leader, or revenge, or the imperative necessity of asserting self (especially self as embodying a nation or people) through acts of power, transcending the fear of death and creating awe at courage in the face of annihilation. The defence of the narrow place against odds is the classic site of the heroic poem (Thermopylae, Maldon, Roncesvalles, Hlidarendi). Women are important because of their essential role in the action, as part of the urging towards power, possession and revenge which are the source of action, not as ideals or as objects of adoration. Men fight for them because otherwise the women will be killed, raped, or forced into subjection, not because they will be upset.

Romance deals in adventure not survival. The hero is not desperately defending his homeland but chooses to go out from a secure bastion of wealth and privilege (such as the Arthurian court) to seek adventures in which the values of chivalry and service to ladies will be submitted to test and proved. 'The series of adventures', as Auerbach puts it, 'is thus raised to the status of a fated and graduated test of election; it becomes the basis of a doctrine of personal perfection.'[17] Courage is still important, but now in the service of an ideal code of values, not as a necessity for survival: in theory that code could require cowardice of the hero (as in Chrétien's *Lancelot*). The action is no longer 'real' or historical; there are elements of the marvellous; geography is vague; time is unreal. Castles spring up as needed, and open meadows suddenly appear in the otherwise all-encompassing forest when space is needed for a joust between knights-errant. The knight is not impelled by dynastic or territorial ambitions, but chooses to go out on adventures because that is how he proves the values by which he lives – proves his reality, his identity, in fact. Feats of arms, arbitrary in themselves, are the means to self-realisation. Action has no exterior real motivation. Inconvenient reality is evaded: wounds are healed with magic ointments, life protected with magic talismans. Confrontation with death is vital in heroic literature; in romance, death is something that happens to other people.

ARTHURIAN ROMANCE IN FRANCE

The first full chivalric romances of love are those of Chrétien, but the first transition from epic to romance was in the earlier twelfth-century adaptations of classical stories to the new ethos of romance. The classical epics of Troy, of Thebes, of Aeneas, of Alexander, are all transplanted to a medieval setting: Hector and Achilles, in the *Roman de Troie* (*c*.1160) of Benoît de Sainte-Maure, become chivalric knights fighting for their lady-loves, and a completely new love-story is invented for a hitherto obscure son of Priam called Troilus and a shadowy Trojan lady called Briseida (later Criseida, in the versions of the story by Boccaccio and Chaucer). Even the story of Thebes has a romantic episode interpolated, though fortunately there is no attempt to romanticise the relationship of Oedipus and Jocasta.

But it was the Arthurian story that provided the richest opportunities for exploitation as love-romance, especially once Chrétien had announced the dominance of the theme of idealised passionate devotion in the relationship of Lancelot and Guenevere. The 'historical' Arthur had been placed at the centre of European story-telling by Geoffrey of Monmouth, whose Latin prose *Historia regum Britanniae* ('History of the Kings of Britain'), written for his Anglo-Norman patrons in 1130–36, elaborated an extraordinary career of conquest for Arthur as a national hero. This came at the end of a largely invented chronology of British kings from the time of Brutus, who fled from Troy after the sack of the city by the Greeks and established an eponymous kingdom called Britain. Geoffrey's history was heroic, martial, militaristic, based on Celtic legends, a little history, and the author's rich powers of invention, and its purpose was to supply England with a national history and a myth of national emergence such as would suit its new Norman overlords. It is, in terms of the literary narratives that derive from it, and their power in articulating the political and cultural assumptions of those for whom they were written, right up to the present day, one of the most influential books ever written – over 200 manuscripts survive – and it generated in England a powerful tradition of nationalistic chronicle-epic poetry in the *Brut* of Layamon (*c*.1230) and the magnificent alliterative *Morte Arthure* of *c*.1400.

But Geoffrey's *Historia* had already been 'romanced' into French verse by the Jerseyman Wace, who presented his *Roman de Brut* to Eleanor of Aquitaine, Henry II's queen, in 1155; and in France the Arthurian legend, transplanted from its national origins, began to accumulate to itself an enormous range of associated legends, many of Celtic origin, such as the Tristan story and the Grail story. One of the great merits of the Arthurian hyper-narrative was that Arthur, whose role as a national hero was less appreciated outside England, could be relegated to a secondary role while his court became the place from which knight-heroes rode out on adventures and the Round Table became the symbol of all the chivalric ideals that they set out to test. The Arthurian story provided an authenticating mythology for all kinds of stories of love and chivalry, and drew into its orbit most of the romances of Chrétien as well as the *lais* (short romances of love, with a strong element of fantasy and magic and a melancholy lyricism, usually ending unhappily) of Marie de France (*c*.1200).

Many such Arthurian romances were written in France in the late twelfth and early thirteenth centuries to satisfy a growing fashionable taste among an increasing leisured class of listeners and (soon) readers. The romances of Chrétien, and the long romance of Perceval and the Grail (*Perceval, ou Le Conte du Graal*) that he left unfinished at his death, are examples. *Perceval* is in some ways the archetypal chivalric love-romance: beginning with the adventures of Perceval, the rustic brought up in ignorance of his noble birth, it incorporates the romance version of the Grail story, the Bleeding Lance and the Fisher King who cannot be healed, and then moves on to Gauvain (Gawain), whose adventures (with the Perilous Bed as well as the Bleeding Lance) occupy the second half of Chrétien's unfinished (and unfinishable) romance. There are a number of continuations, some running to tens of thousands of lines, in which sometimes Perceval and sometimes Gauvain take the lead. The continuators worry little, it seems, about knitting the whole narrative together or bringing it to a seemly close.

There are also many other verse romances: some, such as the *Joseph d'Arimathie* of Robert de Boron, enlarge on the legend that the Grail (the chalice which Christ used at the Last Supper and which was used to scoop up his blood at the Crucifixion) was brought to Glastonbury by Joseph of Arimathea; others, more numerous, relate Gawain's adventures and often slightly comic and improper misadventures in love.

Such verse romances are often associated with a listening audience. Prose romance, especially when it is presented in handsome manuscripts with pictures, seems to be more appropriate to a reading audience. Such manuscripts began to be produced early in the thirteenth century: the earliest illustrated prose *Lancelot* may be Rennes, Bibliothèque Municipale MS 255, made in Paris (*c*.1220–30) and associated with the royal court. Manuscripts of this kind soon got to be very large and splendid, with many pictures, though with generalised scenes (of combat, siege, procession, meeting) rather than scenes adapted to specific episodes – a sign of the pressures of mass-production. Such manuscripts were made for lesser knights as well as aristocratic buyers. A fine *Lancelot*, now New Haven, Yale University, Beinecke Library MS 229, was made for Guillaume de Termonde (d. 1312), son of the Count of Flanders, while another is mentioned in an inventory of the possessions of Jean d'Avesnes, Count of Hainault (d. 1304). In the fourteenth century, many manuscripts of these romances were made for French noblewomen, and they are the commonest books recorded as having been owned by members of the English aristocracy. The earliest dated *Lancelot* manuscript is BN MS fr.342, made in 1274, the scribe apparently a woman.

Arthurian romance swept Europe, and a form so fashionable could not escape clerical appropriation. An early example is the vast prose *Perlesvaus* (*c*.1200). Subsequently, a number of authors and compilers, working *c*.1215–30 under the spiritual direction or influence or inspiration of Cistercian teaching, gathered the sprawling mass of stories into a single vast broadly chronological cycle known as the 'Vulgate' cycle (because in French not in Latin) of Arthurian prose romance. It survives in many forms and many manuscripts, and occupies eight large volumes in the single rare modern edition. The nucleus was the magnificent *Lancelot* (*c*.1210–20, the one in the illustrated manuscripts mentioned above), to which was prefixed an account of the early history of the Grail (the *Estoire del Saint Graal*, how the chalice that had contained Christ's blood was brought to England by Joseph of Arimathea) and the story of Merlin, and followed up with the *Queste del Saint Graal* (the story of the quest for the Grail by the knights of the Round Table) and the *Mort Artu* (the story of the death of Arthur). Later the extensively expanded legend of *Tristan*, from a completely different set of sources, with the loosest connection with Arthur, was added (*c*.1225–35). It provided an anticipatory sub-plot, with another cuckolded king, for the doomed love-affair of Lancelot and Guenevere. The cycle was reshaped around 1230–40, and in truth it would be idle to pretend that it ever had an 'existence' as a fixed and coherent work, variations from which could be analysed and classified. Such has been an implied assumption of some modern scholarship, working with models derived from the technologies of print and the taxonomies of science, but the evidence is not easily assembled to bear it out.

The case, it might be noted in passing, is rather similar with the other large contemporary narrative cycle being produced in French (*c*.1175–*c*.1250), the *Roman de Renart*, another vast sprawling assembly of narratives that defy analysis into anything but 'branches' (loose collections of tales having the same cast of characters). *Renart* is the antithesis of *Lancelot*; probably also written by clerical authors and read by well-educated audiences, though in their looser moments, it is a beast-epic, or collection of beast-fables, in which the only motive of existence is survival and the satisfaction of appetite (including the appetite for trickery). Smartness, quickness of wit, ruthless exploitation of an opponent's weaknesses, are the qualities to be admired, not love, honour, truth and loyalty. All the values of chivalric romance are subjected to obscene and witty mockery. In one of the early scenes Reynard tries to seduce Hersent, the wife of Ysengrin the wolf, using much of the conventional language of romance (he calls her his 'lady-love' and much else besides). When she gets stuck in the small opening to his lair, he 'rapes' her from behind (i.e. like an animal) and later demonstrates further his power over her by beating and urinating upon her cubs. His defence when he comes to trial is that he acted out of passion, and love forgives all. Like the *fabliaux*, tales of coarse comic sexual intrigue popular among the same audiences in France and subsequently throughout Europe, *Renart* stands in a self-consciously antipodean relationship to romance.

The central purpose of the compilers of the Vulgate cycle is most evident in the incorporation of the Grail story as an integral element in the larger narrative, with an entirely new significance given to the Grail itself. In the unfinished poem of *Perceval* or *Le Conte du Graal* attributed to Chrétien, the Grail is a vaguely mysterious object connected with a maimed Fisher King who will be healed when the Grail is won. Already at this point all the features of the story so beloved of Jessie L. Weston and T.S. Eliot are there – the Waste Land, the Fisher King, the Hidden Castle with its Solemn Feast, the mysterious Feeding Vessel, the Bleeding Lance, and the Cup. But in the Vulgate cycle the Grail became the object of a quest for spiritual perfection in which the knights of the Round Table could not but fail, because of their investment in the world and in women, and in which a new hero had to be invented who would win it, Galahad, son of Lancelot. Galahad wins the Grail and therefore leaves the fellowship. The failure of the knights of the Round Table in the Grail quest was the demonstration of the irredeemably fallen state of secular chivalry. Where other individual writers might see in the story of Lancelot and Guenevere a human meaningfulness, even a tragic conflict of high ideals of love and honour, the Vulgate compilers saw a lesson to be learnt concerning the nothingness of worldly desire. At the end, the deaths of Arthur, Lancelot and Guenevere are enclosed in consoling pieties; Guenevere ends up in a nunnery and Lancelot in a monastery and both explicitly repudiate worldly love.

But these large strategies of appropriation, though they may attempt to redirect the narrative toward different goals, cannot change its essential nature as the record of the whole life of adventure taken up in the cause of love and chivalry. The vast expanses of the cycle, encompassing the exploits of scores of named knights, have a complexity, an irresolution, that make them resistant to a single interpretation. Characters appear, disappear and reappear, story-lines cross, run parallel, loop around each other, and are sometimes suspended for long periods. The narrative technique of *entrelacement* ensures that something exciting is always happening but nothing is ever concluded and no one ever seems to get anywhere – Lancelot is always in love with Guenevere, always going away, always coming back; Tristan is always in love with Isolde (one or the other), always going away, always coming back; Palamides is always in pursuit of the mysterious *bête glatissant*. There are endless single combats, conducted according to a set pattern, as strict as the steps of a dance. When any two knights meet in the forest, in no time they will have fewtered their spears and hurled together like thunder so strongly that both their horses will be rashed to the earth. Then they will avoid their saddles and dress their shields and draw their swords and fling together as wood men or lash together with great strokes and foin like two bulls or wild boars and give many strokes, maybe fight for two hours, until one gives the other such a buffet that he kneels on his knees, whereupon the first, who is usually Sir Lancelot, will unlace the helm of the defeated knight and threaten to strike off his head unless he will agree that Guenevere is the fairest of all ladies – if the defeated combatant is lucky, that is, for otherwise he will not even get the chance to do this because he will already have been cloven to the shoulder or the navel or some other final-sounding part of his anatomy.

It is not surprising that the world of medieval Arthurian love-romance, so massively present in these narrative cycles and their derivatives and descendants (which include, in England, Sir Thomas Malory's *Morte D'Arthur* of *c.*1470), has proved such an enduring legacy, and provided such a wealth of stories, themes and images and such a cast of characters for later enjoyment and exploitation. There is no way in which this resource can be 'used up'.

ROMANCE IN ENGLAND

The taste of the English upper classes for fashionable love-romance was satisfied mostly by importation from France. French was still the language of the court, and the cultivated language of polite literary discourse, and even though English began to make way against it after 1300 it remained dominant among the aristocratic reading public until the time of Chaucer.

A particular niche is occupied by indigenous Anglo-Norman romance, composed in the dialect of French that was spoken in England after the Conquest and that gradually grew somewhat apart from Parisian or metropolitan French ('For Frenssh of Parys was to hire unknowe', says Chaucer, rather patronisingly, of his Prioress's skill in this provincial form of French). Anglo-Norman romances like those of *Horn* (*c.*1170), *Fergus* (*c.*1209) and *Fouke Fitzwarine* (1256–64) are generally more interested in action and in stirring stories of the wrongful exile and triumphant return of young princes than in the analysis of fine points of sentiment, though the heroes are always equipped with an appropriate lady-love and wife-to-be (in the same person). Where Anglo-Norman romances have Arthurian heroes or affiliations, which is not often, they follow the French tradition of representing Arthur as a *roi fainéant* rather than as a national hero. The Anglo-Norman aristocracy was jealous of its baronial privileges and reckoned that the king had quite sufficient powers without encouraging him to imitate the national and imperial Arthur. Another keen interest of this newly planted Norman aristocracy was in encouraging the writing of 'ancestral romances' designed to glorify their putative ancestors. In *Gui de Warewic* (*c.*1240), the most famous of these romances, the ancestor of the Beauchamp family, earls of Warwick, turns out to be a famous hero (totally invented) who fought for love and chivalry all over Europe and then came out of eremitic retirement to save England from the Danes, during the reign of the Anglo-Saxon King Athelstan, by fighting in single combat against the giant Danish champion Colbrond.

The French chivalric love-romance trickles down into English by a process of adaptation to a somewhat less sophisticated audience, and Anglo-Norman is similarly adapted, though it has less far to trickle. This English-speaking audience is not low-class or illiterate but increasingly literate and on the margins of courtly society, an aspirant bourgeoisie for whom fashionable romance in English, on the model of French, is a mark of social status and of the status of the language. It is for this audience, with its conventional piety, its appetite for violent and sensational incident, its comparative lack of interest in refined love-sentiment, that the English romancers purveyed. The *locus classicus* of the taste is the Auchinleck manuscript (Edinburgh, National Library of Scotland MS Advocates 19.2.1), made in London in about 1330–40 and containing a great range of romances, saints' legends, pious tales and other poems, nearly all in English. The work that is done here and elsewhere in refashioning French romances into English, and composing new ones, is not contemptible, and the English versions of *Horn* and *Havelok*, both *c.*1290, and new romances (or romances with no known French source) like *Sir Orfeo* (a reworking of the story of Orpheus and Eurydice) show vigour and wit, and dynamic skills in story-telling.

But the differences in the anticipated level of sophistication are evident. The translator of *Gui de Warewic*, coming upon an episode in which the heroine Felice shows the correctly aloof disdain of a courtly mistress towards her wooer Guy, has her explain to her maid (who is puzzled by her behaviour) that she is following the correct procedure: 'That's what ladies do, don't you know?' she says, offering the sort of naive recital of 'correct' notions of social behaviour that one associates with the uninformed but anxious. *Li Biaus Desconeus* ('The Fair Unknown'), a French romance by Renaud de Beaujeu (*c.*1190), centres on the passion of the hero for an irresistibly desirable woman, with many fashionably *risqué* love-encounters. In the English version, *Libeaus Desconus* (*c.*1350), she becomes a sorceress who traps the hero into a liaison by her magical wiles. 'Alas, he ne hadde y-be chast!', laments the author, clearly wishing that his hero had confined his attention to dragons and Saracens. Where there is not enough fighting, or where some favourite act of violence is lacking, the English redactor will throw some in, adding a tournament and a giant-fight, for instance, in *Sir Launfal* (a version of the delicate Arthurian romance of *Lanval* by Marie de France), and a wholly gratuitous dragon-fight in *Beves of Hamtoun*, a version of the Anglo-Norman *Boeve de Haumtone* (1154–76).

Clerical influence was always obviously stronger in English culture than in French (a product of more efficient centralisation of pastoral power), and it remained strong after the English language had reasserted its role as the language of elite literary culture during the mid to late fourteenth century. The greatest of all English Arthurian chivalric love-romances, *Sir Gawain and the Green Knight* (*c.*1390), turns this clerical inheritance to superb advantage. Written in the north-west of England in a difficult dialect, and surviving in only one manuscript (BL MS Cotton Nero A.x), it works with the Gawain of traditional French romance, a womaniser and a paragon of courtesy, to set a new and exquisitely unanswerable problem in knightly ethics. Gawain takes up a challenge by which he promises to cut off the head of a huge green knight and to have his own cut off in a year's time. The huge green knight, as might be expected, survives decapitation, and Gawain has to keep his promise. Then, staying at the castle of Bercilak the next Christmas on his way to his fatal assignation, he gets involved in another 'game', an exchange of winnings (rather than heads) over three days whereby he stays at home with the lady of the castle while Bercilak goes out hunting and they give each other the day's winnings when they meet in the evening. Gawain, with the greatest tact and courtesy, resists the seductive offer of the lady's person, but accepts from her, and does not give back to the lord, a magic girdle which will save his life in the coming encounter. He survives a feinted decapitation, but when the lights go up it turns out that the whole thing was a plot to tempt him into a betrayal of his honour and the honour of the Arthurian court. Gawain is mortified. He has been trapped in an impossible situation, an infernal narrative machine to demonstrate the contradiction at the heart of the chivalric code. Should he seek at all costs to preserve his promise to the lord, or his chastity, or the single-minded devotion to the Virgin blazoned on his shield, or his reputation for courtesy, or his life? He does his best, and he doesn't do badly, but 'not doing badly' is not enough for a knight of romance and he ends the poem in a frenzy of self-denunciation. Quite self-consciously, it seems, the romancer has arranged the story so as to put to the test the compromise between fashionable love-courtesy and devotion to Christ and the Virgin (Gawain bears a pentangle on his shield as a symbol of his fivefold devotion) that had long maintained chivalric love-romance in its precious and uneasy equilibrium. Also, Gawain is now in a world in which the traditional questions asked of a questing knight are put in terms of a material-ised world of real feelings and fears, real internal conflict, and magnificently real landscapes. The winter landscape through which Gawain rides on his quest, the rough rock-strewn hill-terrain of the hunts, the snow-covered and mist-capped hills of the last journey to the Green Chapel, are not part of Gawain's quest for self-realisation and knightly identity: they are really there.

ROMANCE IN CHAUCER

Chaucer, despising the Arthurian legends as hackneyed and out-of-fashion, but recognising the rich potential of love-romance for the investigation of the different obligations of the inner and the outer, the public and the private, took up Boccaccio's poem, derived from the *Roman de Troie*, of the ill-fated love of Troilo and Criseida. *Il Filostrato* ('The one laid low by love'), written about 1338, soon after Boccaccio left Naples for Florence, is a new kind of love-romance, urban, sensual, passionate, lyrical, with an undertone of cyn-icism about the idealised code of love. The love-affair of Troilo and Criseida is conducted with an appropriate orchestration of sighs and protestations, but with no hesitancy or lady-like reticence on Criseida's part. It is a thoroughly 'modern' kind of romance, and Boccaccio introduces a go-between, Pandaro, a worldly-wise confidant of both lovers who lubricates the machinery of contrivance and makes everything seem a little less *comme il faut* than *ce que c'est*. In *Troilus and Criseyde* (1381–86), Chaucer restores much of the tradi-tional delicacy of the love-code, as it was understood in French romance, and makes of his Criseyde a *domina* who is infinitely reluctant to be persuaded into a love-affair, scrupulous of her honour and reputation, subtly conscious throughout of the freedoms she has and the constraints under which she is laid, and in the end relapsing with an almost self-consciously self-dramatising pathos into the embrace of Diomede. The poem becomes not only a celebration of passionate romantic love but also an exploration of the structures, inbuilt and external, voluntary and involuntary, within which an individual becomes obedient to the codes of such love. Pandarus is given an altogether greater richness, a comic self-consciousness, an awareness of how his actions might be perceived, a Falstaffian inventiveness and resource. He is also a character of somewhat doubtful integrity, and to some extent acts out within the narrative the author's own questions about the role of the poet-narrator in such a story – about his commitment to truth, his knowledge, his complicity with his creations, his trustworthiness. Chaucer avoids the more obvious questions about the compatibility of the life of idealised love-service and the life of Christian virtue by accepting the pagan and pre-Christian Trojan setting of the story, but the anxiety about such questions – which had sustained chivalric love-romance in its precarious 'Gothic' poise of contrary tensions – breaks out in the final stanzas, where the story and the witness it offers to the intrinsic worthwhileness of human love are repudiated and the love of Christ recommended as the only true form of love.

Chaucer's other main adaptation from Boccaccio, the Knight's Tale (the first tale of the *Canterbury Tales*), which he takes from Boccaccio's twelve-book epic of Theseus, the *Teseida*, is conventionally classified as a romance. It does indeed concentrate on the story extracted from Boccaccio's epic of the love of the cousins Palamon and Arcite for Emelye, but Chaucer's real interest is less in love and chivalry than in the experimental situation that the story provides for the investigation, on lines suggested by Boethius's *Consolation of Philosophy*, of the freedom of action that human beings have in a world ruled by apparently arbitrary circumstance. Truer to the conventions of love-romance, and specifically of the gentler manner of the Breton *lai* as popularised by Marie de France, is the Franklin's Tale. This story sets questions about the mode of love-romance such as Chaucer, always critiquing, reflecting, interrogating, testing, seems unable to refrain from asking about conventional forms of narrative. It concerns a marriage which is set up on the basis of equality and mutual loving respect – and therefore an implied rejection both of the idolatrous code of love and the conventional view of the husband's sovereignty in marriage – but which is threatened when the wife, Dorigen, makes a rash promise (which she is sure cannot be fulfilled) to an amorous squire that she will grant him her love if he removes the rocks that threaten her husband's safe return from abroad. The rocks of course are duly removed, Dorigen must keep her promise, as her husband insists, for truth's sake, and it is now the marriage that seems to be on the rocks. Romance supervenes, and all ends happily, but not before Chaucer has made us wonder again whether even a Utopian 'modern' marriage will not find husband and wife falling into traditional roles of master and servant when the marriage comes under pressure.

Romances continued to be copied and read in England in the fifteenth century, a few new ones were translated from French or composed, and there was to be an 'Indian summer' of chivalry in Malory's Arthurian compilation, but there was some sense of the exhaustion of the traditional form. Chaucer's truest romance, the one that obeys most strictly all the rules of the form, is *Sir Thopas*, a ludicrously comic parody of the inanities of minstrel-romance that he attributes, with sublimely ironic self-deprecation, to 'Chaucer the pilgrim' on the Canterbury journey.

GERMANY

German courtly culture reached a high degree of sophistication, partly under French influence, in the princely and episcopal courts of Bamberg, Cologne, Eisenach, Mainz, Naumberg, Nürnburg, Regensburg, Strassburg and Würzburg, during the reigns of the Hohenstaufen emperors Frederick I (1152–90) and Frederick II (1218–50). The material appurtenances of courtly culture (castles, clothes, food, weapons) became more elegant and expensive, courtly feasts and other ceremonial occasions such as tournaments became more grand, and the cultivation of courtly ideals of knighthood, womanliness and love – as well as the poets who celebrated them – became more extravagant and self-conscious. A new excitement was introduced into the intercourse between the sexes by the invention of made-to-measure clothing, into which men and women would be tightly laced (this is the pre-buttonhole era). Konrad von Würzburg, in his *Engelhard* (c.1280), has a nice description of the effect: 'The shirt was tailored after an unusual cut and clung so tightly to her splendid body that one could have sworn the lovely lady was entirely naked and bare above the belt'.[18] But we should not get too carried away by the refined elegance of the recital. These castles were still cold and draughty places with very few latrines: a beautiful young lady is described in *Die halbe Birne* as stepping quietly outside the palace-gates in order to relieve herself, and it's not suggested that this is unusual. And the wonders of the court feasts are to be set against the practical admonitions of courtesy books such as Tannhäuser's *Hofzucht*, where the noble audience are told not to blow their noses into the tablecloth. Where are they to blow them? On their sleeves or other parts of their clothing, of course.

But the possible crudities of real castle-life fade from sight in the idealised glow of Arthurian romance, early imported from France in the verse-translations of Chrétien de Troyes by Hartmann von Aue, whose *Erek* (1190) and *Iwein* (1202) are inspired by high ideals of courtly conduct and sometimes primly resistant to Chrétien's irony. The *Parzival* (c.1210) of Wolfram von Eschenbach is a free translation, with much added material, of Chrétien's *Perceval*. The masterpiece of medieval chivalric love-romance, it gives much-needed focus to the sprawling French work by the use of thematic anticipation and echo, by offering motivation to seemingly random episodes, by introducing an ideal-ised lady, Sigune, who figures symbolically at key-moments in the hero's Grail quest, and by setting up Gawan (Gawain) as the paragon of courtly conduct in opposition to Parzival, in whom the courtly code is identical with the life dedicated to God. There is a strong emphasis on religious and ethical teaching, and Wolfram turns aside completely from Chrétien's story in his Book IX to take his hero on a visit to the hermit Trevrizent, who explains the true meaning of the Grail as the 'stone of humility'. Wolfram also provides an ending for the story in which Parzival is admitted by the guardians of the Holy Grail at Munsalväsche ('the mount of Salvation') and crowned King of the Grail with his wife Condwiramurs and his son Loherangrin. If there is, in medieval chivalric love-romance, a spectrum running from amorous libertinism to high eroticized spiritual devotion, *Parzival* is at the extreme latter end.

Gottfried von Strassburg's *Tristan*, also written in about 1210, is likewise suffused with the sentiment and language of piety, but in a manner hinting always at irreverence. It is a highly sophisticated work, full of ironic and other tricks of narration that remind one of Chaucer. Gottfried was a well-educated member of the urban patriciate of Strassburg, one of the largest cities of Hohenstaufen Germany, and probably either a 'ministerial' (like Chaucer) or an episcopal official. His version of the Tristan story is derived from the *Tristran* of Thomas (of which only a fragment survives), composed for Eleanor of Aquitaine in about 1160, one of two twelfth-century French versions of the Tristan story (the other is by Béroul).

Gottfried begins with a statement of his primary purpose, to write for those who are expert in love's sorrows, an elite of melancholy. 'I do not mean', he says 'the world of the many who (as I hear) are unable to endure sorrow and wish only to revel in bliss . . . I have another world in mind which together in one heart bears its bitter-sweet, its dear sorrow, its heart's joy, its love's pain, its dear life, its sorrowful death, its dear death, its sorrowful life. To this life let my life be given, of this world let me be part, to be damned or saved with it.'

> ein ander werlt die meine ich,
> diu samet in eime berzen treit
> ir süeze-sur, ir liebez leit,
> ir herzeliep, ir senede not,
> ir liebez leben, ir leiden tot,
> ir lieben tot, ir leidez leben . . .[19]

As the priest intones the liturgy before offering the bread of the eucharistic sacrifice, so Gottfried intones the liturgy of his Prologue before offering the bread of the lovers' sacrifice in the form of his story, which will give life to noble lovers.

Tristan is freed from some of the customary obligations to virtuous behaviour by the special nature of the plot of the story, in which love inflicts itself upon him through the magic love-potion. Gottfried comes close at times to speaking of the life of Tristan as a martyrdom for the sake of love, his life that of a man of sorrows who shed his blood for love. This is literally true in the extraordinary scene where Tristan, having been bled companionably in the same room as Isolde, tries to leap from his recovery-bed to hers (to avoid stepping in the flour that King Mark has had spread on the floor to detect any impropriety) and bursts open all his veins and fills her bed with blood. If this seems outrageous, Gottfried has more. Isolde, faced with the ordeal of the red-hot iron when the truth of her story about the incriminating evidence of the bedful of blood is to be tested, is worried:

> She feared for her honour and she was harassed by the secret anxiety that she would have to whitewash her falseness. With these two cares she did not know what to do: she confided them to Christ, the Merciful, who is helpful when one is in trouble. With prayer and fasting she commended all her anguish most urgently to Him. Meanwhile she had propounded to her secret self a ruse which presumed very far upon her Maker's courtesy.

The ruse is that Tristan, disguised as an old pilgrim, shall carry her across a ford and, when he falls over, she shall fall on top of him. Then she can swear truthfully that she never lay with any man but her husband – and the old man they all just saw. Christ permits the trick to succeed, we are told, because he is as accommodating to any who pray to him as a lady's close-fitting garment.

When Mark finally banishes the lovers, they retire to the forest and the 'Cave of Lovers', where they live in solitude and perfect bliss, nourished, like the Desert Fathers, on love and desire. The cave is a tabernacle in which the souls of the lovers come into communion on the altar, cut from a slab of crystal, which is their bed. There can be no doubt that in describing the grotto Gottfried is drawing deliberate comparisons between the love of Tristan and Isolde and the rapt eucharistic communion of the Christian mystic. It is not a serious attempt to set up an 'alternative religion', nor is it merely a game, but rather an extravagant display and codification and ritualisation of the emotions associated with sexual love. There is furthermore the daring suggestion that in noble hearts what was usually regarded as illicit love could be elevated to a high idealism, far from the sordid practicalities that surrounded marriage, and lofty in its obedience to the single imperative of dedication to love, for women as well as men (though all the time, of course, as we see in Gottfried's remarks about women, it was in the service of male libertinage).

Tristan is one of the great poems of the Middle Ages, persistently subtle in its ironies, full of panache in its exercise of the skills of the romancer (the descriptions of jousting are both brilliantly vivid in themselves and also simultaneously a critique of the conventional rhetoric of such descriptions), and as penetrating as Chrétien or Chaucer in the analysis of the human heart (Isolde's 'secret self'). The scene where Mark spies on the lovers, who have been forewarned of his plot, is well known as a favourite subject for illustration and an epitome of the theme of the story as it is told in French prose romance. In Gottfried, this famous scene of voyeurism becomes something more. It is often talked about in terms of prurience, concealment, and the oppressive surveillance of the male gaze. But in truth it seems more pathetic than anything, with Mark apparently determined to find out what he doesn't want to know (one is reminded of Othello's response to Iago's offer of ocular proof). It is also, though, more subtly, a fulfilment of his deepest desire, which is the creation of intimacy with the lovers, both of them, through the manipulation of distance: there are for him, in the tree, as he thinks, no obstacles to the fantasy of closeness, the fantasy of access to the secret other life, a 'true' one.

Gottfried's approach to the high idealised code of sexual love, with its rhetorical self-consciousness, bravura wit and pervasive irony, is very different from that of his contemporary Wolfram, and is a valuable corrective to the seriously ecstatic excesses of the nineteenth-century cult of medieval romantic love, as in Wagner's *Tristan*.

EUROPEAN CHIVALRIC LOVE-ROMANCE

French chivalric romance spread throughout Europe. The tastes of the French-speaking aristocracy of Flanders and Brabant were mostly well satisfied by French versions of Arthurian romance, though the 'romancing' of classical epic is well represented in the Middle Dutch poem of *The Garden of Troy* (*tPrieel van Troyen*) by Segher Diengotgaf (active in the early thirteenth century). It is a charming elaboration of an imagined episode in the story of Troy which the prolific Jacob van Maerlant later incorporated in his own Troy-book (*c.*1263). A truce is declared in the siege and the knights of Troy (all of whom, it is said, are fighting principally for their lady's love) retire to a garden for a pleasant afternoon wooing their ladies – or trying to woo them, for none is successful. The aplomb of the ladies in politely putting them off is quietly delicious, especially Helen, who pretends that Pollidamas's whispered 'Mercy, lady' is an apology for some offence he has committed, and then, when he declares his love too openly to be plausibly misconstrued, calls him to wake up, pretending (to save his embarrassment) that he has been talking foolishly in his sleep. The realities of war and death are not forgotten: they serve to throw into sharper relief the exquisite courtliness of the love-exchange. But there are also Middle Dutch renderings of Arthurian romance, as early as the thirteenth century, that are evidently designed for an aspirant bourgeoisie, much like the contemporary English versions of French romance. They survive in simpler manuscripts, with fewer miniatures, and are less interested in fine points of courtly behaviour and sentiment than in broadly playful treatments of Arthurian subject-matter. Gawain, with his *penchant* for slightly comic adventures with women, is a favourite character: in an interpolation in the Middle Dutch version of the prose *Lancelot* he is transformed into a midget lover so that he can find out the true nature of his mistress Ydain.

In addition to romance versions of classical stories, there are also many chivalric love-romances newly based on Celtic and eastern and other originals, such as the popular romance of *Floire et Blancheflor*, translated from the French into many languages. But the inheritance of chivalric love-romance is dominated, in Europe generally as in England and Germany, by the Arthurian story. There are translations and adaptations in prose and verse of the romances of Chrétien and the Vulgate cycle in Spain, Portugal, the Netherlands and Italy, and frequent familiar reference to the persons and events of the story in art as well as literature. In one of the most famous episodes in the *Divina Commedia*, Francesca's spirit, in the second circle of Hell, recalls for Dante the moment when she and Paolo kissed, and so fell into mortal sin, when they read together of the first kiss of Lancelot and Guenevere – 'we read no more that day', she says (*Inferno*, v.138).

The most striking witness to the widespread diffusion of Arthurian romance is in Norway and Iceland, where, side by side with the flourishing of the most vigorous indigenous saga-tradition in Europe (rivalled perhaps only by Ireland), there are also thirteenth-century translations into the prose of the sagas of some of the most important French Arthurian verse-romances, including *Ivens saga Artuskappa*, *Erex saga*, and *Parcevals saga*, all based on Chrétien. There are also adaptations of Thomas's *Tristan* and of two of Marie de France's *lais*, but no translation of any of the romances from the prose cycles.

Subjects from Arthurian romance were also favourites throughout Europe in all forms of interior decoration, furnishings and *objets d'art*. One of the most famous single pieces of medieval goldsmithing is a salt-cellar belonging to Louis, Duke of Anjou, depicting the episode in the story of Tristan (an episode already mentioned in the discussion above of Gottfried's *Tristan*) in which King Mark, up in a tree, eavesdrops upon the lovers, who have been forewarned of his presence. The incident was often selected for representation: in a single image it seems to capture the complexity of motive and emotional sympathy at the heart of the romance, where the wronged king does something mean-spirited and degrading to find out the truth, and the lovers play clever tricks to deceive him further. It was a good subject for dinner-table conversation.

Elsewhere, well-preserved wall-paintings at the castles of Rodenegg in the south Tyrol (*c*.1225) and Schmalkalden in Thuringia (*c*.1230) tell the story of Yvain, hero of the romance by Chrétien de Troyes (if 'hero' is the right word for a knight who completely forgets his promise to return to his wife within a year and who has to perform a prolonged chivalric penance in order to be restored to her favour). Such paintings focus the story as a series of images, acting as a visual reminder for those who know the story and perhaps adding something of their own, for a picture is rarely a simple pictorial 'equivalent' of a text. One of the favourite subjects for illustration in manuscripts of *Yvain* is the episode in which Yvain, riding in hot pursuit of a knight whom he has fatally wounded (the knight is the husband of the lady that Yvain proceeds immediately to woo and win), follows him through the castle-gate and has his horse cut off just behind the saddle by the descending portcullis. What thoughts might this bizarre scene have provoked of the male sovereignties that were put at risk in such a marriage?

THE POETRY OF COURTLY LOVE

There was another way altogether in which the idealisation of sexual love could find literary expression, more sophisticated, less vulnerable to vulgar appropriation. The germinal work was the *Roman de la Rose*, which survives in over 300 manuscripts, many of them finely illustrated, and was by far the most widely disseminated and widely read secular poem of the Middle Ages. Guillaume de Lorris (d. 1237) wrote the first 4,058 lines, in which he virtually invented the courtly poetic genre that was to sweep all Europe before it, the allegorical love-vision in the form of a dream recounted by the poet-dreamer in the first person. His poem tells of a young man's first discovery of the fashionable courtly world of sexual love (portrayed allegorically as a walled garden), his delight in its dancing and singing and flirtations, and his first experience of falling in love, represented allegorically as seeing his lady's (his own) eyes in the well of Narcissus and being struck by Cupid's arrows. There follow his allegorical encounters with the various obstacles in the pursuit of a successful love-affair, particularly the inhibitions placed upon the lady's natural warmth of response (*Bel Acueil*, 'Fair Welcome') by her sense of social obligation and fear of what people may say (*Daunger*).

Guillaume's *Roman* is a poem of considerable erotic suggestiveness, with seductive descriptions of young female dancers and a sense of summery freedom and the daring abrogation of the usual moral laws, of young people flocking to 'fleet the time carelessly, as they did in the golden world'. Twelve-year-old Youth kisses freely and unashamed in public with her lover and Richesse leads by the hand her young man, a gigolo who loves living well. After dancing their *caroles*, the company retire to the shade, where the grass grows velvet-soft for the better enjoyment of love-play.

There was great delight and a sense of audacity in seeing court life presented in this uninhibited way, as there must always be in the representation of general sexual pleasure as innocent of moral and social consequence. There was delight, too, in seeing all the stages of falling in love (a look, a word, a kiss are in turn all the lover desires, would be worth all the world to him, etc.) given the dignity of literary-personification allegory, and military-fortification allegory too: Bel Acueil is to be imprisoned in a great tower guarded by Daunger because 'he' allowed the Lover to kiss the budding Rose. Aspects of psychological and sexual experience difficult to talk about directly in polite society, and perhaps inaccessible to other forms of discourse, can be hinted at covertly through allegory. Much else can be suggested too – the mystery and ambiguity and seamy side of sexual love as well as its vigour and delight. There is much to scandalise and excite a courtly audience and much to argue about and discuss.

Some forty years after Guillaume's death, his unfinished poem was 'completed' in a further 17,722 lines (1268–74) by Jean de Meun, a university-trained scholar. Jean de Meun does complete the allegorical love-story after a fashion, in his last thousand lines portraying the lady, already distributed among her several faculties and totally depersonalised, as a fortress successfully stormed, in a passage notable for its violent sexual imagery. Jean actually has his own garden to set against the garden of Love, and it is, not unexpectedly, a paradisal garden presided over by the Good Shepherd and dedicated to the cultivation of spiritual virtue. But he was generally less interested in continuing the allegorical love-story than in using the impetus and popularity of Guillaume's work as the opportunity for a display of learning, casuistry and scatological wit, and for indulging his sardonic ill-temper in university gossip and in the abuse of his fellow-clerics. His continuation, much of which is in the form of very long discourses by characters with names like Reason, Nature and Genius, is a kind of non-alphabetical encyclopaedia in the vernacular, in which everything gets mentioned somewhere.

The combination of these two extraordinary poems, both of them highly original, was extremely influential (Chaucer did a translation of at least part of the first half of the poem), and the fashion for allegorical dream-visions of love swept through Europe. Sometimes the dreamer-narrator is the lover whose desires and fears are acted out in the scenes and tableaux of the dream; sometimes the dreamer-narrator is the observer of the love-complaints and love-dramas of others (this is Chaucer's preferred mode). The form was exploited in France by Machaut, Deschamps and Froissart, in England by Chaucer, Lydgate and several anonymous Chaucerian poets, and in Italy by Boccaccio. In Spain, where the great chivalric love-romance of the late Middle Ages, *Amadis of Gaul*, was already circulating in the late fourteenth century prior to being first written down in Portuguese as *Amadés de Gaula* by Vasco de Lobeira in the fifteenth century, there was the *Libro de Buen Amor* of Juan Ruiz, a poem of love like no other, of which more will be said in Chapter Four.

COURTLY LOVE-LYRICS

Along with romance and allegorical dream-vision in the cult of love went the love-song, usually the lover's complaint to his lady of unrequited love, or of her scorn and coldness, or of the pains of departure or absence. These are the best themes for development, since there is less to be successfully said about love's contentment and satisfactions, and it is as 'themes for development' that the European love-lyric should principally be seen. The first cultivation of such love-lyrics was in Latin and Provençal in the twelfth century, and the style spread quickly to northern France, Germany (in the lyrics of the Minnesinger), Italy, Spain (where the dialect of the first love-lyrics was Galician-Portuguese, because of the connections of Galicia with France through the pilgrim route to Santiago) and the rest of Europe.

In Italy, the first cultivation of courtly love-lyric was among troubadours like Rambertino Buvarelli (d. 1221), who sang in Bologna in the Provençal language. But a group of learned poets from various regions of Italy gathered at the court of the Emperor Frederick II in Naples in the 1230s and 1240s and began to write love-poems in Italian in imitation of the Provençal mode. One of them was the notary Giacomo da Lentini, who can be credited with the invention of the sonnet. Later, at Florence, there was a group of lyric poets who, taking their lead from Guido Guinizelli of Bologna (*c*.1230–76), developed what Dante called the 'sweet new style' (*dolce stil nuovo*) in love-poetry, a style free from superfluous ornamentation and rhetorical display and expressive of the inward spontaneous heart of love. The group included Lapo Gianni,

Cino of Pistoia and Guido Cavalcanti, who explored in his poetry some of the darker and more enigmatic moods of love. All were admired and surpassed by Dante, who brought a stronger sense of personal experience into his love-poems by placing them in a narrative setting in the *Vita nuova*.

NOTES

1. A 'cathedral' is strictly speaking the church of a diocesan bishop, and some large churches (for example, abbey-churches) are not cathedrals. The distinction is not usually of vital importance in a discussion of Gothic architecture: both cathedrals and churches will be discussed in the following pages.
2. Suger's writings are edited and translated by Erwin Panofsky, *Abbot Suger on the Abbey Church of Saint-Denis and its Art Treasures* (Princeton, 1946; 2nd edn, ed. Gerda Panofsky-Soergel, Princeton, 1979).
3. The comparison is made by Peter Meyer, *Europäische Kunstgeschichte* (1947), and quoted in Florens Deuchler, *Gothic* (London, 1989), p. 20.
4. When it is said that a church was 'begun' or 'completed' at a certain date, what is meant is not unambiguous. A church may be said to be begun when the decision is taken to build or rebuild, or when the plan is drawn up, or when the first foundations are laid; it may be said to be completed when the choir is ready for consecration, or when the church is dedicated, or when the nave is finally closed, or when the last external or internal ornament is added. Several or many years may elapse between one event and another.
5. There is an edition and translation of Gervase's text by Charles Cotton, Canterbury Papers No. 3, Cambridge, 1930; also a more accessible translation in F. Woodman, *The Architectural History of Canterbury Cathedral* (London, 1981), pp. 91–8.
6. This image is from Wim Swaan, *The Gothic Cathedral* (London, 1969), p. 30.
7. *The Tale of Beryn*, ed. F.J. Furnivall and W.G. Stone, EETS, ES 105 (1909), lines 147–73.
8. *Cleanness*, in Malcolm Andrew and Ronald Waldron (eds), *The Poems of the Pearl-Manuscript* (London, 1978), lines 1456–88.
9. The pages on English illumination in this chapter are specially indebted to the surveys of Nigel Morgan, Lucy Freeman Sandler and Kathleen L. Scott (see Guide to Reading).
10. The examples that follow are taken from Michael Camille, *Image on the Edge: The Margins of Medieval Art* (London, 1992), pp. 21, 30, 24, 40, 111–12, and the general argument here is much indebted to Camille's book.
11. Otto Pächt, 'A Giottesque Episode in English Medieval Art', *Journal of the Warburg and Courtauld Institutes*, 6 (1943), 51–70.
12. Madeline Caviness, 'Patron or Matron? A Capetian Bride and a Vade Mecum for her Marriage Bed', *Speculum*, 68 (1993), 333–62.
13. Panofsky's discussion of the Boucicaut Master is in *Early Netherlandish Painting: Its Origins and Character*, 2 vols (Cambridge, Mass., 1953), I, pp. 53–61 (see especially pp. 58–9).
14. Millard Meiss, *French Painting in the Time of Jean de Berry: The Boucicaut Master* (London, 1968), p. 70.
15. Much of the material of this paragraph is drawn from David Wallace, *Chaucerian Polity: Absolutist Lineages and Associational Forms in England and Italy* (Stanford, 1997), pp. 45–7.

16. A.J. Denomy, *'Fin' Amors*: The Pure Love of the Troubadours, Its Amorality and Possible Source', *Mediaeval Studies*, 7 (1945), 139–207 (p. 175).

17. Erich Auerbach, *Mimesis: The Representation of Reality in Western Literature* (1946; trans. Willard Trask, 1953; Garden City, NY, 1957), p. 118.

18. Quoted in Joachim Bumke, *Courtly Culture: Literature and Society in the High Middle Ages* (first published in German, 1986; trans. Thomas Dunlap, Berkeley and Los Angeles, 1991), pp. 142–3 (and see pp. 111 and 197 for further references in this paragraph).

19. For this quotation from the Prologue, see Roger Sherman Loomis (ed.), *Arthurian Literature in the Middle Ages: A Collaborative History* (Oxford, 1959), p. 148; the translations here and below are from the translation of Gottfried's *Tristan* by A.T. Hatto (Harmondsworth, 1960).

4

Fragmentations

Gothic is an equilibrium of contrary stresses, a moment of rest at the intersection of restlessly competing forms. This is the aesthetic impression it conveys, in architecture, sculpture, painting and literature. In a great Gothic cathedral, it seems hardly possible that this vast space has been humanly engineered; soaring arches and piers are visibly at the limit of their constraining power; collapse is imminent. There is what Ruskin calls, in 'The Nature of Gothic', an 'energy of fixedness', 'an elastic tension, and communication of force from part to part'.[1] In a large multiple-storeyed stained-glass window, or a complex *Beatus* page, there is such a reaching for pictorially communicated meaning that the different elements seem to be barely able to be contained within the overall design. In the interlaced or polyphonic narrative of a high Arthurian romance, reading is like walking a high-wire or taking part in a trapeze act: everything is always just out of reach, not quite holding together, in imminent danger of falling apart into meaninglessness but never falling. When one or other element in the choreography of forms seeks dominance, the balance of forces – which is always potentially a stressful and restless condition, and not at all necessarily a harmony – shifts and fragments, or assumes a new configuration.

'Equilibrium of contrary stresses' is also a way of talking about the blending in the Gothic of the spiritual and the human. If one were to talk about Romanesque art, with its aggressively unearthly, rigidly dehumanised, syntactically repetitive forms, as the spiritualisation of the spiritual, it would make the way clear to talk of Gothic as the spiritualisation of the human – in the sculpture at Chartres, in the Vulgate *Lancelot*, in Dante's Beatrice, in early Gothic painting. A version of this form of Gothic would be the humanisation of the spiritual, whether in the robust plasticity of Giotto's holy figures or in the emotional figuring of the person of Christ or the tender emotions of the Virgin in Gothic devotional painting. Always, though, there is some agitation, some energy seeking release, at the heart of Gothic, in the contrary pull of the human and the divine. When that tension is released, when the human becomes capable of being represented as the human unmediated by the experience of the divine, or when the divine soars off into the transhuman, Gothic loses whatever it has of an essential nature.

These, in terms of form and meaning, are the fragmentations of which this chapter speaks, after some discussion of relevant social and economic changes. It is not a dramatic story: the structures of thought, form and feeling that maintained Gothic remained more or less intact at the mid-fifteenth century, some of them surviving well into the early modern period, some until the Romantic revolution, some (such as the attitudes to sexuality, sexual love and gendered identity that the medieval period was largely reponsible for fostering) until quite recently. It is more a matter of cracks and fissures in the façade, an interesting craquelure in the varnish, a disturbance of the balance. Nothing collapsed.

Plague, Poverty and Unrest

The circumstances and immediate effects of the Black Death of 1348–49, and the temporary prosperity brought by depopulation and labour shortages, were outlined in Chapter One. The more general economic effect of the Black Death was to loosen manorial ties by encouraging estate workers to go off in search of the higher wages which were now available because of the shortage of labour. Employers and landowners tried to resist these developments, and to restrict mobility and wages, and these oppressive restraints were triggers for popular revolt in France (the Jacquerie of 1358) and England (the Peasants' Revolt of 1381), but they had in the end no choice. The labour market was becoming more powerful than the webs of customary obligation that had characterised the old manorial economy, and the already increasing practice of commuting estate services for money rents assisted in the process. While wages rose because of the shortage of labour, and then stabilised, prices fell, because of the surplus in production. The acreage under cultivation shrank, but it was the best land that remained, only the marginal land which had been ploughed during the days of overpopulation being abandoned. The proportion of arable land shrank, and much more land was given over to viticulture (in the south) and stock-raising to cater for the expanding urban populations. The Black Death did not cause all these changes – they had been taking place before – but it did accelerate them and consolidate their effects.

Partly for these reasons, the impression of change in the later fourteenth century, the sense of an old and stable and nostalgically idealised order being threatened, eroded and fragmented, is strong. Money became more and more the medium through which social as well as economic relationships were mediated, acting as a solvent upon older forms of obligation and covenant – much to the distress of traditional moralists like Langland and Gower and to the delight of observers of the urban scene like Boccaccio (in the *Decameron*) and Chaucer (in the *Canterbury Tales*). The barriers between social classes became more permeable, and successful merchants could now buy their way into the aristocracy: the consequence was a greater emphasis upon the symbolic boundaries of the classes (to protect both the old and the *nouveau*), as for instance in the promulgation of sumptuary laws to regulate the kinds of clothing appropriate to the different ranks of society. Throughout Europe, in assemblies and processions and other public gatherings, different ranks had their own assigned role and place and could be identified by the nature and colour of the costume they wore. Social stability and the political order were threatened, it was thought, by the adoption of clothing as a form of personal ostentation. In 1401 the bourgeois of Bologna were given two days to submit the gowns they possessed to inspection by a commission charged with enforcing a law regulating luxury in clothing. Over 200 garments were seized, on the grounds of excessive ornament (silver stars, gold fringes, pearls, precious stones), fur linings and hems, and exotic colours.

There was an increase in migration to the towns, which began to compete with the old agricultural economy in the encouragement of a new European capitalism. Indirectly, one of the far-reaching changes of the Black Death was that it helped to concentrate capital in a smaller number of hands and thus to encourage mercantile adventurism. The new availability of capital led to the growth of more investment in trade and commerce by new families of entrepreneurs – the Fuggers of Augsburg, the Stromer of Nürnberg, the Bladelin of Bruges, the De la Poles of Kingston-upon-Hull.

Ordinary workers were not so fortunate. The new mobility of rural labour, as well as the disruption caused by depopulation and the breakdown of local rural crafts, led to an influx of poor people into towns, where they would hope to find employment in the textile and other industries. They did so, but at a level of remuneration that left them poorer than they had been before and without the traditional support systems available in the older type of community. A new class of chronic urban poor was created who were less idealistically regarded than the more inconspicuous rural poor, and who were seen less as an opportunity for charitable almsgiving than as a threat to social order. In the twelfth and thirteenth centuries it had been possible to relieve some of the distress of poverty within a network of structures of ecclesiastical and civic almsgiving. After the Great Famine of 1315–17 these programmes of charity were overstrained and began to collapse. As they collapsed, and it began to seem impossible to cope with the increasing numbers of the poor, the ideology of poverty shifted: from being an involuntary version of the poverty that was every Christian's ideal state of life ('If thou wilt be perfect', said Jesus, 'go and sell that thou hast, and give to the poor . . . and come and follow me', Matt. 19:21) it became an offence, a deficiency of will, a product of idleness.

Pauperism had its roots in the rural economy, and there was probably a larger overall number of very poor people before the Black Death of 1348–49 than there was afterwards, for the simple reason that there were more people to be poor, perhaps twice as many in the worst-afflicted regions. But the most devastating effects of the new kinds of chronic poverty were seen in the towns, with the wave of immigration that followed the Black Death. There was employment for all at first, with the stimulus of underpopulation and labour shortage, but within 20 years urban poverty began to emerge as a new and large-scale phenomenon that could only be dealt with by treating it as a form of criminality, except in the case of the old-fashioned 'deserving poor' (widows, the infirm, cripples). Urban poverty was not spread through a traditional community such as was able and socially prepared to sustain and relieve the poor. There was now, in the towns, in Lille, Bruges, Florence and London, a depressed class of part-time, casual, under-employed and unemployed workers, many of them unskilled, many of them recent immigrants, many of them likely to turn to begging, vagabondage, prostitution or crime. The textile industry was a particular breeding-ground for the new poverty, for it was one in which many unskilled workers were needed in the 30 or so operations involved in the preparation of wool for cloth-making. It was the kind of work that could be put out to people, particularly women, working part-time and on piece-work at home. The employer saved on overheads, the employee was a captive of the system. William Langland, in the final version of his *Vision of Piers Plowman* (*c*.1380–90), has a harrowing picture of the woeful lives of such women, harassed by landlords, 'charged with children', and eking out a bare living in the most meagre employment (C-text, IX.70–87). He is one of the very few who recognises the existence of the new class. Dante had celebrated the marriage of St Francis of Assisi to Lady Poverty in the *Paradiso* (XI.57–81) – St Francis, of course, was the son of a rich merchant, and had a *choice* – but any celebration of ideal poverty now had to avert its gaze even more strenuously from the encompassing realities. This did not prove difficult, and any modern assessment of the phenomenal increase in the prosperity of the late medieval town would have to recognise the barbarism upon which it was founded.

Heresy and Mysticism

The shock of the Papal Schism (1378–1415), and the growing inability of an institutionally fossilised church to accommodate reform or to channel the powers of fervent spiritual devotion, led to reformist movements directed against the established church in both England and Bohemia. These movements were larger, better organised and more threatening than the sporadic movements of sectarian dissent that had always been part of the experience of the medieval church, and they anticipated the fragmentation of the western church at the Reformation.

In England, John Wyclif (*c*.1330–84) put forward increasingly extreme views on sacerdotal privilege, on secular dominion, on disendowment, and on the doctrine of the Real Presence in the Eucharist. Wyclif was an Oxford theologian, and wrote in Latin: no doubt his opinions could have been contained within the structures of scholastic theology and perhaps would have been in the past. It was when his views began to be disseminated in the vernacular that they began to be perceived as a real threat, and that his followers, called Lollards (idle mumblers, or 'lollers', or sowers of tares [Lat. *lolia*] among the good corn of faith), began to be seriously persecuted: the statute for the burning of heretics (*De heretico comburendo*) was enacted in 1401, just after the first burning in England of a heretic, William Sawtry.

It was the threat to the established church and the privileges of the priesthood that led to the condemnation of Wyclif's opinions and the persecution of the Lollards. The debate concerning the Real Presence – whether Christ's body and blood are really or only symbolically present in the consecrated bread and wine of communion – was in a sense theological hair-splitting, but to deny the Real Presence was to deny to the priest a specially miraculous power of re-enacting Christ at the consecration, and was seen as an attack on priestly privilege. Likewise, to recommend the disendowment of the church and the dissolution of the religious orders was a direct attack on the institutional edifice of the church; to oppose tithe-paying and the excommunication of offenders was another encroachment; to assert that inner contrition before God was all that was necessary for penitence and that oral confession to a priest was superfluous struck at the priest's sacramental prerogative; to demand that the scriptures should be available in the vernacular (the Wycliffite translation of the bible was the great achievement of English Lollardy) was to question the church's monopoly upon the mediation and interpretation of their meanings. Lollard extremists came close at times to declaring the efficacy of a direct relationship between man and God, without the mediation of the church, or of saints, shrines and pilgrimages.

Some members of the English aristocracy seem to have looked with favour for a while on the Lollard movement, whether out of genuine reformist zeal or because of the attraction of the Wycliffite doctrines of secular dominion (that the church was under the secular jurisdiction of the king) and disendowment, but they soon came to realise that church and state must stand together. Heterodox opinions were a threat to the stability of both, and so must be declared heretical because seditious. The persecution of the Lollards by the Lancastrian kings was a response to what was perceived as a real danger, though it was also a way of reinforcing the political authority of the new dynasty. The Lollard movement was decapitated and driven underground, where it had a vigorous if inchoate life through the fifteenth century, to put out new growth at the Reformation.

The followers of Jan Hus, the Bohemian reformer, shared many views with the Wycliffites, on the sacramental role of the clergy and on disendowment, for instance, but where the Lollards lost their base among the upper classes, the Hussites drew their strength from those classes. It was part of a national movement against German influence, and an assertion of lay rights in church affairs. After Hus was executed at Constance in 1415, the Hussites set up an independent church, and an army of sorts under the knight John Žižka harried Austria and Franconia (in central Germany) until 1434. Eventually, by the *Compactata* of Basle (1436), the more moderate Hussites, or Utraquists (permitted to receive communion in both kinds, *sub utraque specie*), reached an accommodation with the Catholic church.

An easier option, for those faced with the institutional sterility and rigidity of the church, was the retreat inward into more private forms of affective devotion, with much concentration, and more than hitherto, upon the humanity of Christ, the suffering, the wounds – opportunities for the exercise of feelings that had no issue in desires for reform. Even more removed from any form of action that might go against the orthodoxies of the institutional church (such as had been earlier contained in the face of the challenge of Franciscanism) was the increasing cult of mysticism, of sophisticated forms of meditative practice that detached the individual from all communion with his or her fellow-believers in the rapt search for communion with God. Mystical writers were very conscious of the potential neglect of sacerdotal privilege and the rights of mother church that might attach to their solitary practice. The English author of the *Cloud of Unknowing* (*c.*1390) makes it very clear that his treatise, though it is in the vernacular, is intended only for a small group of specialised initiates in the life of contemplation, and not for the general Christian community, and is in that sense as 'safe' as it would be if it were indeed written in Latin. Julian of Norwich (1342–*c.*1418) is careful, in her *Revelation of Divine Love*, to assert her obedience to holy mother church, her respect for the priesthood, her role as a medium in bringing God's truth to others. Jan van Ruusbroec, or Ruysbroeck (1293–1381), the most influential and widely translated of the Flemish mystics, was similarly circumspect. In his masterpiece, *Die gheestelike brulocht* ('The spiritual espousals'), he deliberately set out to counter the libertine beliefs of the Brethren of the Free Spirit, who were sure that their elect status exempted them from all normal forms of religious obedience.

A particular form of devotional piety was the *devotio moderna*, established in the Low Countries in the late fourteenth century under the influence of Gerhard Groote (1340–84), a Carthusian monk who established a community at Deventer in northern Flanders called the Brethren and Sisters of the Common Life. They avoided persecution, did much practical work and produced many books (in this respect at least they were like the Lollards). The involvement of a Carthusian monk in the foundation of the community reminds us of the role that the Carthusians played, as an order of monks vowed to a particular austerity of life, and comparatively untouched by the worldliness of the older orders, in the new devotion. They gave it both spiritual focus and political respectability. The high Franciscan masterpiece of affective devotion, the *Meditationes vitae Christi* (*c.*1340), was translated into English (1410) by Nicholas Love, the prior of the recently founded (1396) Carthusian house at Mount Grace in Yorkshire. It was specifically approved by Archbishop Arundel as an orthodox and anti-Lollard document, was disseminated in 40 or more manuscripts, and was widely influential.

Chivalry and Society

Like the church, the closely bonded community of the nobility and gentry showed the strain of adapting to change. In England, there was increasing nervousness among the old aristocracy about the intrusion into their ranks of upstart royal appointees such as those favoured by Richard II, and about the more obtrusive political role being played by the urban merchant-class. The codes of conduct which knights and ladies aspired to and were accustomed to admire in the mirror of chivalric love-romance were increasingly brought into question by being juxtaposed with the realities they had obscured. Those who read or listened to *Troilus and Criseyde* or *Sir Gawain and the Green Knight* could no longer come away from the experience with a glow of satisfaction at belonging to a society that lived by such values. Chivalry, whatever had been its power in the past as an influence in creating class solidarity, social aspiration and civility of behaviour, was changing. The practice of commuting knight-service (the duty of fighting and providing troops when required by one's liege-lord) for money ('bastard feudalism') was becoming increasingly common – like the practice, at a lower level of the feudal hierarchy, of commuting tenant-service for rents. Much of the panoply remained, and there was much genuine attachment to the ideals of chivalry on the part of historical individuals and in the increasingly nostalgic literature of chivalry throughout the fifteenth and well into the sixteenth century, but the core values of chivalry were no longer the main inspiration of social idealism. The knight was already often a justice of the peace and a member of parliament, and was well on his way to becoming the high-ranking civil servant and 'governor' of Tudor times.

Even warfare was changing. Wars had been the proving-ground of the mettle of chivalry, and the English and French knights who fought against each other at Crécy and Poitiers were bound closely together by the kind of combat in which they were engaged. Knights and squires expected to be captured and ransomed and to live to fight the same opponents another day: the fighting in which they engaged was a form of social bonding. Froissart no doubt idealises the life of the chivalric warrior-knight during the Hundred Years War, and embroiders and even invents episodes in which that life can be shown to advantage, but his *Chronicles* are also a record of the realities of battle and of the ideals of courage, generosity, loyalty and comradeship that sustained men amidst those realities. It was technology that helped to bring about change, and gunpowder and firearms that completed the transformation of war into a professionalised activity in which the ideals of a transnational chivalric community were no longer often in evidence. Soldiers shared no close bond now with those against whom they were fighting, only the same chance of getting killed.

Tournaments underwent a comparable change. They had been a prominent form of chivalric activity in the thirteenth and fourteenth centuries, and often a tournament would be arranged between combatant knights during interludes in an ongoing war. They could be lethally dangerous, especially if fought between groups of knights who had other reasons for hostility than the formal passage of arms. But in the fifteenth century the tournament became a form of theatre, in which every artifice was employed (tipped lances, armour so heavy that little movement was possible, strict rules of engagement) to reduce the risk of serious injury and every opportunity taken for display, ritual, and the exhibition of wealth. The Order of the Golden Fleece, founded at Bruges by

Philip of Burgundy in 1430, had a somewhat different function from the Order of the Garter founded by Edward III in 1349. Like gunpowder, the artifice of tournament created *distance*, and accelerated the fragmentation of the idea of a chivalric community.

Local and Programmatic Realism in Art and Literature

The search for a new 'realism' is often what inspires developmental histories of medieval painting, literature and the other arts. The desire is to find the precursors of the forms that are perceived to have become established in the Renaissance or later and that have come to be regarded as normative. Histories of painting are full of excited discoveries of the first hints of this or that optical innovation – the first cast shadow, the first night-scene, the first snow at the Nativity, the first experiments in fixed-point perspective and recession in depth. Observations of this kind are not incorrect, yet they can give a distorted picture of what medieval artists were trying to do as well as of what they did. Local realism, accuracy in the representation of natural objects or individual nature, has a function in the economy of Gothic. A change takes place when it becomes detached from the ordering of elements that gave it, and to which it imparted, meaning.

The leaves of Southwell are a case in point. These carvings (*c*.1310), in the vestibule of the chapter-house at Southwell Minster in Nottinghamshire, of leaves of oak, maple, vine, hawthorn, rose, hop and ivy, are done in exact imitation of nature, as are similarly precise carvings at Exeter, Lincoln and York of about the same period. Hailed by Pevsner[2] as a revolution in perception, and the beginning of a new recognition of the real world, these carvings are more likely to have been the result of a passing fashion, the taste of a particular carver or group of carvers, a joy in the possibilities offered by a new set of tools and drills. The fashion passed, and more formal and ornamental foliage carving, more obviously in accord with the prevailing iconographic programme, became again the norm. The whole style of carving at Exeter, for instance, changed with the arrival of new craftsmen in 1308.

In fact, the kind of local realism evidenced at Southwell had long been present in illuminated manuscripts, in coexistence with generally decorative or symbolic page-programmes. The margins of such manuscripts are full of beautifully observed flora and fauna, particularly birds, as in the picture of birds gathering at an angel's call in an early fourteenth-century Apocalypse (BL MS Royal 19.B.xv, fol. 37v), where hoopoe, magpie, kingfisher, wren, great woodpecker, goldfinch, bullfinch, woodcock, stork, crane and parrot have all been identified. Likewise, the Holkham Bible Picture-Book (BL MS Add.47682) of *c*.1325–30 has a Creation scene (fol. 2v) showing plants, animals and birds, some of them carefully observed, piled up in the picture plane in a completely formalised manner, as if they were stacked on shelves, against a patterned background.

Local realism was always a possibility. The sketchbook of Villard de Honnecourt has drawings of the towers of Laon, the windows of Reims and the maze at Chartres that are all part of his business as an architect, but it also has careful studies, for no such reason, of a snail's shell, a bear drawn from life, a beautiful swan with a curving neck. There are very accurate drawings of birds in Frederick II's *De arte venandi*, and a strong tradition of naturalistic animal portraiture in northern Italy, especially Lombardy, which comes to its perfection in the sketchbooks of Michelino da Besozzo, Giovannino de' Grassi, and Pisanello. One of the most tenacious artistic traditions in Italy was that of the *Theatrum Sanitatis* or *Tacuinum Sanitatis*, texts deriving from Arabic sources via Byzantine manuscripts, describing the medicinal properties of plants, animals and minerals, and illustrated with minutely accurate portrayals of flora and fauna done with neither foreground nor background in a totally unrealised landscape. An important change, anticipating the integration of accurately portrayed creatures and plants in a habitat and therefore in a composed landscape 'scene', is when they begin to be shown living or growing in a piece of landscape, sometimes with rain falling or sun shining and human figures going about their business. An example painted in the style and workshop of Giovannino de' Grassi, and sharing the characteristics of his sketchbook, is in the Biblioteca Casanatense in Rome (MS 4182).

The hegemony of the symbolic code, and of the allegorical and typological system of associations through which every representation of the natural world – in manuscript marginalia, sculptural bas-reliefs, roof-bosses, bestiaries, herbals – became part of the bible of meaning, can probably be overemphasised, but certainly it existed. 'Art', says Emile Mâle, 'was at once a script, a calculus and a symbolic code.'[3] It was a form of sacred writing, a 'veritable hieroglyphic', with its own coded systems of representation. Sinuous circling lines are sky, horizontal undulating lines are water; a tree, represented by a stalk surmounted by two or three leaves, indicates that a scene takes place on earth; a tower pierced by a doorway is a town. There are set attributes for characters such as saints which enable them to be recognised without being 'seen', and the layout of scenes and the positioning of figures within them is of immediate doctrinal significance – the orientation of the saved and the damned at the Last Judgement, the table-setting at the Last Supper. An artist, like a priest not in a state of grace, could communicate sacramental meaning even if he could not draw very well.

But once images were pursued for the aesthetic satisfaction that they could give in and of themselves, allegory, which had been such an apt instrument in a world ordered by analogies and systematic hierarchies, began to disintegrate, and the literal level, instead of existing in subordinate relation to the allegorical, moral and anagogical levels in the fourfold medieval hierarchy of meaning, assumed primacy. The process is a long and subtle one. In terms of composition, representational precision of the most unmannered kind was for long contained within a pre-existing programme, and did not offer itself as a component in a newly composed world of experience. Even presented with the human and unsymbolic solidity of Giotto's figures, the programmes do not weaken. The specially English taste for naturalistic ornithology continues in the Pepysian Sketch-Book and the Sherborne Missal of the fifteenth century. But dedication to the representation of observed reality, and of human figures realised as solid forms in relation to each other and in their spatial environment, with the commitment to human experience, drama and emotion that is then necessarily involved, was bound to disturb the precarious equilibrium of Gothic.

Yet the process of reconfiguration is a subtle and prolonged one, discontinuous, with much movement to and fro. It takes time for habits of perception and expression, established over many centuries, to refashion themselves or to be refashioned, and the development of the formulae and techniques associated with representational realism – compositional integrity, consistency of detail, referential truth to observed reality – is slow, and often resisted. In Italy, a clear statement about the primacy of depth of perspective and solidity of representational illusion was being made by painters like Masaccio and Masolino, but northern painters of the fifteenth century, whilst bathing delightedly in the new freedoms of perspectival illusionism and naturalistic observation, were sometimes reluctant to allow the new forms to stand without adding some explicit visual comment.

Two paintings by Jan van Eyck show how the balance was preserved. The Turin–Milan Hours is part of a manuscript originally made for the Duke of Berry (the *Très Belles Heures de Notre Dame*, described in Chapter Three above) that went unfinished to Holland and was decorated by several Netherlandish artists. This part was subsequently divided: part went to Turin, part to Milan. The Turin part was burnt in 1904; the Milan part was later (rashly, it may seem!) deposited in Turin, in the Museo Civico. The masterpiece of the Turin–Milan Hours is the Birth of John the Baptist (fol. 93v) attributed to Jan van Eyck, and perhaps done in 1422–24 when he was in the service of John of Bavaria, Count of Holland-Bavaria (Fig. 60). It is the use of light that transports the picture to a new world – not just an aesthetic effect, like the Boucicaut Master's experiments with aerial perspective or the night-scenes of the *Très Riches Heures*, but an emotional one, a confirmation of humanity, a setting for warm and companionable activities. One can almost hear the clink of ewers, the cry of the baby: it seems 100 years ahead of its time. But in the bas-de-page, the baptism of Christ, as a parallel scene, with its deep space merging into the tone of the vellum itself, restores the main picture to the world of religious significance in which it has its fullest reality.

In another painting, the Virgin in a Church (1425–27), now in the Stiftung Preussischer Kulturbesitz in Berlin, Van Eyck portrays the Virgin with every detail of the costumed figure and its occupation of space, every angle of the building and shaft of light, rendered with overpowering realism. Yet the Virgin is majestically out of proportion with her surroundings; she towers almost to the clerestory windows, and the light that transfigures the scene, as we can tell from the meticulously signalled disposition of the church interior, comes from the north, as if to confirm the spirituality, the un-real-ness, of the scene. Other painters, both northern and Italian, will incorporate resistance to the temptations of naturalism in simpler ways: in the Agony in the Garden of Andrea

Figure 60: Jan van Eyck, The Birth of John the Baptist and the Baptism of Christ. Turin, Museo Civico, the Turin–Milan Hours, fol. 93v. 1422–24.

In Van Eyck, miniature painting begins to evolve in the manner that was eventually to upset the balance between the flatness of the page and the suggestion of depth in the framed painting, between the naturalistic commitment to the world and the symbolic commitment to the spirit. Here, the balance is perfect still between a fully developed secular Flemish interior, seen as if through an open wall, and a Baptism that rests on the page-surface and asserts an unequivocally spiritual order. The text is *De ventre matris mee* ('From my mother's womb'), a prayer from Isaiah 49 used in the Office of St John the Baptist (see Fig. 55).

Mantegna, painted in Padua in 1454 and now in the National Gallery in London, a small band of unlikely-looking putti-angels stand on a platform of cloud in front of the praying Christ holding the instruments of the Passion, while in the Adoration of the Shepherds of Hugo van der Goes (c.1480) in the Gemäldegalerie of the Staatliche Museen in Berlin, prophets draw curtains as if to display the 'scene' of the Nativity. In both cases, the purpose seems to be to reinforce a piously meditative reading of the picture which the emphasis on 'appearance' may seem to belie.

Sometimes, it is not the painters who provide the comment, but the commentators. The increasing commitment of later artists to a painterly realism is evident, for instance, in revealing little details that got added to familiar scenes as they were more fully materialised through the artistic imagination. The Nativity scene in the Paris Hours of René of Anjou (BN MS lat.1156A, fol. 48) shows Mary testing the bath-water with her hand while she holds the suckling babe in her other arm. Why did he need a bath?, the theological purist might ask, but, fortunately for the painters whose art was producing a need for answers to such questions, there was an answer. The baby Jesus had to have a bath so that he could symbolically cleanse the water for all future baptisms.

Nativity scenes are particularly receptive to the influence of affective devotion, and to that perception of the human in the divine that encouraged a greater range of expressivity in the representation of the human feelings of the Virgin as mother. Likewise, in the Annunciations of the developing International Style, there is, amid much decorative elegance, a sense of human response rather than immediate transfiguration in Mary, a sense of perturbation and hesitation such as we see in the 1333 Siena altarpiece of Simone Martini (see Plate V) or the slightly later Annunciation altarpiece (1339) by the same painter in the Musée Royal des Beaux-Arts in Antwerp. In the robust altarpiece of the Annunciation by Melchior Broederlam in the Dijon museum (1399) there is a strong sense of human contact, with the responses of Mary identified more and more as the reactions of a human being to an unexpected and rather alarming visitant (see Fig. 32). The range of these reactions is elaborately developed and subtly coded in fifteenth-century Annunciations. In a different Marian scene, an altar-painting by Rogier van der Weyden (c.1400–1464) of Christ appearing to his mother (c.1445), now in the Metropolitan Museum of Art in New York, there can be seen the fully heightened form of the expressively represented encounter. At the same time, the rich suggestions of the human are counterpoised by non-realistic reminders of the iconographic programme of which this scene is part: Christ's Resurrection is viewed through the window of the room in which the appearance to Mary takes place, while scenes from Christ's early life are displayed in the archivolts of the forward framing arch (Fig. 61). Of such a painting it might be said, as Panofsky so memorably said of Jan van Eyck, 'No residue remains of either objectivity without significance or significance without disguise'.[4]

Something similar can be seen in the cycles of mystery plays, representing for outdoor performance scenes from the story of the bible and the life of

Christ, which began to be more fully developed in the fifteenth century. In Spain, France and Germany they remained largely under the control of the church, and were acted out at fixed stations by professional players. In England, the cycles of plays that were developed in the towns and cities of the north – York, Wakefield, Chester, Newcastle, Beverley – were often put on by the craft-guilds under the supervision of the municipal oligarchy, as in the classic case of York, and acted mostly by amateurs performing on pageant-waggons that were pulled through the city and that stopped for performance at various fixed stations. The overall text of the plays was under clerical control, but the mode of production meant that a good deal more freedom was taken with the introduction of comic and realistic episodes, Noah's wife represented as a noisy termagant, for instance, or Cain as a rough Yorkshire farmer, or Joseph as a querulous cuckold, or the shepherds of the Annunciation as poor, cold, grumbling, ground-down peasants. But suddenly they become the shepherds of the bible-story. The general effect, of a collision of two modes of representation, is not dissimilar from that of some fifteenth-century Nativities, with their awkward lumpy figures, the midwives pushing forward, the thatched cottage with its shattered walls, the Child radiating light at the centre. The truth that is struggling for emergence is in the particulars as well as in the broad symbolic programme.

Gothic Poise and Disequilibrium in Literary Texts

The kinds of equilibrium that have been described as characteristic of Gothic art, and the challenges to which they were subject, can be perceived too in some literary texts of the fourteenth century. In Dante's *Divine Comedy*, a powerful sense of the human is held steadily in orbit by an equally powerful sense of the divine order. It is an equilibrium that is embodied in the poem's narrative landscape. There is, as Muscatine has argued,[5] a perfect Gothic tension and poise between two kinds of locus of action, one of which uses spatial references (such as the aerial journey through the spheres) to organise and clarify types of conceptual and spiritual relationship, while in the other a personal perspective of height and depth, of falling and climbing, a locus of action both immediate and true, represents psychological and emotional experience. The combination of these two perspectives is powerfully controlled so as to maintain an equilibrium.

In Langland's *Piers Plowman* (*c*.1370–90), a poem of similarly encyclopaedic ambition in the representation, through the experience of the dreamer-narrator, of the spiritual odyssey of mankind, this balance begins to break down. The urgent realities of personal experience and social indignation demand a more immediate form of representation, human figures kick away the restraints that hold them in the network of transhuman signification, the allegory runs into dead-ends, turns on itself, collapses, and seeps in and out of the space and time of the poem's narrative. There is no consistent perspective, no spatial

metaphor which is tied into a constant subjective reality. There may be something in this of Langland's individual mode of vision, and a desire to break down stubborn categories into which the perception of reality had stiffened; or there may be some reflection of a contemporary social crisis, in which traditional codes of behaviour, class-structures, hierarchies, social relationships were seen to be threatened by the universal solvent of cash and the money-economy.

The contrast between Dante and Langland is instructive of changes in perception and representation that can often be located or focused in the third quarter of the fourteenth century. Chaucer offers a different kind of contrast with Dante, since, unlike Langland, he can definitely be shown to have known the *Divina Commedia*. His response to Dante, in the *House of Fame*, is not exactly a parody of the aerial journey through the spheres (though there are moments, when the poet-dreamer looks nervously down as the eagle carries him upward in its claws, when it comes close), but it is an explicit repudiation of the Dantean spatial metaphor in which the journey and ascent correspond to a spiritual ascent. Chaucer goes up, misses the point of the eagle's discourse, keeps wanting to be back home, and eventually finds himself in the House of Rumour, which is just like home. The reality that he seeks and wants to write about is not transcendental truth but ordinary experience.

In literary texts, allegory had long been available, not just as a strategy for interpreting the Old Testament, but as a literary technique in original compositions through which the literal and spiritual worlds could be held in some kind of fixed relation. The literal level, though it appealed to the elementary and necessarily preliminary desire for the recognition of the familiar, could be cracked open like the shell of a nut so as to reveal the kernel of spiritual meaning and doctrinal truth – a double lesson in the folly of trusting to external appearances and the importance of seeking spiritual meaning. Allegory confirmed the systems of analogy upon which Christian doctrine was made to rest – God/man, king/subject, man/woman, reason/passion, the well-ordered mind/ the well-ordered commonwealth, the political body/the human body. As a literary technique, it could be dynamically creative, as in Langland's *Piers Plowman*, or deadeningly predictable. Guillaume de Deguileville's *Pèlerinage de la vie humaine* (1340) is the low point and epitome of medieval allegory, extremely popular in France and England throughout the rest of the Middle Ages, and one of three such life-allegories that its author wrote. It is an allegory of the journey of man's life in which the meanings of the narrative episodes and motifs can be read off even before the literal narrative has established an inclination to do so. The dreamer meets Venus, who is not portrayed

Figure 61: Rogier van der Weyden, Christ appearing to his Mother. New York, Metropolitan Museum of Art. Right panel of an altarpiece, 63.5 × 38 cm. *c*.1445.
The encounter is viewed through a doorway, on the archivolts of which are portrayed scenes from Christ's life, while through the window of Mary's oratory can be seen a deep landscape and the moment of Resurrection. The overpowering sense of human presence and the space of the real world combines with the many iconographic reminders that call the observer to meditation.

as beautiful and simultaneously ugly, nor beautiful at first sight and ugly at second, nor beautiful before and ugly behind (all of them ways in which the allegorist might have sustained an elementary interest in the narrative), but simply ugly, because of course she represents, that is, 'stands for' (*id est*), Lust. When the dreamer meets Memory, she has eyes, as we might have guessed by now, in the back of her head.

But before long it was the literal level that was to assume pre-eminence, and the underlying spiritual meanings that were going to become more difficult to extract. This can happen in Langland, where the power of the narrative can sometimes overwhelm its ostensible didactic purpose, and it can happen too in secular allegory, where the gardens of love become less the allegorical sites of an elegant psycho-drama and more like real places where real people are harbouring thoughts of real seduction. In the fifteenth-century illustrated manuscripts of the thirteenth-century *Roman de la Rose*, the gardens are irresistibly the arbours and parterres of fashionable aristocratic estates, the allegorical figures of the dreamer and Bel Acueil and Daungier more and more the fashionably clad actors in a contemporary love-affair. The small gate in the wall of the garden of Love guarded by Idleness is not so much the allegory of social privilege and indulgence as a ridiculously small gate in the wall of a real garden. The allegorical 'meanings', when they need to be drawn, collide with the culturally belated pictorial representation.

In non-allegorical literary works of the later Middle Ages, a similar balance of elements, a similar equilibrium, can be detected, likewise made precarious by the pressures towards representational realism. In manuscript-painting, as has been seen, a high sophistication of naturalistic representation can coexist with a predominantly symbolic programme and not disturb the Gothic equilibrium. The full-page miniatures of the Boucicaut Master (discussed in Chapter Three above) are under visual restraints of various kinds which temper the naturalistic exuberance of the style and draw it into consonance with the iconographic code; the calendar-pictures of the Labours of the Months in the *Très Riches Heures*, though released from most such compositional restraints (as described in Chapter Three above), are still surmounted by the arc of the zodiac, and the chariot of the sign of the month passing through it, as a reminder of the overseeing ordinance of the Ruler of the heavens. The final emancipation of this style from its iconographic programme, or, to put it in a different way, the final collapse of this order of representation, will only come in the early sixteenth-century imitations of the *Très Riches Heures* calendar-pictures in the Grimani Breviary (Venice, Biblioteca Marciana MS lat.1.99, *c*.1510), where the scenes stand independently.

Chaucer's *Canterbury Tales* may stand similarly at some juncture between equilibrium and disequilibrium such as is evidenced in early fifteenth-century French manuscript-painting. The 'naturalistic surge' of Chaucer's poem has often been remarked upon – the individuality of his characters, the naturalistically unfolding drama of the pilgrimage, the overpowering substantiality of the narrative settings. But even within the tales that are most devotedly substantial, such as the coarse comic tales told by the Miller and the Reeve, there is still a cavalier inconsistency of representation – even of elements that are evidently of prime importance to the realisation of the narrative, such as the exact layout of the houses of John the carpenter (in the Miller's Tale) and Simkin the miller (in the Reeve's Tale) – that would suggest an only partial commitment to an aesthetic of the naturalistic. Chaucer's narratives exhibit a vivid apprehension of place and subjective space, in so far as the plot requires them, but they are not integrated into a coherent compositional locale.

The same is true of the *Canterbury Tales* as a whole. Chaucer has chosen here a framework which seems to demand naturalistic organisation in terms of space and time, and he tempts us to impose such an organisation by many hints and allusions to places on the way between London and Canterbury and to the time of day, and above all by the extraordinary degree of local dramatic realism in the exchanges among the pilgrims along the way. But the attempt to evolve a consistent itinerary and diary framework for the *Tales* has been a frustration for those scholars who have tried it, for the rules of the realistic novel do not apply. Chaucer seems to have valued the illusion of the roadside drama created by the pilgrimage framework, and fostered it to some extent, but he was very ready to abandon it when other matters seemed more pressing. Perhaps he knew (like Shakespeare) that to seek an absolute consistency of character-representation, or of setting and spatial reference, would encourage naturalistic deductions such as would ultimately collapse the illusion altogether. It is not a matter of design: Chaucer did not leave the *Tales* in a state of deliberate disorder because he consciously recognised the limitations of naturalism; it is rather that his habits of mind, artistic motives and methods of work made certain kinds of organisation, the lack of which seems to us inexplicable, seem to him unimportant. Maybe they were to him literally unthinkable.

But these are not the only ways of talking about the disintegrative tendencies of late medieval narrative poems. Chaucer's tale-collection, and Boccaccio's *Decameron* before it, may seem models of order compared with the earlier *Libro de Buen Amor* ('Book of True Love') of the Castilian poet Juan Ruiz, a 7,000-line narrative poem in monorhymed septenary quatrains (1330–43) telling the story of the usually ill-fated attempts of the 'Archpriest of Hita', supposedly the author himself, to obtain a woman.[6] It has to be a woman of the right rank and station, not just any woman, and he spends some effort trying unsuccessfully to fight off the attentions of mountain cowgirls who waylay him in the mountain passes determined to exact their *peaje*, or toll. A nun would be ideal, and one of the old bawds he employs is called *Trotaconventos* ('Convent-trotter'), also known as *Buen Amor*. She excites him with stories of nuns' skill in lovemaking and their readiness to prepare whole tablefuls of aphrodisiac sweetmeats and candies for their lovers. The sophisticated erotic gaming is reminiscent of Latin and Provençal poetry rather than the love-poetry of the clerically dominated vernaculars of northern France and England, but the real character of the poem is Ovidian. Something of the joyousness of unfettered sexuality is suggested in the licentiousness of the poem, but it is an illusion that depends on treating women as despised objects, and the mask of courtliness does not hide a well-rooted clerical misogyny reminiscent of Jean de Meun (*Trotaconventos* is a kind of Spanish version of *La Vieille* in the *Roman de la Rose*).

It is a witty and outrageous display-poem, lively, dramatic, packed with detailed observation, darting from subject to subject, which the author claims to have composed while imprisoned by order of the Archbishop of Toledo. The autobiographical story acts as a frame for an anthology of narrative and lyric forms from Latin and Romance sources, with some admixture of Jewish and Arabic influences. The form of the poem as a whole may be indebted to the *maqamat*, an Arabic-Jewish genre of fictitious autobiography. Mixed in with the author's amours, as illustrations, *exempla*, digressions, and digressions within digressions, are moral reflections, songs to the Virgin, beast-fables (a large number of these), *fabliaux*, debates, love-songs, an elegy for *Trotaconventos* (or rather a vehement denunciation of Death), a begging poem, a parody of courtly pastoral, an account of the Seven Deadly Sins with exemplary fables, an allegory of the Labours of the Month portrayed as male personifications, a parodic appropriation of the prayers at the canonical hours to the suit of the lover, a song in praise of little women (*chicas*), a song about the clerics of Talavera (warning them of an edict of the pope that they are to keep no concubine), and a lengthy inset mock-heroic allegorical epic (stanzas 1,067–1,209) of the battle of Lady Lent (*doña Cuaresma*) and Lord Flesh (*don Carnal*). The latter's troops are chickens and partridges, capons and hens, ducks and widgeons, armed with frying pans and cooking pots. They fight against inedible and indigestible foods and the consequences of overeating. In the middle there is what seems a perfectly serious digression on the importance of true penance.

The most disintegrative element in the collage is the author, and Chaucer's *Canterbury Tales* come very much into mind for comparison. Like the latter, the *Libro* exists in variant forms showing evidence of authorial revision. Inconsistency, ambiguity, inventive freedom are the character of the work, and its narrator is a blur of shifting viewpoints and roles. Parts of the poem are not there: songs are promised but appear in no manuscript and clearly the poem had a fresh existence in each reading or recital. The climactic seduction of Lady Plum (*doña Endrina*), in a central episode based on the twelfth-century Latin comedy of *Pamphilus and Galatea*, is the only success the Archpriest has in the whole poem: it comes at a point where 32 stanzas are missing, as if in a novel by Laurence Sterne. An opening prose homily explains how human beings need to understand the sinful love of the world to which they are subject by having many examples of its power – models of sinning – put before them. *Intellectum tibi dabo* ('I will give thee understanding'), he says, citing Psalm 32:8, and it is up to the reader to use that understanding properly ('Blameth nat me if that ye chese amys', we hear Chaucer saying, *Canterbury Tales*, I.3181, as if echoing this tongue-in-cheek piety). It is all a matter of interpretation. His book, says the author, is a musical instrument – it is up to the reader to play it: 'How so you tune me, well or badly, I'll resound in kind' (*bien o mal, cual puntares, tal te dirá çiertamente*, st. 70).

The International Style

The 'International Style' of Gothic has been frequently mentioned in the preceding pages. It is interestingly placed at the fault-line of some of the shifts in
style that have been discussed, which in turn depended upon shifts in the
perception of man's relation to his physical and spiritual environment. It is
the name given to a style, in painting and sculpture above all, that dominated
the artistic vocabulary of cultural centres throughout western Europe in the
period from about 1390 to about 1430 – Paris, Dijon, Avignon, London, Prague,
Cologne, Milan, Florence – and the tastes of bourgeois patrons as well as
the still dominant aristocracies of Burgundy, Berry, Bavaria, Habsburg and
Luxemburg. It is marked by patterns of exchange in which precise identification of provenance by style becomes difficult: ivory Virgins are exported
from France to Italy, Italian panel-paintings are found in England and the
Low Countries, German goldsmiths work in Venice, Florentine embroidery
turns up in Hamburg. Artists migrate, and contribute to the homogenisa-
tion of style – Simone Martini (at an earlier date) from Siena to Avignon, the
Netherlandish Claus Sluter to Dijon, Hermann Scheerre from the Rhineland
to London.

It is a style of mannered elegance and artifice, privileging surface in a way
that made it particularly appropriate for tapestries, where the elegant arrange-
ment of figures against a background of delightfully observed plants and flowers
and little animals suited both the style and the medium very well. But it was
not a style from which spiritual meanings are necessarily emptied out. The
cult of the surface can indeed tend towards a love of elegance and ornament
for their own sake, but it can also, through the precarious fragility of its
images, suggest a precious, private, refined kind of spirituality, as in the Siena
Annunciation altarpiece (1333) of Simone Martini, a forerunner of the International Style (see Plate V), or in Melchior Broederlam, or, as we have seen, in
the Wilton Diptych (see Fig. 8) and the later work of manuscript-painters like
the Limbourgs, the Boucicaut Master, John Siferwas, Hermann Scheerre and
'Johannes'.

The International Style, like Gothic, is a name for a moment rather than a
movement, and Broederlam can stand as an example of the style in its emergence and almost instantaneous urge to transformation. His most famous
work is in the two painted wings that he did for a sculpted altarpiece installed
in 1399 and now in the museum at Dijon (see Fig. 32). These panels show the
Annunciation and the Visitation on the left and the Presentation and Flight
into Egypt on the right, both pairs of scenes portrayed side by side with
'space-box' interiors juxtaposed with external landscapes with spiralling
'broken terrace' rock-structures derived from Italian painting. Broederlam looks
back to Pucelle and the miniaturists but also forward, precociously, to fully
developed compositions set in space with monumental figures. He is a perfect
exemplar of the International Style.

The famous painting of St Eustace by Pisanello (c.1400), now in the National
Gallery in London (Fig. 62), is a particularly rich example of the precarious

Figure 62: Pisanello, St Eustace. London, National Gallery. Panel painting. *c*.1400.
St Eustace has a vision of Christ crucified in the antlers of the stag he is pursuing.
In Pisanello's picture, the moment of vision retains its transfiguring power against
the delights and visual temptations of the landscape and its exquisitely realised animal
inhabitants. The scroll in the foreground helps with the creation of aesthetic distance.

potential of the style. The legend tells how the Roman general Placidas was
hunting a large stag when it turned at bay and he saw a cross and image of
Christ between its antlers. God's voice spoke in the stag, 'O Placidas, why
pursuest thou me . . . ?', whereupon Placidas fell or dismounted from his
horse, knelt before the crucifix and was converted to Christianity. Pisanello's
picture shows many touches of spatial realism and hints of sophisticated
perspective (as in the representation of animals facing away from the observer,
always a piece of joyful optical trickery on the part of painters), but the
general purpose of the composition seems to be to fill the picture space, and to
throw up a mass of quite realistically observed detail onto the surface of the
picture. It is characteristic of the International Style to bring this kind of
local and fragmentary realism into enigmatic conjunction with an only partly

organised spatial assembly, thus creating that effect of rich medley frequent in the style.

In the use of terms like 'partly organised', or 'hints of perspective', there is the suggestion that progress is somewhere being made towards full organisation and fully developed perspective, and an evolutionary narrative might look to sixteenth-century paintings of the subject by Albrecht Dürer and Annibale Carracci to see the full Renaissance development of the *paysage composé*. The familiarity of such paintings is comforting, but it would be possible to argue that the fashion for picturesque landscape contributes to a sterilisation of vision. The mystery of Pisanello's picture, the quality of vision so apt to the subject, is partly a result of a deliberate denial of the prosaic composing power of three-dimensional perspective. Perhaps this mode of painting was intrinsically better able to communicate certain kinds of momentary and evanescent spiritual experience.

A painting by Giovanni di Paolo, of St John going into the Wilderness (*c*.1450), also in the National Gallery in London, can be read in the same way to make a similar point concerning a precarious moment of poise (Fig. 63). It portrays St John riding into a rocky unearthly landscape of improbable scimitar-like rocks, familiar from Giovanni's illustrations for *The Divine Comedy*. Beneath, totally out of scale, is a landscape of neatly cultivated fields and pink houses, themselves 'properly drawn', as we say, according to the laws of perspective. Clearly, we are not dealing here with a clumsy attempt to create a unified composition but with a deliberate divorce (related to the theme of the picture, which is that of preparation for spiritual vision) between things of the world (the phenomenal world of perspective) and things of the spirit (the numinous world of wilderness). The function of the landscape is to embody that distinction and to enforce it not merely by inverted perspective (that is, making things bigger according to their importance rather than according to their nearness to the observer) but by paradoxical perspective, in which two kinds of landscape are juxtaposed for symbolic and spiritual purposes. We might compare this painting with the St John in the Wilderness of Geertgen tot Sint Jans (*c*.1485), in the Staatliche Museen, Preussischer Kulturbesitz, in Berlin. Here, nothing is allowed to disturb the unity of the composition, which recedes through avenues of exquisitely drawn trees and lush vegetation to a distant perspective of the heavenly Jerusalem. A new world has been discovered, but an older one, and a certain moment of vision, are fragmented beyond recovery.

Death

Death had been, as one might say, 'contained' within the iconographic programmes of Gothic. In the fifteenth century it began to leak into representation in a manner that was sometimes less orderly, though one should not think of a general descent of the late Middle Ages into a macabre obsession with decaying corpses. It is, at least partly, a matter of changes in fashion and technique.

For one thing, the extended programmes of mural decoration in fourteenth-century churches gave opportunity for a wider range of scenes of death, not necessarily more graphic but certainly more personal. Scenes of the Last Judgement showing the torments of Hell awaiting the sinful after death had long been a familiar presence in churches – in the tympanum over the west doorway, in the west window, in the painting over the crossing – and were a constant and terrible reminder of mortality. A painting of the Torments of Hell by Taddeo di Bartolo in the Collegiata di Santa Maria Assunta at San Gimignano (c.1390–1400) shows the sins, represented as persons and allegorically named, being tormented in Dantesque style with reminders of their sin (Fig. 64). Usury is swallowing quantities of hot coins pouring from a devil's anus, Avarice is being strangled with the draw-strings of his money-bags, a sodomite is being sodomised by a devil with a long rod that goes in at his anus and comes out from his mouth. The scene is graphic, but the figures are allegorical simulacra of damned souls, remote as persons from the observer, who experiences the scene as a lesson in the consequences of sinfulness not as a personal reminder of the terror of dying. So it is at an earlier date in Giotto's Last Judgement in the Arena (Scrovegni) Chapel at Padua (c.1305), where the tormented little figures are, for such a painter of the human figure, notably unhumanised. Death was a lesson to be learnt, and it was a lesson best learnt as the experience of a visual thunder-clap of shock and horror. It is interesting that Purgatory is rarely represented in painting or literature, except in the *Divine Comedy* and illustrated copies of that poem. The reason is perhaps that Purgatory mitigated the starkness of the opposition of Heaven and Hell and in offering what might seem to some sinners an escape-lane from disaster might carry the message of penitence less powerfully.

A different kind of representation of death, and a foretaste of the fifteenth-century preoccupation with personal mortality, can be seen in the *Triumph of Death* painted in 1347 in the north gallery of the Campo Santo burial ground at Pisa (*Campo Santo* means 'Holy Field' and was so called because the soil was brought from the hill of Calvary by the Crusaders). It is a famous and spectacular celebration, as one might call it, of the power of Death, done in the traditional grand narrative of common human mortality (Fig. 65). On the right a female figure with bats' wings comes flying down through the air bearing a scythe and aiming for a group of aristocratic young men and women sitting comfortably under some trees. The upper part of the composition shows the souls of the recently departed being fought over by angels and black

---

Figure 63: Giovanni di Paolo, St John the Baptist going into the Wilderness. London, National Gallery. Panel painting. c.1450.

St John emerges from an archway firmly set in one world of (earthly) reality, drawn by the artist to match the perception we have of the natural world, and passes into another world of spiritual (unearthly) reality characterised by broken-terrace structures and beaked rocks that defy the prosaic composing power of the three-dimensional imagination. The painting records the crossing of a threshold from worldly seeing to spiritual vision.

winged demons, while at the upper left some desert saints go quietly about their business (death holds no terrors for those who live truly holy lives). But at the lower left there is a more unusual scene. Three young men on richly caparisoned horses amid a company of horsemen come upon a row of three coffins containing corpses, two of them shrouded, one a skeleton: they are the dead bodies of the three young men. It is the scene of the Three Living and the Three Dead, which was becoming increasingly common in texts and images (an earlier example is in the Psalter of Robert de Lisle, BL MS Arundel 83 [II], c.1310, fol. 127r) as a means of enforcing the lesson of mortality in a more personal way. 'As I am now, so will you be.' This, says the corpse, is *your* body.

There is a natural tendency to associate changes in the representation of death with the catastrophic European experience of death during the Black Death of 1348–49. Such a holocaust must, one assumes, have prompted some morbid reflections, some desire to exorcise or extirpate the horror. It was not so, either in literature or art, and Millard Meiss, in an influential book, *Painting in Florence and Siena after the Black Death* (1951), has attempted to explain why. Visual language, he says, became for a while more abstract and old-fashioned, and the innovations of Giotto and others in the representation of the human form were not followed up. Artists perhaps took refuge from the all-too-real experience of human mortality in a greater austerity and transcendentalism, a tendency to distance God from the world and not to see the divine embodied in the human. Meiss's conclusions carry weight, but some have been questioned, and there is more caution to be exercised, generally, in relating developments in literary and artistic representation directly to historical events, however cataclysmic. The influence of events can work itself out in many different ways, some of them irrecoverably hidden from view; works of art are rarely faithful in their allegiance to one or other mode of representation; and meanwhile there are more pragmatic issues to be reckoned with in the effects of changes in the systems of patronage, in technology and technique, and in fashion.

The most famous late medieval death phenomenon is the Dance of Death, or Dance Macabre, which is first recorded as having been portrayed in the church of the Holy Innocents in Paris in 1423. A series of sculpted panels shows Death as a skeleton or decomposing corpse laying his bony finger on the arm of figures representing the 'estates' of society, as if inviting them to join a dignified processional dance. Verse-inscriptions in French accompanied the panels, giving the words of Death's invitation and the reply of the victim. The place became a resort of fashionable society and hell-fire preachers. The

---

Figure 64: Taddeo di Bartolo, Torments of Hell. San Gimignano, Collegiata di Santa Maria Assunta. Wall-painting. *c.*1390–1400.

The mural offers no respite from the artist's ugly and inventive imaginings. In addition to Usury (*Usurrio*), Avarice (*Avaro*) and Sodomy (*Sotomitto*), all mentioned in the text, Adultery (*Avultera*) can readily be picked out middle right (a couple are flogged by a devil, while another devil gropes a woman), and Lust (*La Lussuria*) at bottom right (a devil rides astride a long-tressed woman).

English monk-poet John Lydgate saw the panels on his stay in Paris in 1426 and did a translation into English, adding new stanzas of his own. Subsequently, around 1430, he did a revised version at the request of John Carpenter, town clerk of London, to be inscribed, with appropriate illustrations, on the walls of the cloister (pulled down in 1549) in the Pardon churchyard of St Paul's.

The origin of the 'Dance of Machabre', as Lydgate calls it, is much debated, but the likeliest explanation is that the word *macabre* (properly trisyllabic) is derived from a Hebrew word meaning 'grave-digger', and refers to a death-dance introduced by Jewish burial societies into France in the thirteenth century, a kind of undertakers' pantomime. Whatever its origin, the dance was very popular in the fifteenth and sixteenth centuries, and provided material for much visual illustration, as well as texts, culminating in the famous series of woodcuts done by Hans Holbein the Younger to accompany a text published at Lyons in 1538. Often associated, as by Johan Huizinga in his influential book on *The Waning of the Middle Ages* (1926), with a general spirit of morbidity and decadence in the later Middle Ages, it was in fact firmly in the tradition of mortality literature, its purpose being to remind folk of the inevitability of death so that they can repent and reform in time. The threat of death is a salutary one, an invitation to learn the art of dying well, and the correct answer to Death's summons comes from those – the Carthusian monk and the Hermit in Lydgate's poem – who understand that the death of the body is the portal to heavenly bliss. They say to Death, in effect, 'At last: I have been waiting for you all my life'. Preparing to die well placed a heavy burden of penitential discipline on the ordinary individual, but there was a compensatory satisfaction to be taken in the power of 'Death the leveller' to create a certain democratisation of death. It was not in the literary texts, but in the increasingly graphic pictorial representation of the person of Death, and the horribly contrasting 'normalness' of his victims, that the Dance Macabre comes to have its power to shock people into a more personal awareness of bodily death and some anticipatory frisson, at least, of 'the macabre'.

Another factor in the increasingly graphic and personal representation of death, and the disturbance of the symbolic order in which death was to be deliberately *used* as a reminder of mortality and a corrective to worldly pride, was the increasing availability of more lifelike (or deathlike) representations of dead persons. Charles V and his sons showed considerable interest in funerary portraiture as well as in having lifelike portraits of themselves inserted into books they had commissioned, and death-masks were beginning to be used for

Figure 65: Pisa, Campo Santo, The Triumph of Death (left side). Wall-painting. 1347.
On the left, the legend of the Three Living and the Three Dead; on the right, the Triumph of Death, bearing a scythe. Above, on the right, devils contend for the souls of the newly departed, while on the left hermit-saints go quietly about their business, free from the terror of death that afflicts the worldly. The frescoes in the Campo Santo were badly damaged in 1944 during Allied bombardment.

Figure 66: Lincoln Cathedral, tomb of Bishop Richard Fleming (d. 1431).
    This is one of the earliest cadaver-tombs, with decaying corpse below and the Bishop, in his robes, with crozier, above. Such tombs acknowledge the power of 'Death the Leveller', and the promise of a kind of democracy in death; but only the rich could afford them, and they represent less an act of humility than a spectacular performance of self-humiliation. The individual self is being asserted even in death.

funeral effigies. Later came the cadaver tombs, or *transi* ('I have passed on') tombs, double-decker tombs in which the finely arrayed funeral effigy on the top deck sleeps over its vividly realistic decayed cadaver on the lower deck. Such tombs (Fig. 66) are mostly confined to England and France, and the earliest seems to be that of Cardinal Jean de Lagrange (d. 1402) at Saint-Martial in Avignon. The *transi* tomb prepared in 1424–26 for Archbishop Henry Chichele, apparently the earliest in England, was erected in Canterbury

Cathedral where he could contemplate it in life from his archepiscopal seat. The cadaver tomb was an ostentatious act of humility: since only rich people could afford such elaborate tombs they were necessarily a form of display. It was also a fashion, the spread of which can be traced, and, as far as technique was concerned, a predictable exploitation of the developing forms of naturalistic representation. But the fashion for *transi* tombs is also connected with a more vivid sense of the importance of the individual as an individual, not as a member of a collective or a particular manifestation of the divinely implanted soul-in-a-body. It provoked meditation on death and mortality, but it also provoked a specially personal response to the fact of bodily death. The tomb says, in the manner of the Three Dead to the Three Living, 'Here am I as I was and am; as I am so shall you be'. A sense of the indivisibility of body and soul which had permeated twelfth- and thirteenth-century thinking and inspired the serenities of human figure sculpture at Chartres, Reims and Bourges (as well as curious questions concerning the need to know whether animals would, at the Last Judgement, have to regurgitate the people they had eaten so that their bodies could be reunited with their souls) began to be less strong in the later Middle Ages. The body, in association with a more individualised notion of the self, had come to take on a more personal and real existence. This is *my* body.

There are similar evidences of a preoccupation with the personal reality of death, with 'my own dead body', in a manuscript owned by René of Anjou (1409–80), the London Hours (BL MS Egerton 1070), which was first painted *c.*1409–10 but came into his possession only after 1430. On fol. 53r he caused to be inserted a picture of himself as *Le roi mort*, crowned, naked, cadaverous, his stomach open and full of worms, and holding a scroll inscribed *Memento homo quod cinis es et in sinere [cinerem] reverteris* ('Remember, man, that thou art dust and that to dust thou shalt return'). René's manuscripts of this period, which include writings of his own, some of them illustrated by himself, embody several such reflections upon his recent unhappy career, but it is unusual to find the medieval preoccupation with death given so very personal an embodiment in the image of the self's certain dissolution.

Though there appears to be no direct connection, the picture is reminiscent of the most famous representation of a dead man in a book of hours, the scene of the Commendation of the Soul ('*In manus tuas . . .*') in the *Grandes Heures de Rohan* (BN MS lat.9471, fol. 159r) of *c.*1420 (Fig. 67). The naked pathetic emaciated corpse lies stretched on a cloth among bones and skulls while the Archangel Michael and a devil combat for his soul (in the form of a small infant). God looks on with infinite pity, the scroll from his lips promising a place in heaven after a due time of purgatorial penance. The same sense of the pitying humanity of the divine is present in the Christ in Judgement in the same manuscript (fol. 154r). Christ, as the Man of Sorrows, bleeding, crowned with thorns, old, white-haired and white-bearded, worn-out, in pain, almost naked under his cloak, looks on in pity as naked figures rise from their graves and a clothed man with long dark hair and beard sits crouched in anguish. His presence, presumably as a representative of those left alive at the Judgement

Figure 67: Paris BN MS lat.9471 (the *Grandes Heures de Rohan* [Rohan Hours]), fol. 159r. Commendation of the Soul, from the Office of the Dead. *c.*1420.

The dying man commends his soul to God in the words of Psalm 31:5: 'Into thy hands, O Lord, I commend my spirit; thou hast redeemed me, O Lord, God of truth' (*In manus tuas domine commendo spiritum meum; redemisti me domine deus veritatis*). God replies reassuringly in French, 'For thy sins thou shalt do penance. At the day of judgement thou shalt be with me' (*Pour tes pechiez penitence feras. Au jour du jugement avecques moy seras*). The devil who has seized the dying man's soul seems to have little hope against the band of armed angels who surround and attack him.

Day, gives an unutterable pathos to the admonitions of mortality. It is instruct-ive to know that the manuscript was made for Yolanda of Aragon, widow of Louis, second Duke of Anjou (1377–1417), mother of Louis the third duke (1403–34) and of René the fourth duke (1409–80), and one of the most powerful women of the 1420s. She moved quickly to have her daughter Marie married to Charles the Dauphin when he became heir-in-waiting to the throne of France in 1422.

Another manuscript, the Hours of Catherine of Cleves (New York, Morgan Library MSS M.917 and M.945, Dutch, c.1440), shows an extraordinary degree of realism in the borders of its text-pages, with their continuous concatenations of fish-eating-fish-eating-eel (the greedy oppressor swallowing the poor?). But this illusionistic perfection has a different and disturbing effect in the page (fol. 99v) that shows the body of a man being prepared for burial, a miniature illustrating an additional office of the Dead. The rigid, shrunken, grinning corpse is being displayed in a winding-sheet by two grim-faced at-tendants in a beautifully lit chamber, with a central window looking out on a landscape, and within a text-page bordered with delicate rinceaux (foliated scrolls) of ivy-leaves and pictures of fruit and flowers.

On a more homely level, there was a great expansion in the production of cheap block-books on the 'Art of Dying' (Ars moriendi), that is, the art of dying well through penitential preparation. Increasingly popular from about the time of the Council of Constance (1414–18), and anticipating by some decades the introduction of printing with movable type, these block-books (books with whole pages printed from single incised wooden blocks) with woodcut illustrations were popular and widely disseminated. They can be associated with an increasing sense of the 'particular judgement' of the indi-vidual at the moment of death (as distinct from the general Last Judgement on all souls), and of the need to prepare assiduously as an individual for such a promise of salvation. But the availability and comparative cheapness of the technology may have preceded or generated or interacted with the 'need'.

NOTES

1. John Ruskin, 'The Nature of Gothic', in *The Stones of Venice* (1851; ed. J.G. Links, New York, 1960), p. 174

2. Nicholas Pevsner, *The Leaves of Southwell* (Harmondsworth, 1945).

3. Emile Mâle, *The Gothic Image: Religious Art in France of the Thirteenth Century* (first published in French, 1910; trans. Dora Nussey, London, 1961), p. 22.

4. Erwin Panofsky, *Early Netherlandish Painting: Its Origins and Character*, 2 vols (Cambridge, Mass., 1953), I, p. 180.

5. Charles Muscatine, 'Locus of Action in Medieval Narrative', *Romance Philology*, 17 (1963), 115–22.

6. See *The Book of True Love, by Juan Ruiz, The Archpriest of Hita*, ed. Anthony N. Zahareas, trans. Saralyn R. Daly (University Park, PA, 1978).

5

New Identities

Nothing remains in stasis and nothing, strictly speaking, is new in cultural history, and the catchpenny title of this chapter is in some respects misleading. But the disentangling of the threads of the Gothic weave produces more than loose ends. It is some of these materials of change that will be spoken of as 'identities'.

The 'Growth of the Individual': Portraiture and Writing

The idea of the 'individual', inseparably body and soul, bounded by the body, personally responsible to God at the Last Judgement, was perfectly well understood in the Middle Ages. Metamorphosis, hybridisation, metempsychosis, body-hopping, shape-shifting, all so common in the stories that came down from classical and pagan sources, were anathema, and had to be understood as forms of diabolical possession. Ovid's *Metamorphoses*, with its extravagant, free and playful treatment of human/animal transformation, had to be brought under the strictest allegorical and moral control through the supply of scholarly commentary. Ovid's stories, whether because of or despite such prohibitions, remained a source of fascination for medieval audiences, and were frequently retold in the vernaculars, as were the stories of lycanthropy that began to circulate around 1200 (as in Marie de France's *Bisclavret* and other werewolf romances). The provisionality of the body and the leakiness of the self's boundaries were uneasy, disturbing and exciting presences even though individuality, the boundedness of the individual as a body-and-soul, was an absolute theological necessity.

There is the part played too by the confessional self. The individual Christian was constantly summoned to acts of self-analysis and self-examination which, though they were performed within certain pre-existing structures of understanding (how could it be otherwise?), were nevertheless a profoundly important stimulus to individuality of consciousness. In literature, the 'confessional' monologue was the most important entry writers could find into the revelation of the inner self. Conducted at first, as in the confession of Faux-Semblant (Hypocrisy) in the *Roman de la Rose*, as a formal allegorical exercise in the display of motifs and attributes of sinfulness, it became a means to speaking from within about certain kinds of inner experience that were otherwise unable to be conventionally coded, as in Chaucer's Wife of Bath and Pardoner.

So it is hard to agree that individuality as such is 'unmedieval', that the individual in the Middle Ages was, systematically more than in other periods, a position in a hierarchy or an intersecting point in a set of constraining circumstances, that people in the Middle Ages had no individual personality. It seems ridiculous even to think of arguing such a case, though such ideas have provided a platform for early modern cultural historians to launch their opinions concerning the emergence of the individual in the sixteenth century. Yet there are ways in which individuality came to be more thought about in the later Middle Ages, became more a subject of discourse and representation, perhaps partly because the modes of discourse and representation were themselves changing, often for other related and unrelated reasons.

A fashion, for instance, for portraits 'from the life' began to appear in late fourteenth-century France in paintings commissioned by or done for Charles V and his sons. Images and portraits the subjects of which were intended to be recognised, such as pictures exchanged or sent between lovers, are a stock motif of romance, and are conventionally described as being so lifelike that the person seemed to be there present, alive and breathing, but such portraits existed only in fantasy. Royal portraits in particular were supposed to conform in appearance and gesture to the image of the divinely ordained office. But about 1360 a change began to come about, first of all in France. John, Duke of Berry, frequently had his portrait inserted, done to the life, in pious and reverent poses in his manuscripts, and his father, Charles V, appears on fol. 2r of a *Bible historiale* (The Hague, Meermanno-Westreenianum Museum MS 10.B.23), where he is shown being given the bible, with some flourish, by his (smallish) chancellor, Jean de Vaudetar, who had the book made for him in 1371 and holds it open at the first page of Genesis. The picture is by John of Bruges, also known as Jean Bondol, who worked in Paris for the dukes of Berry and Anjou as well as for the king. The comical beak-like nose is a strong argument for lifelikeness: it could hardly be part of any idealising programme. Berry's brother Philip the Bold, Duke of Burgundy, has his portrait in the D below the Annunciation on fol. 13v of the book of hours made for him about 1370 (Cambridge, Fitzwilliam Museum MS 3–1954). In Bohemia, in about 1375, the Emperor Charles IV allowed a lifelike statue of himself (contemporary descriptions of his person are not flattering) by the sculptors of Peter Parler to be placed among the dynastic series of statues on the triforium in Prague Cathedral.

Another example of this desire to be remembered as an individual person (and not necessarily an attractive one, in the traditionally idealised way) is the increasing use of death-masks in the making of funeral effigies, as for example that which was made of Charles V in 1364 and that which was incorporated in the elaborate burial ceremony for Bertrand du Guesclin in the royal necropolis at Saint-Denis in 1380. In England, the contracts for the effigies of Richard II and Queen Anne, for their tomb in Westminster Abbey, drawn up in 1395 after her death, specify that they are to *contrefaire* or 'portray' (imitate the appearance of, 'counterfeit') the two sovereigns.

Portraiture generally began to have as its goal the representation of the subject in an unidealised way. There is a great gulf between the Wilton Diptych, made not much before 1400 (Fig. 8), and Jan van Eyck's *Madonna with Chancellor Nicolas Rolin* (c.1433), now in the Louvre. At whatever stage in Richard's life the Diptych was made for him, he is represented as an attractive young ephebe, beardless, unblemished, perhaps as he was idealised to have been at his coronation. The Chancellor Rolin is as he was and for ever is, heavy, formidable, forbidding: the point that the artist and patron want to make is that such a man, foursquare in his power in the world, *still* has himself portrayed kneeling before the Virgin and Child (Fig. 68). The history of portraiture in the fifteenth century is of the development of ever subtler means of combining the necessary flattery of the patron's power with the artist's desire to use the new techniques of individual portrait-painting.

Writers are of course specially important for the investigation of the 'growth of the individual', since they were responsible for the discourse in which that process, whatever it is, would be carried forward and remembered. Author-portraits are an interesting record of the change in understanding. Earlier author-portraits are blandly uninformative and standardised: an undifferentiated person, soberly clad, sits at a desk by himself writing or at a lectern reading to an audience. By the late fourteenth century a greater sense of the author's individuality is sought for. In a frontispiece (fol. D), done in grisaille in a manuscript of his poems made at his own instructions in about 1370 (BN MS fr.1584), Guillaume de Machaut (c.1300–77) is portrayed, in a Pucelle-style open-sided room or 'space-box' (Fig. 69). Here he receives the God of Love and allegorical figures of Sweet Thoughts, Pleasure and Hope, all elegantly dressed, while in the background a prettily stylised landscape climbs to the top of the frame, with clumps of trees and a pond in which ducks, only their heads visible, appear to be drowning or struggling for life. It is an important author-portrait, and an important manuscript in the history of secular book-illustration. Machaut's face is quite vividly modelled, as if from life.

Much more striking, and often acclaimed as the first 'true portrait' in England, is the picture of Chaucer that Thomas Hoccleve caused to be inserted in manuscripts of his *Regiment of Princes* (1411–12). In the midst of a memorial eulogy of his revered master, he declares that the image of the poet is so fresh and vivid in his memory that he will have a likeness of him painted in the margin,

> That they that han of him lost thoght and mynde
> By this peynture may ageyn him fynde.[1]

Figure 68: Jan van Eyck, Madonna with Chancellor Nicolas Rolin. Paris, Louvre. Panel painting. *c.*1433.

Chancellor Rolin, Chancellor of Burgundy (d. 1462), who commissioned the picture, is the dominant presence within it, despite the reminders of divinity in the hieratic pose and gesture of the infant Jesus and in the imminent coronation of the Virgin. Outside the arched opening of the oratory, two figures stand on a balcony looking outward, away from the foreground scene of piety, upon the wide prospect of a prosperous city. The world is much with us in this picture.

Figure 69: Paris, BN MS fr.1584 (poems of Guillaume de Machaut), fol. D (frontispiece). *c.*1370.

This frontispiece accompanies a Prologue that Machaut wrote late in life to introduce manuscripts of his collected works. The ageing poet sits in his study to receive the God of Love (*Amours*), who presents to him Sweet Thoughts (*doux penser*), Pleasure (*plaisance*) and Hope (*esperance*), the qualities in lovers that have been celebrated and encouraged in Machaut's love-poetry. The illustration is by a famous and prolific artist of the time known as the pseudo-Bondol, who did similar pretty landscapes for two fine manuscripts of Nicholas Oresme's French translations from Aristotle (*c.*1370).

One can detect elements of possible idealisation in the portrait, in the sober garb and serious demeanour of the poet and in the rosary that he carries, but one presumes that Hoccleve's claim that the portrait was a likeness, and was intended to remind people what Chaucer actually looked like, would have fallen rather flat for those who were still able to remember him if it had not been reasonably accurate.

There are ways too in which the individuality of writers as writers came to be more emphatically asserted in the later medieval period, perhaps as certain conventions of expression were exhausted or transformed, though it is always possible to overstate the degree of novelty in such phenomena. It is tempting, for instance, to see in Chaucer or in Hoccleve a quizzical and ironical self-consciousness that we might wish to signal as modern, and that we might wish to differentiate, as being not entirely prompted by and contained within the literary artifice, from another kind of equally subtle and sophisticated self-consciousness in Chrétien de Troyes or Gottfried of Strassburg or the authors of the *Roman de la Rose*.

But the French poet Rutebeuf (1248–77) would give us pause. Known only by this name ('rude ox'), which he continually alludes to and plays upon, and unknown apart from the poems attributed to the name, he has a 'modern' kind of enigmatic poetic presence. He wrote polemically about contemporary events, and especially about the struggle in the University of Paris between the secular masters and the mendicants, but he also wrote a series of poems – about a spiritual crisis, a failed marriage, a life of misery and destitution (*La Complainte Rutebeuf*), a 'conversion' – in which an authentic personal voice of urban disaffection and disillusion seems to be speaking, one that is not heard again in French poetry until François Villon (1431–63). Much of Rutebeuf's poetry is so obviously explicable in terms of patrons and commissions, the desire to please and the desire to earn money, that the unusualness of these other poems, taking what is claimed to be personal experience as their subject, is all the more marked. Whether or not they are autobiographically 'true', the personal poems suggest an interest in individual experience and consciousness that had not often before found expression.

In later poets, this self-conscious use of the enigmatic relation of the poet's inner and outer life as the subject of his poetry became more widespread. Machaut and Chaucer are different from their predecessors in the manner in which they provoke interest in the person behind the *persona*. Authors were becoming more self-conscious about the trope of the fictive *persona*. John Gower, fearful that the earnest 'I' of the *Confessio Amantis* (who actually names himself as John Gower) will be mistaken for the real John Gower, enters a nervous Latin marginal note when he first introduces Amans, the first-person Lover – 'Here the author pictures himself in the *persona* of one of those others whom love holds in its power'.

Authors were also more daring in their claim to be recounting their own personal experiences. While Dante describes a purely visionary journey that he couldn't possibly have made, William Langland used what purports to be the narrative of his own real spiritual life as the dream-structure of *The Vision of Piers Plowman.* He imitates the conventions of traditional spiritual autobiography, in which the experiences of doubt, crisis, search and revelation would be arranged in a suitably edifying narrative order, but he uses them in a distinctly idiosyncratic way that suggests the immediacy of personal discovery. It is this emphasis on the unique importance of the personal experience that is new. It is unlikely to be in its entirety an accurate record of personal experience – the very existence of such a category of record, even in the most intimate diaries in code, is doubtful – but it is not entirely conventional or made up.

Thomas Hoccleve (1368–1426) is a particularly interesting example of a poet who made his own life often the subject of his poetry, since in so far as the autobiographical references in his poems (to his job, his annuity, his acquaintances) can be checked against the documentary record they seem to be remarkably accurate. An early poem like *La Male Regle* (1405–06), a confession of his 'Badly Ruled Life', is not unusual in its theme nor in its assumption of naiveté and bumbling good nature, but it has an unexpected edginess, a sense of the personal that seems excitingly surplus to the requirements of the genre. In the long 'autobiographical' sequence at the beginning of the *Regiment of Princes* (1411–12) and in the *Complaint* and *Dialogue with a Friend* that he wrote in later life as part of a writing 'sampler' (1421–22), he talks about the problems and disappointments of his life in a way that lays bare a certain raw nerve. In the *Complaint*, he gives a detailed account of a kind of nervous breakdown that he suffered in 1416. 'Madness' usually appears in medieval writing in the service of some moral or narrative theme: the madness inflicted by God on the sinful (Nebuchadnezzar), the madness of thwarted love (Lancelot, Tristan), the 'madness' of those who have no care of the world (Langland's 'lunatyk lollares'). It is rarely observed, least of all by the sufferer, as closely as it is by Hoccleve. He has a reason to speak of his breakdown (to prove that he is recovered, and able to write again) and he draws in the end a conventionally consolatory moral from it, but in the meantime there is a perhaps new sense of individual consciousness in his description of his attempts to prove to himself that he 'is himself', his examination of his behaviour in public, his return home to look in his mirror and say, 'Is this the face of a man who is mad?' Mirrors had traditionally functioned as images of vanity and narcissism (a lady looking at herself in a glass, or the Lover in the *Roman de la Rose* falling in love when he looks down into the well of Narcissus), or else in the Latin form, *speculum*, and its translations, as names for pieces of writing, metaphorical mirrors that one looked into for a truthful reflection not of oneself but of some body of knowledge – history, nature, true kingship, salvation. But mirrors had not before been the means to define identity, to prove the existence of the individual as a whole and integrated person. There is anticipation here of the modern notion that the mirror is the means through which the body is integrated as a self, the means through which the self is produced, and the reassurance of selfhood.

It is in the person of the lover, perhaps, that the late medieval poet explores most consistently subtly the idea of an individual consciousness. Generally speaking, medieval love-poems are not expressive of personal feeling, nor do they have an individual 'voice': they are part of a larger world of shared thought and experience, and the poet's job is to embroider and work variations upon familiar themes. The beginnings of a different ambition, towards a tender and personalised expressiveness, are present in the *dolce stil nuovo* of Dante's predecessors, but it is the integration of the series of love-poems into a narrative framework (in Dante's *Vita nuova*) or into a suggested narrative (in Petrarch's *Canzonieri*) that makes them most vividly suggestive of an individualised experience of love. Dante's Beatrice and Petrarch's Laura are not so much the occasions of this new kind of poetry as the necessities of it.

Many love-poems in the conventional style continued to be composed, but from now on the most ambitious poets wanted to explore the illimitable inner world opened up by the organised sequence of love-poems. Machaut's *Le voir dit* ('The True Story') tells of the elderly poet's love-affair with a young noble-woman who especially admired his music. The rhymed narrative is interspersed with prose letters and many songs copied down and exchanged between the lovers: it is like the journal of a love-affair, done from the point of view of a narrator who understands nothing for sure of what is going on in his lady's head, and not much of what is going on in his own. The fiction is so authentic-seeming (note the title) that a sense of a real individual self is created.

The poems of the Flemish poets Jan van Hulst and Jan Moritoen in the Gruuthuyse manuscript of *c.*1400, perhaps the greatest *chansonnier*, or song-book, of medieval Europe, have been likewise attached, in the manner which is always so persuasive to the modern reader, to a real-life story in which they themselves figure as individuals. And when Charles of Orléans was in prison in England (1415–40) after being captured at Agincourt, he learnt English and had a series of his English poems and his English translations of his French poems organised into a narrative sequence and copied into what is now BL MS Harley 682. The familiar themes and conventions of courtly lyric are skilfully manipulated, but there is also an individually confected poetic 'voice', in which colloquialisms, sharp questions, interpolated exclamations and stac-cato repetitions are used to convey the impression of strong feeling barely restrained by convention (in a manner somewhat anticipating Wyatt). As always, it is probably not helpful to look in real life for the experiences described nor the ladies addressed in such poems.

The Private Self

The idea of the individual, though hard to define, is evidently tied up with the material realities of privacy and the idea of private space and the private self. Private spaces were becoming more common in the fourteenth century. Houses, especially the houses of rich city-dwellers in Italy and elsewhere, were now being organised as a series of spaces of varying degrees of intimacy, rather than as central communal spaces with few if any specialised withdrawing-rooms. Bedchambers were being locked or more securely bolted, and conver-sations could take place between intimates that had previously been conducted in a more formal and ritualised way in public or semi-public. Other places, too, that had once been public and communal were being divided up and partitioned off as private spaces. The chantry-chapel is a particular kind of example. William of Wykeham (d. 1404), Bishop of Winchester and Richard II's long-serving chancellor, had his chantry set up in the nave-aisle of Winchester Cathedral at just the place where he had been accustomed as a boy to pray before an image (see Fig. 44). So a portion of a great communal space was annexed to a bit of private biography.

Private experiences began to be written down, in memoirs and forms of autobiography. In the various kinds of 'spiritual autobiography', as also in the *Book of Margery Kempe*, the private experience of self was largely absorbed in a traditional and purposeful discourse of communion with God that has the rhetoric of intimacy but the intention of being made public. In other genres, though it would still be true that memoirs and diaries such as we would call private did not start to be kept (or to be kept and to survive) until after the end of the fifteenth century, the experience of a private self began to find a more direct expression. The Emperor Charles IV, in addition to permitting a lifelike statue of himself to be set up in Prague Cathedral, also wrote a Latin 'autobiography', or self-eulogy, the *Vita Caroli*, which records some private events that have no apparent exemplary value. Buonacorso Pitti of Florence, early in the fifteenth century, wrote an account of his travels – a conventional enough genre – which soon breaks with tradition and offers a frank account of a love-affair, a murder, and a vendetta in which he was involved, none of them particularly creditable, and ends with the author's success in business and politics, his travels quite forgotten. He is not giving an account of the world but of himself.

From about 1360, too, first in Italy and then in France and other countries, more and more personal letters were being written. Much that they contain is purely practical, but the writing of such letters in the vernacular, especially where there is no intermediary scribe, invokes a new kind of self-consciousness. They were now, too, becoming more truly private: in Machaut's *Le voir dit*, the exchange of love-letters between the ageing poet and the young woman must be kept secret, and the narrator makes a point of emphasising that he did not read aloud or share the contents of the letters with his intimates, as must be presumed to have been the usual practice. 'I seized and opened the letters', says the poet, 'but the secret that lay within was not revealed to all, because I read them between my teeth' ('les lisoie entre mes dents', that is, silently).

Painting, too, began to record moments of feeling that might be called individually self-expressive, windows into the private heart, in traditional scenes long portrayed in a formalised way. The expression of grief on the face of Mary in Giotto's Lamentations over the Body of Christ in the Scrovegni Chapel at Padua (1304–06) is powerful but conventional, as are the expressions of maternal grief in his Massacre of Innocents in the same series of frescoes. But Giotto's portrayal of the meeting of Saints Joachim and Anna (Mary's mother) at the Golden Gate, also in Padua (Fig. 70), manages, through the reaching out of the couple's hands as they meet together after a long and painful

Figure 70: Giotto, The Meeting of Joachim and Anna at the Golden Gate (detail). Padua, Scrovegni Chapel. Wall-painting. 1304–06.

According to a legend in the Apocrypha, made widely known in the immensely popular collection of saints' lives known as the Golden Legend (*Legenda aurea*), Joachim was forced into exile by the priests of the Temple because his wife was barren and he was unable to make offering. His faith and humility were recognised by God, who gave Anna (St Anne) a child (Mary) and brought him back out of exile. Upon his return to Jerusalem Joachim was met at the Golden Gate (the gate at which Christ entered Jerusalem on Palm Sunday) by his wife and servants. A sacred moment is also a moving witness to human love.

absence, a moment of tender feeling more affecting as a testament to ordinary private human love than anything prescribed or needed by the exemplary narrative. Saint Anne, in other pictures, looks upon her daughter with grave tenderness as she teaches her to read. It is in the subsidiary figures of the biblical and apocryphal narrative that painters can reveal best the inward self.

The 'Man of Letters'

The careers of poets and writers had long been tied to the service of courtly patrons or the church. What they wrote, apart from minor effusions, was what they were expected to write. The great Italian writers of the Trecento, Dante, Petrarch and Boccaccio, were the first to establish, or re-establish, the notion of the *vocation* of the poet, the service that he performed not as an entertainer or a propagandist but as a member of the community at large, in which he spoke as a philosopher and a representative of the wisdom of the past, including the classical past. All three were attentive to their reputations as poets, none more assiduously than Petrarch, who had himself crowned poet laureate in the presence of his patron, Robert, King of Naples, when he was 36, and again in the following year (1341) before the Roman Senate on the Capitoline. He concocted a ceremony in which he delivered an oration on the value of poetry and the high status and fame in history of the poet, an oration constructed on the principles of the medieval sermon but with quotations from classical writers rather than the bible. It was, from one point of view, the beginning of the Renaissance; from another, it was a supreme act of self-promotion. Perhaps it had to be both. In the manuscript of Virgil that he caused to be made for himself and so fortunately recovered after it was stolen (Fig. 56), Petrarch for many years (1348–72) inscribed, as if in a bible, the names of persons dear to him who had died, including (on the reverse of the frontispiece) a moving epigraph to Laura:

> Laura, celebrated for her own virtues and by my poems . . . appeared to me for the first time in my earliest adolescence, in the Year of Our Lord 1328, on the sixth day of April, in the morning, in the church of Santa Clara in Avignon; and in the same city, in the same month of April, on the sixth day of the month, at the same time in the morning, in the year 1348, she was taken, while I was in Verona . . .

In this way he consecrated his love, his beloved and his poetry, in the imagined presence of the greatest poet of antiquity, to his life and the memory of his name as a poet.

In other countries, the older structures of patronage prevailed longer, but there were exceptions. Richard II was a noted patron of the arts, and attempts have been made to link him with Chaucer. Chaucer was a member of his court, certainly, and received royal patronage in the form of employment, annuities and grants. But the jobs were not sinecures, and there is no sign in Chaucer's poetry, nor in the manuscripts that survive, of such characteristic tributes and recognitions as are usually thought to be the proper return for patronage. *The Legend of Good Women* is playfully submitted to Queen Anne, and *The Book of the Duchess* must surely have been done under Gaunt's auspices, but there is no mention of Richard II. On the contrary, the circle of readers that Chaucer acknowledges, even in the courtly poem of *Troilus and Criseyde* (namely, John Gower and Ralph Strode), is that of men much like himself in status – civil servants, lawyers, country gentlemen, diplomats – and not that of the royal and aristocratic entourage. Chaucer pretends, of course, to the incompetence of a professional entertainer, toying with the image of himself as a poor hack, but more properly what he gives evidence of is the emergence in England of the 'man of letters' – educated, independent, and bound to no service. John Gower (d. 1408) is not dissimilar: he seems to choose his patrons, rather than they him, and he discards Richard, one feels, not because Richard failed to reward him but because he did not come up to John Gower's expectations as a king.

Women Writers

Though there is some debate about the matter, the role of women through the later medieval centuries does not seem to have undergone much change or amelioration, except perhaps in the immediate post-Black Death period, when their labour was needed and their status for a while improved. Generally, they were chattels, could be bought and sold in marriage, and their legal rights were largely subsumed in those of their fathers and husbands. A woman was her father's daughter (or a ward of court) until she became her husband's wife. She was always someone's possession. This at any rate was the official view, and the one promulgated in a written culture dominated almost entirely by men, and it became more rather than less rigid during the thirteenth and fourteenth centuries. Individual women, especially wealthy women, could of course exert considerable power and influence in courts and households, and negotiate positions of authority for themselves within the prevailing structures, and the fourteenth century saw more *femmes soles*, whether spinsters or widows, setting up in business on their own account. Chaucer's Wife of Bath, though in many respects a figure of fantasy, has her roots in contemporary economic reality as a business-woman.

The limitations placed upon their education (they were rarely taught Latin) and the constraints imposed by a traditional patriarchal culture meant that women did not often emerge as authors, though the continued constraints of that culture in modern scholarship have obscured from view, until recent years, some of the few that there were. More and more, it is coming to be thought that love-poems spoken in a woman's voice and once presumed to be a form of male ventriloquism are actually by women, and that devotional writings directed at women, like the superb group of prose texts written in the south-west midlands of England around 1225 and including the *Ancrene Wisse* ('Guide for Anchoresses'), may be, if not written by women, yet essentially the product of female textual communities. There are also writers like Marie de France, in the early thirteenth century, whose accomplishment calls into question any easy assumption that constraint meant exclusion or that a woman could not make her way in the world of writing.

Still, there were few of them, and women appear even less frequently as artists. The crafts of mason, sculptor, painter, goldsmith, were male preserves, jealously guarded, and few women's names emerge from the record except for a few scribes and illuminators and those engaged in traditionally female crafts such as embroidery (Mabel of Bury St Edmund's appears in the record of Henry III's commissions). But wealthy women played a considerable part in medieval culture in commissioning or acting as the recipients of commissions for illuminated manuscripts, both religious and secular, just as they did in their role as patrons, audiences, readers and owners for romances and devotional writings.

Nuns and other female religious were exceptional among medieval women in having access to learning and scholarship (though not often to Latin) and in being accepted as writers. From the time of Hrotsvitha (Roswitha) of Gandersheim in the tenth century and Hildegard of Bingen in the twelfth, they had played a significant part in religious and devotional writing. Some of it was routine men's work done by women, such as the Anglo-Norman saints' lives written by what seems to have been a flourishing group of nuns around 1200 at Barking Convent near London, one of the oldest houses for women in England. Some of it was far from routine, inspired by an extreme and ardent fervour, a passionate devotion to the wounded and mutilated body of Christ and to the eucharistic body, and an emphasis on the female body and on bodily feats of fasting and lactation such as were rare or impossible in the devotional writings of men.

The most prominent of these holy women were Bridget of Sweden and Catherine of Siena. Bridget (c.1303–73) was the daughter of a Swedish nobleman, and she married well and had eight children, but after the death of her husband in 1344 she had the first of the visions in which she saw herself married to Christ and commanded by him to found a new religious order. She went to live in Rome in 1350, and her new order of Brigittine nuns received papal approval in 1371. Her visions, which she received in Swedish, were put into Latin by her confessors and published as the *Revelaciones* after her death. They often take the form of dialogues between herself (always referred to as 'the Bride of Christ') and Christ, Mary or the saints. Her devotion tends to the pragmatic and didactic, and she was an outspoken supporter of papal policies, which made her at times a controversial as well as an influential figure.

Catherine of Siena (1347–80), daughter of a dyer and the 24th child in a family of 25, also played a key public role in contemporary religious politics, and corresponded with popes and bishops. Her letters, her written prayers, and her *Dialogue concerning Divine Providence* survive in written form from her dictation in Italian (such women were not illiterate, but they were less accustomed to writing than men, and they usually had male clerks as scribes). Catherine's own (dictated) writing is explicit enough about her extravagant inedia, her eucharistic craving, her compulsion to suffer, but the most extreme examples of her passion to discipline appetite are in the biography that was written by her Dominican confessor, Raymond of Capua. It is here that we find described the most singular feats by which she sublimated her distaste for food into a spiritual exercise – thrusting her mouth into the putrifying breast of a dying woman, or drinking the pus from a leper's sores ('no food or drink ever tasted sweeter or more exquisite', she told Raymond).[2]

Perhaps not in this case but in others there is a suspicion that the lives of these holy women were sometimes manipulated by male clerics who were close to them and who encouraged them in their more sensational acts of devotion, or invented them, whether for the purposes of winning fame for themselves or in the service of doctrinal disputes that needed eucharistic freak-shows. Some of these devout women left a record of their lives and visions in their own vernacular writings, such as Mechthild of Magdeburg (d. 1282), who wrote in the Swabian dialect of German, and Margaret Porete (d. 1310), who wrote in French her *Mirror of Simple Souls*, a lyrical and erotic celebration of the ascent to divine love which led to her condemnation as a heretic in 1300 and eventual burning. Mechthild of Hackeborn (d. 1298/9) and Angela of Foligno (d. 1309) both dictated their visions in their vernacular dialect to their confessors for translation into Latin. But a number of these devout women are known only from the *Vitae* written by their clerical biographers. The life of Margaret of Cortona (d. 1297) was told by her confessor Juncta Bevegnati, and James (Jacques) of Vitry (d. 1240) and his disciple Thomas of Cantimpré were the tireless professional biographers of the female devout and tell us all we know of Mary of Oignies (d. 1213) and Christina Mirabilis (1150–1224). The latter truly deserved her name ('Christina the Astonishing'): she fled humans, couldn't bear their smell, lived in trees or on church-roofs like a gargoyle, threw herself into fires and cauldrons, howling terribly, hung herself on gallows, stretched herself on racks, haunted the graves of the dead, stood for days in the icy waters of the Meuse. To express her grief over the fate of sinners, she wept and wailed, twisted her body into contortions, bent her fingers back as if they were boneless, and cried out as if with the pangs of childbirth.[3]

In England, not ignorant of but not deeply influenced by these continental holy women, there were two female religious writers of exceptional interest. Julian ('Juliana') of Norwich (1342–c.1416) was a devout woman who on 13 May 1373 had a series of sixteen visions, to meditation upon which she devoted the rest of her life, as she describes in her *Revelations of Divine Love*. The *Revelations*, or 'Showings', survive in two versions, an early shorter version and a later version much expanded with additional contemplative material as Julian 'worked' upon the meaning of her sixteen visions. Julian shares fully in the desire to identify physically and emotionally with the humanity of the suffering Christ, but she also conducts her meditations in a methodical, step-by-step and rational-seeming way ('like a man'), and reaches out to her fellow-Christians as someone who has a responsibility to share with others what she has been granted by God.

Margery Kempe (1373-c.1440), who once went to see Julian at her anchorhold in Norwich to seek her advice, was a well-to-do bourgeois wife and businesswoman in Lynn, in Norfolk, who after bearing fifteen children developed a distaste for sex and wished to be wedded only to Jesus Christ, who visited her frequently. She went about England and Europe for many years on mission and pilgrimage, at first with her husband, and was frequently in trouble with the authorities. Being a wandering woman who seemed to be preaching, she was accused of Lollardy as well as gross impropriety, and was brought for interrogation before the archbishops of both York and Canterbury. Late in life she dictated her account of her life to scribes, and it survives in a single manuscript as *The Book of Margery Kempe*. Long dismissed as the autobiographical rambling of a noisy and unaccommodating and hysterical woman, it has come to be recognised, with the advent of feminist criticism, as a work of courage and originality, shaped to the author's purpose of justifying her life as an independent unvowed religious woman. She challenged the exclusively male authority of the church and violated every prohibition by which men tried to keep women silent ('I would thou were closed in a house of stone that there should no man speak with thee', said one old monk, no doubt speaking for many).

Secular women writers were rare, almost non-existent, at least in the record, and the career of Christine de Pizan (c.1364–c.1431) is unique. She has been called the first professional woman writer in Europe, the first, that is, who was not a nun or religious and who made her living from her writing. In this she was extraordinarily precocious: she had no women predecessors, and there had been few men who could be called professional writers, as we have seen. Her role was to some extent forced on her by circumstance. She was the daughter of Thomas of Pizan (from Pizzano, a small town near Bologna, not from Pisa), who was early in her life appointed as physician-astrologer at the court of Charles V of France. She was brought up at the French court, married young (in 1379) and had three children in short order. But Charles V, her father's patron, died in 1380, and her father and her husband were both dead by 1389, and she was left with a young family, as well as her mother and a niece, to provide for. Since she did not wish to remarry or to enter the church and abandon her family, and since no suitable appointment was available at court for a woman, she turned to her pen for support and began to look for patrons.

She wrote prolifically in many genres, and her writing nearly always expresses a woman's point of view: she did not challenge the patriarchal order, but she did not simply write 'like a man'. Her early love poems, such as the *Cent ballades d'amant et de dame* ('A hundred ballades of a knight and a lady'), are written in different voices, men's and women's, and in *L'epistre au Dieu d'Amours* ('The letter of the God of Love'), dated 1399, she protests against the slanders put upon women by men and defends women against their accusers.

Warming to her role as a public poet and advocate of women, Christine turned to prose and wrote *L'épistre d'Othéa* ('The letter of Othea', 1400), an exhortation to the practice of political moderation based on wisdom, inventing for the purpose a goddess of wisdom, Othea, who dispenses the good advice. The work is an important turning-point in Christine's career, and is constructed in a novel fashion as a compilation of fables from mythological and encyclopaedic sources, each introduced in a verse quatrain and then explained and allegorised at length. It is like a commentary on a newly discovered text.

Christine also took an earnest part in the debate concerning the *Roman de la Rose* (1401–02). Though in some respects a literary and intellectual game, at least for the male participants, the debate also acted to focus attention on some important literary questions: the connection of literature with morality, whether literary texts should portray people as exemplary models of behaviour, whether obscene language had a place in literature, and – of particular interest to Christine – whether the *Roman* presented a false and slanderous picture of women. Supported by Jean Gerson (1363–1429), the famous scholar and Chancellor of the University of Paris, Christine opposed the arguments of prominent intellectuals like Jean de Montreuil, Provost of the city of Lille, and the scholar-bureaucrats Pierre and Gontier Col, who claimed that the *Roman* was not defamatory of women or that if it was it didn't matter. Taking a now-familiar moral high ground, Christine argued that to defame women in literary texts had serious moral and social consequences and encouraged men to behave badly towards them.

Christine went on to write *Le livre de la cité des dames* ('The book of the city of ladies', 1404–05), perhaps her major work, or at least the one that has received most attention from modern feminist readers. In it she complains of the neglectful treatment women have received in a tradition of writing dominated almost exclusively by men, and proceeds to compile a catalogue of women worth remembering, a city inhabited by women whose worth and virtue are a repudiation of the slanders of men.

The *Cité des dames* was in prose, and Christine was now active in a whole series of such works of edification and advice. She did a life of Charles V (1404) for Philip the Bold, Duke of Burgundy – the first time that she had been summoned by a powerful patron to his palace and received a direct commission. She also wrote treatises on women's conduct in society, *Le livre des trois vertus* ('The book of the three virtues', 1405–06), and, as her sphere of interest and activity widened, on the art of warfare, *Le livre des faits d'armes et de chevalerie* ('The book of deeds of arms and chivalry', 1410).

But the court-culture in which she had flourished was disappearing. As Charles VI's periods of insanity grew more frequent, and Henry V's armies began to force their way to the gates of Paris, the French court fell apart, plagued by bloody feuds between the Burgundian and Armagnac rivals for regency. Christine fell into a series of lamentations at the sad state of France, exhortations to good government and peace between the factions, and, finally, hopes for a better life in the hereafter, in *L'épistre de la prison de vie humaine* ('Epistle concerning the prison of human life', 1418). In 1418 she left Paris for a nearby convent, where she spent her remaining years in silence, apart from an outburst of patriotic rejoicing at the achievements of Joan of Arc and the crowning of Charles VII at Rouen in 1429, the verse *Ditié de Jehanne d'Arc*.

Christine de Pizan's career was extraordinary. She was not only the first woman to write and be successful at writing for her career, but also, for a long time, the last. She wrote in many genres, verse and prose, and, in a literary culture where innovation was not always fashionable, invented some more. She also took a major part in the 'publication' of her work, organising the preparation of manuscripts with a keen eye to the relation of text and image and an even keener one to potential patrons. Christine presented her *Epistre d'Othéa*, a work intended as a 'mirror for princes', to four different patrons: the French king and the dukes of Berry, Burgundy and Orléans. Each manuscript has a slightly different programme of illustration, supervised by Christine, adapted to be particularly meaningful to the individual patron. She did the same with several subsequent works, and showed, amongst many other qualities, an extraordinarily sophisticated understanding of the political economics of cultural exchange.

The Artist

We shall look in vain in the Middle Ages for any emergent identity of 'the artist' as a specially sensitive and tormented soul seeking fulfilment in self-expression, but there are some changes that can be remarked. Though the 'anonymity of Gothic art' is a pious fiction, and architects, sculptors and painters – from Hugues Libergier and Erwin von Steinbach to Johan Siferwas and Hermann Scheerre – quite often signed their work, or indicated that they wished to be remembered as the maker, the role of such artists was still as functionaries and master-craftsmen. Froissart's praise of André Beauneveu, the Duke of Berry's sculptor and painter, as a supreme artist is praise of a man who was very good at doing what he was told to do. Jean de Beaumetz, who acted as the Duke of Burgundy's artistic adviser, was officially his *valet de chambre*, a kind of household functionary, as was Pol de Limbourg in the household of the Duke of Berry. Architects were always master-masons and bureaucratic officials, supervising the work of building in all its departments of activity.

But in Italy, quite early on, a change became apparent. Giotto di Bondone (1266–1337) was treated as a new kind of artist, celebrated soon after his death by Boccaccio and others for his special power of deceiving the eye into thinking that what it sees in his paintings is real. This is not true of Giotto's paintings, nor is it anything that a medieval painter would have thought worth achieving: it is a trope of eulogy in the praise of painters, familiar from classical writers such as Pliny, and important in marking the entry of a medieval painter into the classical pantheon. It singles Giotto out as a supreme 'artist'. Giovanni Pisano, with his Latin inscriptions of self-eulogy below the narrative reliefs on his pulpit at Pisa, clearly considered himself to belong in the same select company. When Duccio di Buoninsegna was commissioned in 1308 to do the *Maestà* for the central altar of the cathedral at Siena, it was as an already-famous artist that he was invited to do the work, and in his workshop that it was prepared, to be transported thence in 1315 with great ceremony to its home in the cathedral (it is now in the Palazzo Pubblico, as a 'work of art'). The increase in the commissioning of panel-paintings in churches from the late fourteenth century was partly due to an increasing sense of the intrinsic value of a painting by a great master, of the desire that it should be portable rather than entrusted to a potentially damp or decaying wall.

There were also changes in the details of commissions for paintings that indicate a changing conception of the artist.[4] The earliest such commissions that survive in writing are insistent upon the use of certain expensive colours and materials – ultramarine (made from powdered lapis lazuli, imported from the Levant) and gold especially. The contract drawn up in 1408 for Gherardo Starnina to paint frescoes of the Life of the Virgin in the church of San Stefano at Empoli is meticulous about blue: the ultramarine used for Mary's cloak is to be of the quality of two florins to the ounce, while for the rest ultramarine at one florin an ounce will do. It is partly a matter of beauty: such saturated blues have a breathtaking violet-blue tinge. But it is also a matter of conspicuous expense in the exhibition of a conspicuous piety. The artist is the instrument of the patron's will.

Later in the century, contracts began to place a value not so much on the expensiveness of the materials as on the reputation and skill of the artist. It may be specified, for instance, that the main artist must paint the main figures and leave to his assistants or the lesser artists of the atelier only the landscape or other background. The contract for some new frescoes in the chapel of St Peter in the Vatican (1447) allowed twice as high a rate of payment to Fra Angelico as to all the three other members of his team (which included Benozzo Gozzoli) combined. This was for a large-scale fresco; when it was a panel painting, the contract might specify that only a single designated painter should work on it. 'No painter may put his hand to the brush other than Piero himself', says the contract (1445) for the *Madonna della Misericordia* of Piero della Francesca, now in the Museo Civico at Sansepolcro.

In this way, the discerning client switched his funds from gold to the artist's brush, and helped in the making of the Renaissance idea of the artist. The humanist commentators on art were also important in helping to bring about this change: they looked for restraint, and affected a classical distaste for excess of display, and they also stressed the special nature of the genius of the individual artist. Alberti, in his treatise *On Painting* (1436), argues that the best artist will use his skill to create an effect of gold through a mix of yellow and white pigments rather than use actual gold: 'To represent the glitter of gold with plain colours brings the craftsman more admiration and praise'.

The Humanist and Book-Collector

In the late fourteenth century many classical stories, such as that of Troy, began to be illustrated for the first time. A new version of the pagan past emerged, in which it was not merely a repertoire of *exempla* to be allegorised for the moral instruction of Christians, but a gallery of ancestral heroes for modern aristocrats, a humanist mythography. The beginnings of a self-conscious revival of admiration for classical learning and antique art are best seen in Petrarch, who had a considerable influence in making people think of the Middle Ages as 'the middle ages' (between an important Then and a newly important Now), inferior, ephemeral, undistinguished, *passé*, and who thus anticipated the characterisation of the period of 'Gothic Europe' as 'Gothic'. Petrarch was a book-collector as well as a scholar and writer, but unlike Richard of Bury (1281–1345), Bishop of Durham, the best model of the older type of book-fancier (his *Philobiblon* is the endearingly undiscriminating confession of an unrepentant bibliophile), Petrarch collected with a purpose. The *Pro Archia* of Cicero that he discovered in a monastery in Liège contained a famous encomium of the *studio humanitatis* that became a key-text for humanist scholars. His later discovery in the cathedral library of Verona of Cicero's *Letters to Atticus* encouraged him and others in the cultivation of scholarly personal correspondence in Latin. Following Petrarch's example, Boccaccio turned up more Cicero as well as Apuleius and Tacitus in the library of the great abbey at Monte Cassino.

Italy had a great advantage over the rest of Europe in promoting classical learning. It had the presence of the Roman past, in its buildings and antiquities and libraries of manuscripts; it also had an urban culture, an admiration for civic government, a respect for the 'orator' as a public citizen, which put Italy in touch with its Roman past. Petrarch inspired Boccaccio, Boccaccio encouraged the humanist scholar and collector Coluccio Salutati (1331–1406), whose library of manuscripts (120 have survived) included rare copies of the Latin love-poets Tibullus and Catullus, and Salutati's protégés included Leonardo Bruni (1369–1444), Niccolò Niccoli (1364–1437), and Poggio Bracciolini (1380–1459). Poggio expanded his horizons during a long spell as papal *scriptor* at the Council of Constance – and not just through his trip to Baden (1414), where he wrote a scandalised and admiring account of the sexual freedoms and luxuries of the town's public baths. On a more professional visit, he went to the monastery of St Gall and found the first complete text of Quintilian's *Institutiones Oratoriae*, the discovery that made him famous. The monks wouldn't let him take it away, but he copied it out in full. He and his friends toured other monasteries and found rare copies of Lucretius, Cicero and Vitruvius. His visit to England (1418–22) was much less exciting.

These enthusiasts didn't have much money and were glad to find a rich and discriminating patron in Cosimo de' Medici (1389–1464), a clever banker and politician whose hobby was book-collecting. He went to Palestine with Niccoli to look for Greek manuscripts and after Niccoli's death paid off his debts by buying all his books and installing them in the library of the convent of San Marco. About this time, inevitably, the world of enthusiastic scholars and book-collectors began to give way to the encroachments of dealers and the professional book-trade. Vespasiano da Bisticci (1422–98) was the new kind of entrepreneur who organised this trade and acted as a book agent and dealer. One of Vespasiano's clients was William Gray (*c*.1413–78), Chancellor of Oxford and a scholar of Balliol, a rich man who toured Europe looking for books. Many were transcribed for him specially and survive in Balliol College library – Cicero, Sallust, Quintilian, Virgil, Pliny. He was typical of the English collectors who tried, with limited success, to keep up with developments in Italy.

Humphrey, Duke of Gloucester (1391–1447), Henry V's younger brother, was another. One of the most important figures in his country's affairs from his brother's death until his own in 1447, he has a reputation as a patron of letters, and he had dealings with many of the writers of his day, including Lydgate, Hoccleve, Capgrave and the anonymous translator of Palladius's *De re rustica* (a Roman treatise on horticulture). He was also an assiduous collector of books, and employed Italian humanist scholars as agents in buying and commissioning books for him, a large number of which he gave or bequeathed to the University of Oxford (the foundation of 'Duke Humphrey's Library' in the Bodleian). He was certainly more successful than his arch-rival, Cardinal Beaufort, who met Poggio Bracciolini at the Council of Constance (1415) and brought him over to England (1418–22). Poggio had a great reputation as a professional 'discoverer' of lost classical texts, as we have seen, but he found nothing to interest him in England, and he told people so when he got back. Humphrey had more success. He took advice from papal officials resident in England, such as Piero del Monte, whom he put in touch with Thomas Beckington, his own chancellor (1420–38). He had an important contact in Zano Castiglione, Bishop of Bayeux, who went to the Council of Basle in 1434 with Humphrey's commission to buy books. Humphrey brought Tito Livio Frulovisi over to England about 1436 to work as his secretary and also got him to write a eulogistic biography of Henry V, the *Vita Henrici Quinti*, and a poem, the *Humfroidos*, in praise of his own (comparatively insignificant) martial exploits in the Calais and Flanders campaigns of 1435–37. Without any great personal taste or learning, Humphrey knew what was expected of a humanist patron and knew the advantage of having educated men working for him. He recognised too that epistolography was a powerful instrument and that it would assist his political and other ambitions if letters from his chancery were in the polished curial style of the Italian Latinists.

Other Italian patrons included Federigo de Montefeltro (1422–82), Duke of Urbino, the Este dukes at Ferrara, the Gonzaga dynasty at Mantua, and the Aragonese kings of Naples. Such collectors paid great attention to their libraries. Leonello d'Este (1407–50) kept manuscripts in a room decorated with figures of the Muses. Pope Nicholas V had his library decorated with paintings of pagan and Christian writers by Fra Angelico in 1449. Federigo's study at Urbino has book-cupboards, still to be seen, with *trompe-l'oeil* pictures of heaps of manuscripts on the doors. It was not just a matter of display: these people were collecting books according to schemes of desirability (of content) thought up by scholars ('I must have a Quintilian') as much as for their lavish execution and conspicuous expensiveness.

The humanist reawakening of interest in classical rhetoric and literature was tied also to the secularism of Italian university education, which was part of its urban culture. Nowhere else in Europe was it possible, yet, to think of the non-Christian classical past as a model for emulation, or to think of history as a process of time in which other things than salvation and judgement were important. History could be differently understood. The idea of anachronism became possible – that another age and culture might have its own self-sufficient meaning and system of understanding, and not be there merely to be allegorised into Christian meaningfulness. Many before the humanist scholar Lorenzo Valla (1406–57) had doubted the authenticity of the 'Donation of Constantine' (a document giving the Lateran in Rome to the papacy, and establishing the state's responsibility to endow the church), and by many it had been denounced, deplored, excoriated, repudiated, denied, but no one before Valla had thought of proving it a forgery on philological grounds. The appointment of this combative scholar, who had been vehement in his denunciations of the church, as a papal secretary in 1447 may be thought of as a kind of victory for humanism, though Pope Nicholas V may have had in mind to contain as much as to reward him.

The Nation

Nationalism, in so far as it may be defined as a nation-wide movement of which most of the population is aware, belongs to the nineteenth century, while the growth of the nation-state (in England, France, Spain, especially) is largely a sixteenth-century phenomenon. But there were recurrent assertions of national power and prestige throughout the medieval period, increasingly strident towards its close, which were eventually to threaten or cut across the Europe-wide social and cultural communities upon which Gothic had rested. Most of these movements were short-lived and had pragmatic local objectives, or were on a small scale (Scotland, Switzerland), but some were to have a longer history. The *Dalimil Chronicle* (*c.*1308–11), written in the vernacular by a member of the Czech nobility, tries to build up a philosophy of Czech history and identity through which Bohemia can maintain an independent existence as a state in opposition to the penetration of German power and influence. The *Chronicle* periodically played a part in subsequent Czech national movements. There was also a cult, from the mid-fourteenth century, of St Procopius, founder-abbot of Sázava monastery, as a kind of national patron-saint, and the Hussites proclaimed themselves a national movement. But Bohemian culture was largely destroyed in the Hussite wars (1422–34), and the Czechs had to wait a long time for their independence.

In England and France, the 'nation' had a longer history. As long ago as Abbot Suger and Louis le Gros (Louis VI), it had been recognised how a great church could serve purposes of national and dynastic prestige. Tombs especially could be a key instrument of royal power and prerogative. The abbey-church of Saint-Denis had long housed the tombs of the kings of France, and

Louis IX, recognising, like Abbot Suger, the importance of a royal mausoleum to the throne of France, had tombs ordered in 1260 for all the rulers who had been buried there from the seventh century (the bodies were all thrown out at the Revolution, though some of the tombs were preserved). Later, Charles V had the great French soldier Bertrand du Guesclin, Constable of France, who died in 1380, buried there, and Charles VI incorporated a magnificent funeral service for him into his Feast of May in 1389. By having him buried in the royal necropolis, they identified the state that du Guesclin had served as embodied in the person of the king. The new practice of incorporating realistic portrait-sculpture in funerary monuments, such as the likeness of Charles V sculpted by André Beauneveu in 1364 (he is the first king of France whose features are known to us), and that of Bertrand du Guesclin (taken from a death-mask) in 1389, is part of this cult of the royal person.

Richard II attempted to do something similar in Westminster Abbey, where many English kings had been buried from the time of Edward the Confessor (d. 1066). When Queen Anne died in 1394, Richard arranged for the manufacture of tombs and magnificent gilt-bronze tomb-effigies for himself and his dead queen, and had them placed in position in the Chapel of the Confessor, to whom he owed a special devotion. The effigies are lifelike portraits, in striking contrast to the bronze effigy of the Black Prince, Richard's father, in Canterbury Cathedral (1376), where the armour is minutely realistic but the face idealised as the epitome of calm, *mesure* and courtesy. Richard proceeded also to allocate burial-places in the abbey-church to his own loyal followers, sometimes moving the tombs of minor royalty and royal minors to less prestigious corners of the choir-chapels so as to make proper space for this new national hierarchy of personal royal servants.

In the fifteenth century, the power of the state in England and France was employed in the creation of a specifically national sense of identity. In England Henry V encouraged the use of English (instead of French and Latin) in official documents, and proclaimed the new war against France in 1415 as a war for the dynastic rights and honour of England in which the English nation was symbolised in the person of the king. He identified English as a national language, as the language of the nation, for the first time with any systematic emphasis: he wrote in Anglo-Norman French, as was customary, to his brothers and officials, but in English to the burghers of the City of London to announce the victory at Agincourt (1415), conscious that national fervour would be stimulated by the use of English and his prospects for the further financing of his French wars enhanced. The Council of Constance, where the delegates from different countries were competing to establish their relative importance as 'nations', offered a forum in which both England and France were encouraged to proclaim their national identity. Henry's instructions to his ambassadors in 1415 made clear the importance of language in this campaign: 'The peculiarities of language', he said, 'are the most sure and positive sign of a nation in divine and human law'. Aside from England and France, Spain and Portugal were other embryonic nation-states waiting to come into their full sixteenth-century vigour.

The People

In the centuries of Gothic Europe, nearly all land that was not wilderness was given over to agriculture, and the vast majority of the population worked as labourers or tenant-farmers on the land. Yet an inevitable omission in a book of this kind is of any substantial record of the culture of this majority. There were folk-tales, songs, dances, song-dances, popular ballads, ritualised plays and processions, ritual objects, ceremonies, and many other forms of cultural production and activity, but, since they were oral, or existed only in performance or were otherwise ephemeral, they have not survived.

Those of which we have any knowledge at all have only survived because they were appropriated by a superior culture and inserted into the record. An unexpected insight into popular culture is given by a particular form of record, that is, by the inquisitional records where the business of the interrogation was to elicit just those aspects of religious belief and practice that might be specifically 'of the people' and judged to be heterodox or heretical. From the time of the early thirteenth-century records investigated by Le Roy Ladurie in his pioneering study of the inquisition in the Pyrenean village of Montaillou[5] to the evidence presented to the commissions established in the fifteenth century to extirpate Lollardy in the English shires, the reporting procedures offer a unique revelation of the nature, sometimes bizarre, sometimes sophisticated, of popular religious belief.

In quite another context, folk-tales and fairy-tales of one kind or another were picked up and used as the materials of popular romance, a bastard form in which old tales of exile-and-return, magical transformation or the 'family drama' were dressed in chivalric costume or larded out with didactic moralising and served up to a pious aspirant bourgeois or lower gentry audience; or else they were gathered by clerical compilers and extravagantly allegorised so that they could be used as exemplary stories (*exempla*) in sermons. Sometimes, a fragment of pre-literate popular culture will protrude and set up some uncanny resonances in its new gentrified or clericalised environment. The foliate heads carved in medieval churches (and other folk-survivals too) make a neat design for a corner of a capital, or a roof-boss, or a misericord, but the branches and leaves growing from the mouth and ears of the human faces are reminders of the 'green men' of vegetation myths, who might not be entirely at home in a church. In a romance like *Sir Gawain and the Green Knight* (England, late fourteenth century), the sophistication of the courtly adaptation cannot entirely close off some trains of thought suggested by green-man transformations.

The popular plays of the later Middle Ages are 'popular' chiefly in the sense that they were made for the people by clerical authors determined on edification. They may have been 'popular' too, for there was little enough in the way of public entertainment, but the idea that they were the expression of the communal faith of 'the people' needs a generous helping of modern sentiment to make it persuasive. What is interesting about them, again, is the way unwritten pre-existing forms of genuinely popular drama get taken up in the mystery plays and morality plays and made into the materials for the dramatic amplification of the biblical story or moral allegory, sometimes with sufficiently odd effects. In the cycles of mystery plays put on at York and Wakefield, the rough-and-tumble of Noah and his wife, the obscene quick-fire repartee of Cain and his unruly servant, the alewife scene in the Chester Harrowing of Hell, are the only record we have of some of the midsummer shows and 'mumming-plays' that are presumed to have been a staple of popular entertainment. The first written record of these shows and plays was not made until the eighteenth century.

Popular culture is thus a difficult subject to talk about, and it is not made easier by some of the 'turf-wars' that have been fought around the subject. One faction wishes to insist on the large contribution made by popular culture to elite forms of culture. Others, perhaps considering themselves less swayed by sentiment, see everything going the other way. The long debate about the origin of the Robin Hood story, and of the fifteenth-century ballads associated with his name, now resolving itself into a general acceptance of 'downwards' cultural diffusion, is an example of the passions and interests that have been vested in the two kinds of approach.

Certainly, there has been some excess of enthusiasm for finding the evidences and traces of 'the folk'. It would be pleasant to think that the form of the *pastourelle*, in which a knight meets a peasant girl and woos her into submission (or sometimes not), is derived from popular songs such as come down in 'Where are you going to, my pretty maid?', but the truth seems to be the other way round. Chaucer and his contemporaries and followers, and French poets too, have a number of poems in which they attach dreams and stories of love to St Valentine's Day, the day on which the birds choose their mates. 'An old folk-belief' seems the obvious explanation of such a rural custom, but the fact seems to be that Chaucer invented the whole idea as an 'occasion' for poetry. The little song about the coming of springtime, 'Sumer is icumen in', with its charmingly frank allusions to the friskiness of young bulls and bucks, seems to fit the image of 'the popular', but it is in fact a sophisticated little part-song, with instructions in Latin for singing it, the only English item in a monks' commonplace-book from Reading Abbey of about 1300.

Only at the end of the Middle Ages, with the increase in the writing down of all forms of previously evanescent oral entertainment, do we start to get more than a fitful glimpse of popular culture. Then, kinds of song that seem indeed to have come from the workplaces and taverns of the people began to break surface, though most have undergone some kind of cultural 'translation', and the process is sporadic.

NOTES

1. *The Regiment of Princes*, ed. Charles R. Blyth (published for TEAMS [The Consortium for the Teaching of the Middle Ages] by Medieval Institute Publications of Western Michigan University, Kalamazoo, Michigan, 1999), lines 4997–8. The most famous of the surviving pictures is that in BL MS Harley 4866, fol. 88r,

which Blyth shows on p. 187 of his edition opposite the text; pictures in other manuscripts are of poorer quality, or else those that should appear have been cut out, or were never put in.

2. These matters are treated at length in the important book by Caroline Walker Bynum, *Holy Feast and Holy Fast: The Religious Significance of Food to Medieval Women* (Berkeley and Los Angeles, 1988). The quotation is on p. 172.

3. See Barbara Newman, 'Possessed by the Spirit: Devout Women, Demoniacs, and the Apostolic Life in the Thirteenth Century', *Speculum*, 73 (1998), 733–70.

4. These paragraphs draw their examples and quotations from Michael Baxandall, *Painting and Experience in Fifteenth Century Italy* (1972; 2nd edn, Oxford, 1988), pp. 11–23.

5. Emmanuel Le Roy Ladurie, *Montaillou: Cathars and Catholics in a French Village 1294–1324* (first published in French, 1975; trans. Barbara Bray, London, 1975).

Glossary of Technical Terms

AMBULATORY: an aisle for walking, especially around the apse or choir of a church

APSE (adj. apsidal): the large semicircular or polygonal, domed or arched extension, usually at the east end of a church

ARCADE: a series of arches at the side of the nave supported on piers or columns rising from the floor (see Fig. 10)

ARCHIVOLT: the inner surface of an arch around a portal, often decorated with concentric bands of moulding or sculptures

BAS-DE-PAGE: the lower margin of the manuscript page

BAY: a section of wall or wall-space between the columns or buttresses of nave, choir or transept

CHANCEL: see CHOIR

CHANTRY CHAPEL: a small chapel (or altar) in a church, endowed for the maintenance of one or more priests to say daily mass for the soul of the donor

CHOIR: the eastern part of a church, beyond the crossing, containing the high altar, and usually reserved for the clergy and the performance of the divine office, and often separated from the nave by a rood-screen; also called the CHANCEL (a term now usually reserved for smaller churches)

CLERESTORY (pronounced 'clear-story'): an upper row of windows above the triforium, and above the external aisle roofs (see Fig. 10)

CROCKET: a small projecting carved ornament, such as a bud or carved leaf, on the inclined side of a pinnacle or gable

CROSSING: the place in a church where the nave and transepts meet

DROLLERIES (French *drôleries*): pictures with odd or fanciful subjects in the margins of manuscripts

EASTER SEPULCHRE: a tomb-like recess in a church where the host was laid on Good Friday in imitation of the burial of Christ, and brought out on Easter Sunday

GRISAILLE: clear glass, usually with conventional non-figurative designs

GROIN: the line of intersection of vaulting-surfaces

MISERICORD: a small projection, often with decorative or figurative carving, on the underside of the hinged seat of a church stall, which, when the seat is lifted, gives support to a person standing in the stall (from Latin *misericordia*, 'pity')

NARTHEX: a vestibule or porch across the west end of early churches (before *c.*1200) separated from the nave by a rail or screen and intended as a waiting area for pilgrims, penitents, etc.

NAVE: the main body of a church, extending from the west door to the crossing (the word is derived from Latin *navis*, 'a ship', the pitched-roof structure being likened to an upturned boat, with the additional suggestion of the ship or 'Ark' of the faith)

NODDING OGEES: ogee arches alternately recessed and projecting.

OGEE ARCH: an arch with two ogee (S-shaped) curves meeting at the apex

RETABLE: a decorative structure behind an altar providing a frame for a picture or sculpted relief

ROOD-SCREEN: a carved stone or wooden screen separating the nave from the choir (chancel), such as became widespread in churches from the fourteenth century onward

SPANDREL: the triangular space enclosed between an arch, a vertical line rising from the springer, and a horizontal line at the level of the apex of the arch

TRANSEPT: either arm, north or south, jutting out from a cruciform (cross-shaped) church at the crossing

TRIBUNE: a vaulted blind gallery above the side-aisle of the nave (see Fig. 10)

TRIFORIUM: an arcaded wall-passage opening towards the nave above the aisle-roofs (or tribune) and below the clerestory (see Fig. 10)

TYMPANUM (plural tympana): the triangular or semicircular space between the lintel of a door and the arch above, and the relief sculpted carving in this space

VOUSSOIR: one of the wedge-shaped blocks of masonry used in the construction of an arch

Guide to Reading

Place of publication is London unless otherwise stated.

History; Cultural History

ABULAFIA, David (ed.), *The New Cambridge Medieval History*, Vol. 5, *c*.1198–
c.1300 (Cambridge, 1999). See also ALLMAND, JONES.

ALLMAND, Christopher (ed.), *The New Cambridge Medieval History*, Vol. 7,
c.1415–*c*.1500 (Cambridge, 1998). See also ABULAFIA, JONES.

BINSKI, Paul, *Medieval Death: Ritual and Representation* (Ithaca, N.Y., 1996).

BLOCH, Marc, *Feudal Society* (first published in French, 1939; trans. L.A.
Manyon, 1961).

CARRUTHERS, Mary, *The Book of Memory: A Study of Memory in Medieval
Culture* (Cambridge, 1990).

CIPOLLA, C.M. (ed.), *The Fontana Economic History of Europe* (1972).

CLANCHY, Michael J., *From Memory to Written Record: England 1066–1307*
(1979; 2nd edn, Oxford, 1993).

DUBY, Georges (ed.), *Rural Economy and Country Life in the Medieval West*
(first published in French, 1962; trans. Cynthia Postan, 1968).

——, *The Chivalrous Society* (collected lectures and essays in French; trans.
Cynthia Postan, 1977).

——, *A History of Private Life*, Vol. 2: *Revelations of the Medieval World*
(first published in French, 1985; trans. Arthur Goldhammer, Cambridge,
Mass., 1988). Evidence mostly from France and Italy.

FORD, Boris (ed.), *Medieval Britain*, Vol. 2 of *The Cambridge Cultural History
of Britain* (Cambridge, 1988).

HEER, Friedrich, *The Medieval World: Europe 1100–1350* (first published in
German, 1961; trans. Janet Sondheimer, 1962). Dated, sentimental and
overwritten, but unique in its attempt at comprehensiveness.

HERLIHY, David, *Medieval Households* (Cambridge, Mass., 1985). Evidence mostly from Italy.

HOLMES, George (ed.), *The Oxford Illustrated History of Medieval Europe* (Oxford, 1988).

HUIZINGA, Johan, *The Waning of the Middle Ages: A Study of the Forms of Life, Thought and Art in France and the Netherlands in the XIVth and XVth Centuries* (first published in Dutch, 1919; first published in English, 1924; New York, 1949). A vividly written study, much criticised for its tendency to colourful generalisation, but still influential.

JONES, Michael (ed.), *The New Cambridge Medieval History*, Vol. 6, *c*.1300–*c*.1415 (Cambridge, 1999). See also ABULAFIA, ALLMAND.

KEEN, Maurice, *Chivalry* (1984).

—— (ed.), *Medieval Warfare: A History* (Oxford, 1999).

LADURIE, Emmanuel Le Roy, *Montaillou: Cathars and Catholics in a French Village 1294–1324* (first published in French, 1975; trans. Barbara Bray, 1975). Pioneering study, drawn from inquisitional records, of the life of a whole community.

LEFF, Gordon, *Paris and Oxford Universities in the Thirteenth and Fourteenth Centuries: An Institutional and Intellectual History* (New York, 1968).

LE GOFF, Jacques, *Time, Work and Culture in the Middle Ages* (first published in French, 1977; trans. Arthur Goldhammer, Chicago, 1980).

——, *The Medieval World* (first published in Italian, 1987; trans. L.G. Cochrane, 1990).

——, *Medieval Civilisation, 400–1500* (first published in French, 1964; trans. Julia Barrow, Oxford, 1989).

LITTLE, Lester K., *Religious Poverty and the Profit Economy in Medieval Europe* (Ithaca, N.Y., 1978).

MATHEW, Gervase, *The Court of Richard II* (1968).

MOLLAT, Michel, *The Poor in the Middle Ages: An Essay in Social History* (first published in French, 1978; trans. Arthur Goldhammer, Chicago, 1986).

—— (ed.), *Etudes sur l'Histoire de la Pauvreté* (Paris, 1974).

MURRAY, Alexander, *Reason and Society* (Oxford, 1978).

ORIGO, Iris, *The Merchant of Prato, Francesco di Marco Datini* (1957). A vivid picture of the world of a fourteenth-century Italian merchant.

PAGE, Christopher, *The Owl and the Nightingale: Musical Life and Ideas in France 1100–1300* (1989).

RASHDALL, Hastings, *The Universities of Europe in the Middle Ages*, new edition by F.M. Powicke and A.B. Emden, 3 vols (Oxford, 1936). Still unique in its attempt at comprehensive coverage.

REYNOLDS, Susan, *Fiefs and Vassals: The Medieval Evidence Reinterpreted* (Oxford, 1994). Revisionist assessment of ideas of feudalism.

SOUTHERN, R.W., *The Making of the Middle Ages* (1953).

STEVENS, John, *Words and Music in the Middle Ages: Song, Narrative, Dance and Drama, 1050–1350* (Cambridge, 1986).

SUMPTION, Jonathan, *The Hundred Years War*, Vol. 1, *Trial by Battle* (1997); Vol. 2, *Trial by Fire* (1999) (continuing).

ULLMANN, Walter, *Law and Politics in the Middle Ages: An Introduction to the Sources of Medieval Political Ideas* (Ithaca, N.Y., 1975).

ZIEGLER, Philip, *The Black Death* (1969). Superseded in some respects, but a powerful narrative.

Religion

BLOOMFIELD, Morton W., *The Seven Deadly Sins: The History of a Religious Concept* (Ann Arbor, 1952).

BYNUM, Caroline Walker, *Holy Feast and Holy Fast: The Religious Significance of Food to Medieval Women* (Berkeley and Los Angeles, 1988).

DUFFY, Eamon, *The Stripping of the Altars: Traditional Religion in England 1400–1580* (New Haven, 1992).

HUDSON, Anne, *The Premature Reformation: Wycliffite Texts and Lollard History* (Oxford, 1988).

KNOWLES, David, *The Religious Orders in England*, 3 vols (Cambridge, 1948–59).

LAMBERT, M.D., *Medieval Heresy* (1977).

LEFF, Gordon, 'Heresy and the Decline of the Medieval Church', *Past and Present*, 20 (1961), 36–51. A compelling account of the church's loss of power to contain and 'canalise', institutionally, new spiritual movements.

——, *Heresy in the Later Middle Ages: The Relation of Heterodoxy to Dissent c.1250–c.1450*, 2 vols (Manchester, 1967).

LE GOFF, Jacques, *The Birth of Purgatory* (first published in French, 1981; trans. Arthur Goldhammer, 1984).

PANTIN, W.A., *The English Church in the Fourteenth Century* (Cambridge, 1955).

REEVES, Marjorie, *Joachim of Fiore and the Prophetic Future* (1976).

SMALLEY, Beryl, *The Study of the Bible in the Middle Ages* (Oxford, 1941; 2nd edn, 1952; 3rd edn, 1983).

SOUTHERN, R.W., *Western Society and the Church in the Middle Ages* (Harmondsworth, 1970).

History of Art and the Arts in General

ALEXANDER, J.J.G., and BINSKI, Paul (eds), *Age of Chivalry: Art in Plantagenet England 1200–1400* (1987). Exhibition catalogue.

BAXANDALL, Michael, *Giotto and the Orators* (Oxford, 1971).

——, *Painting and Experience in Fifteenth Century Italy* (1972; 2nd edn, Oxford, 1988).

CAMILLE, Michael, *The Gothic Idol: Ideology and Image-Making in Medieval Art* (Cambridge, 1989).

——, *Image on the Edge: The Margins of Medieval Art* (1992).

——, *Gothic Art: Glorious Visions* (New York, 1996).

DEUCHLER, Florens, *Gothic*, The Herbert History of Art and Architecture (1989). Short study, useful for the brief informative notes to the 207 plates.

DUPONT, J. and GNUDI, Cesare, *Gothic Painting* (Geneva, 1954).

EVANS, Joan, *English Art, 1307–1461*, Oxford History of English Art, 5 (Oxford, 1949).

FOÇILLON, Henri, *The Art of the West in the Middle Ages*, Vol. 1, *Romanesque Art*; Vol. 2, *Gothic Art* (ed. Jean Bony; trans. Donald King, 1962–63).

FRANKL, Paul, *The Gothic: Literary Sources and Interpretations through Eight Centuries* (Princeton, 1960).

HAUSER, Arnold, *Social History of Art from Prehistoric Times to the Middle Ages* (English version by Stanley Godman and the author, New York, 1951).

HENDERSON, George, *Gothic* (Harmondsworth, 1967).

MÂLE, Emile, *The Gothic Image: Religious Art in France of the Thirteenth Century* (first published in French, 1910; first English translation, 1913; translated for the 3rd edn by Dora Nussey, 1961).

——, *Religious Art in France*, ed. H. Bober, 3 vols (Princeton, 1978–87).

MARTINDALE, Andrew, *Gothic Art: From the Twelfth to the Fifteenth Centuries* (1967).

——, *The Rise of the Artist in the Middle Ages and Early Renaissance* (1972).

MEISS, Millard, *Painting in Florence and Siena after the Black Death* (Princeton, 1951).

PANOFSKY, Erwin, *Gothic Art and Scholasticism* (1951; 2nd edn, 1957). Important on the ideas behind the building of the cathedrals.

——, *Early Netherlandish Painting: Its Origins and Character*, 2 vols (Cambridge, Mass., 1953).

SCHAPIRO, Maurice, *Late Antique, Early Christian and Medieval Art* (New York, 1979).

SITWELL, Sacheverell, *Gothic Europe* (New York, 1969). A very different book from this one.

SWAAN, Wim, *The Late Middle Ages: Art and Architecture from 1350 to the Advent of the Renaissance* (1977).

TOMAN, Rolf (ed.), *The Art of Gothic: Architecture, Sculpture, Painting* (Cologne, 1998). Essays by various hands; magnificent photographs (over 500 of them, all in colour) by Achim Bednorz.

Literature; Literature and Art

BLOCH, R. Howard, *Etymologies and Genealogies: A Literary Anthropology of the French Middle Ages* (Chicago, 1983).

BUMKE, Joachim, *Courtly Culture: Literature and Society in the High Middle Ages* (first published in German, 1986; trans. Thomas Dunlap, Berkeley and Los Angeles, 1991).

BURROW, J.A., *Medieval Writers and their Work: Middle English Literature and its Background 1100–1500* (Oxford, 1982). Invaluable short primer.

CURTIUS, Ernst Robert, *European Literature and the Latin Middle Ages* (first published in German, 1948; trans. Willard R. Trask, New York, 1953).

DRONKE, Peter, *Medieval Latin and the Rise of the European Love-Lyric*, 2 vols (Oxford, 1968).

GELLRICH, Jesse M., *The Idea of the Book in the Middle Ages: Language Theory, Mythology, and Fiction* (Ithaca, N.Y., 1985).

GREEN, Richard Firth, *A Crisis of Truth: Literature and Law in Ricardian England* (Philadelphia, 1999). A wide-ranging study of changing perceptions of the nature of 'truth'.

LEWIS, C.S., *The Allegory of Love: A Study in Medieval Tradition* (1936). Classic study of the allegorical love-vision and love-romance.

LOOMIS, Roger Sherman, *Arthurian Legends in Medieval Art* (1938).

—— (ed.), *Arthurian Literature in the Middle Ages: A Collaborative History* (Oxford, 1959).

PATTERSON, Lee, *Negotiating the Past: The Historical Understanding of Medieval Literature* (Madison, Wis., 1989).

PEARSALL, Derek, and SALTER, Elizabeth, *Landscapes and Seasons of the Medieval World* (1973).

PICKERING, F.R., *Literature and Art in the Middle Ages* (1970). Evidence mostly from Germany.

ROBERTSON, D.W., *A Preface to Chaucer: Studies in Medieval Perspectives* (Princeton, 1962). A valuable if over-dogmatic introduction to Christian iconographic meanings in literature and art.

SALTER, Elizabeth, *English and International: Studies in the Literature, Art and Patronage of Medieval England* (Cambridge, 1988).

TUVE, Rosemond, *Allegorical Imagery: Some Mediaeval Books and their Posterity* (Princeton, 1966). A study of the later medieval illustration of manuscripts of earlier allegorical poems such as the *Roman de la Rose* and Deguileville's *Pelerinage*.

VINAVER, Eugene, *The Rise of Romance* (Oxford, 1971).

WALLACE, David (ed.), *The Cambridge History of Medieval English Literature* (Cambridge, 1998).

ZUMTHOR, Paul, *Speaking of the Middle Ages* (first published in French, 1980; trans. Sarah White, Lincoln, Nebr., 1986).

Architecture

BRANNER, Robert, *Gothic Architecture* (1961).

——, *St Louis and the Court Style in Gothic Architecture* (1965).

FRANKL, Paul, *Gothic Architecture*, Pelican History of Art (Harmondsworth, 1962).

GRODECKI, Louis, *Gothic Architecture*, History of World Architecture (London and Milan, 1978). Specialised study of building techniques.

KRAUS, Henry, *Gold was the Mortar: The Economics of Cathedral Building* (1979).

PEVSNER, Nikolaus, *An Outline of European Architecture* (1943; 7th edn, Harmondsworth, 1963).

RUSKIN, John, 'The Nature of Gothic', in *The Stones of Venice* (1851; ed. J.G. Links, New York, 1960).

STIMSON, Otto von, *The Gothic Cathedral* (New York, 1962). Important on the ideas behind the building of the cathedrals.

SWAAN, Wim, *The Gothic Cathedral* (1969). Superb text and photographs. Introduction by Christopher Brooke.

WILSON, Christopher, *The Gothic Cathedral: The Architecture of the Great Church 1130–1530* (1990).

Illuminated Manuscripts

ALEXANDER, J.J.G. (ed.), *A Survey of Manuscripts Illuminated in the British Isles*. See below under MORGAN, SANDLER, SCOTT.

AVRIL, François, *Manuscript Painting at the Court of France* (New York, 1978).

BRANNER, Robert, *Manuscript Painting in Paris during the Reign of St Louis* (1977).

CALKINS, Robert, *Illuminated Books of the Middle Ages* (Ithaca, N.Y., 1983).

DIRINGER, David, *The Illuminated Book: Its History and Production* (New York, 1967).

HAMEL, Christopher de, *A History of Illuminated Manuscripts* (1986).

HARTHAN, John, *Books of Hours and their Owners* (1977). An excellent introduction to the basic form of the book, with 72 colour plates of selected manuscripts.

MEISS, Millard, *French Painting in the Time of Jean de Berry: The Late Fourteenth Century and the Patronage of the Duke*, 2 vols (1967).

——, *French Painting in the Time of Jean de Berry: The Boucicaut Master* (1968).

——, *French Painting in the Time of Jean de Berry: The Limbourgs and their Contemporaries*, 2 vols (1974).

MORAND, Kathleen, *Jean Pucelle* (Oxford, 1962).

MORGAN, Nigel, *Early Gothic Manuscripts*, Part I, 1190–1250, and Part II, 1250–85 (1988). Vol. IV of J.J.G. ALEXANDER (ed.), *Survey*.

PÄCHT, Otto, 'Early Italian Nature Studies and the Early Calendar Landscape', *Journal of the Warburg and Courtauld Institutes*, 13 (1950), 13–47.

——, *Book Illumination in the Middle Ages* (Oxford, 1986).

RANDALL, Lillian M.C., *Images in the Margins of Gothic Manuscripts* (Berkeley and Los Angeles, 1966).

ROBB, David M., *The Art of the Illuminated Manuscript* (1973).

SANDLER, Lucy Freeman, *Gothic Manuscripts 1285–1385*, 2 vols (1986). Vol. V of J.J.G. ALEXANDER (ed.), *Survey*.

SCOTT, Kathleen L., *Later Gothic Manuscripts 1390–1490*, 2 vols (1996). Vol. VI of J.J.G. ALEXANDER (ed.), *Survey*.

STONES, Alison, *Gothic Manuscripts 1260–1320* (1993).

Index